Design
Principles
for Desktop
Publishers

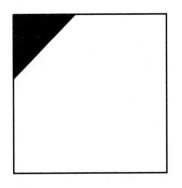

Design Principles for Desktop Publishers

Second Edition

Tom Lichty

Wadsworth Publishing Company
Belmont, California
A Division of Wadsworth, Inc.

Editor: Todd Armstrong
Editorial Assistant: Joshua King
Production Editor: Pat Waldo
Print Buyer: Randy Hurst
Permissions Editor: Peggy Mehan
Text and Cover Designer: Andrew H. Ogus
Copy Editor: Rebecca Magee
Technical Illustrator: Tom Lichty
Compositor: Wadsworth Digital Productions
Printer: R. R. Donnelley & Sons Company, Crawfordsville

*This book is printed on
acid-free recycled paper.*

IP™

The International Thompson Publishing
trademark ITP is used under license.

Printed in the United States of America
1 2 3 4 5 6 7 8 9 10—98 97 96 95 94

Library of Congress Cataloging in Publication Data

Lichty, Tom.
     Design principles for desktop publishers / Tom Lichty. — 2nd ed.
      p.   cm.
     Includes bibliographical references and index.
     ISBN 0–534–23082-2 (alk. paper)
     1. Desktop publishing.   I.   Title.
Z253.53.L53 1994
686.2'2544536—dc20

Table of Contents

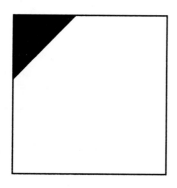

Preface

The best kind of friend to have is one with a sailboat. And my friend Roy not only has a sailboat, he lives in the Puget Sound. There, thousands of coves and harbors offer refuge after those days of maritime activity that always seem to be slightly beyond our competencies. In the asylum below decks, after dinner is consumed and the dishes are washed, our conversation turns to consequential matters: world peace, last week's *Saturday Night Live,* and design.

Which is precisely what happened one August evening in 1986. Contemplating the menacing future of the newborn desktop-publishing movement, we lamented what we perceived as the demise of the printed word: design and typography were falling into the hands of Everyman, and the lowest common denominator would prevail. The entire industry was about to become another episode of *Saturday Night Live,* and we were powerless to defend it.

Or were we?

"You can write a book," offered my shipmate. "You can distill the essence of design into a few pages of common sense and offer it as an antidote to doom." Such a friend. Always anxious to place Fate in my hands and see what I can do with it. I suppose that's why we choose to sail with each other.

Thus, *Design Principles for Desktop Publishers* was born. The book originally appeared in 1988, and being the first of its kind, promptly seized the Best How-To Book Award for the year from the Computer Press Association.

The Owner's Manual for Desktop Design

With this edition, *Design Principles* enters the province of academe. Revised and updated, the book now bristles with exercises and pedagogy gleaned from the nearly five years of seminars and classes I've taught based on its content. Design is a theory, but it's a theory that's best learned through application, and above all, application is what this book has to offer.

Each chapter suggests a number of exercises that students can conduct either independently or as a group. Every theory is illuminated with practical how-to methodology using Aldus *PageMaker* or Quark *XPress*. The book explains not only what must be done but how it's done as well. It's not just the designer's primer, it's the owner's manual for desktop design.

What's in This Book

Here's a preview of what's ahead.

Chapter 1 sets the tone for the book. It addresses the student, defines the reader, and offers an unconditional guarantee.

Chapter 2 discusses the reader, the subject, the system, and the proper attitude—the commonsense aspects of desktop publishing that become so elusive when we're confronted with deadlines, frustration, and the hypnotic stare of the computer screen.

Chapters 3, 4, and 5 explore the essence of our trade: type. When should you use Times instead of Helvetica? How many columns are appropriate? What's this business about kerning? And just who are Hermann Zapf and the Dingbats?

Chapter 6 presents the five basic design concepts: proportion, balance, contrast, rhythm, and unity. Combined with a solid background in typography, these concepts provide the foundation for successful page design.

Chapter 7 addresses the nontypographical elements of design: illustrations. Here we include borders, rules, ornaments, and line art. Best of all, we learn that the principles regarding the use of each are simple and direct.

Chapter 8 casts an eye at photography and offers a strategy for the inclusion of photographic elements in page design. Topics include selecting and framing the subject, placing pictures on the page, bleeds, scanning, and the technicalities of electronic photographic reproduction.

Chapter 9 explores the universe of color. We examine the psychology of color, contrasting colors, complementary colors, spot color, process color, and some of the techniques offered by today's desktop-publishing software.

Each chapter contains numerous principles—design principles for desktop publishers. As principles, they should be considered whenever design decisions must be made. And each chapter offers the hands-on practicality I mentioned earlier, intent on clarifying its subject via hands-on experience.

The "principles" referred to by the title of this book appear like this. They are principles, not rules. Violate them, but violate them with good reason and with knowledge of the infraction. An error of ignorance is usually cause for regret.

The principles of commonsense typography, page layout, illustration, photography, and color are addressed by scores of volumes available in any library or bookstore. The advantage that this book has to offer is one of practicality. It's intended for the student of design who is short on erudition but long on enthusiasm, and is eager to apply every theory learned.

A big thank you to my reviewers:

- Paul Adams, California State University, Fresno

- Van Kornegay, University of South Carolina

- Gary W. Larson, North Dakota State University

- Belinda Peters, Clark Atlanta University

- Don W. Stacks, University of Miami

- Patsy G. Watkins, University of Arkansas

And a special thanks to Kristine Clerkin, Holly Allen, Patricia Waldo, Joshua King, Andrew Ogus, and Joan Olson at Wadsworth Publishing for their support and contributions. Without them, this book would still be a remote aspiration.

Tom Lichty

Introduction

Arrested in mid-enthusiasm, we discover that good design is elusive but not impossible and may, in fact, be nothing other than the usual unusually well done.

I n *Megatrends*, John Naisbitt summarizes the occupational history of the United States in three words: *farmer, laborer,* and *clerk.* Until the turn of the century, farmers constituted the majority of our work force. By the 1920s, the industrial age was upon us, and laborers had their day. In 1979, the information age arrived and the number one occupation became clerk.

We are the clerks.

We mass-produce information. We're so good at it that the volume of information we produce doubles every couple of years. Willard Kiplinger published the nation's first newsletter—*The Kiplinger Washington Letter*—in 1923. Now over 150,000 newsletters are published on a regular basis, a number that's expected to grow by 40 percent per year.

No wonder desktop publishing is so popular.

And with this stupefying growth comes chilling fear: a flood of ineptly designed materials will arrive with the proliferation of desktop-publishing systems, giving the entire publishing industry and everyone associated with it a bad name.

This book addresses that fear.

The Good News and the Bad News

Let's take the bad news first: you're not going to become a graphic designer by reading this book. Drawing may be taught by tutors, but design is learned in heaven. This book alone can't produce a graphic designer any more than a fine piano can produce a musician.

The good news, however, is encouraging: whereas inspired design may be divine, commonsense design is not. Inspired design is the realm of coffee-table books and *Architectural Digest*. As desktop publishers, we produce reports, proposals, overheads for presentation, newsletters, memos, forms, and manuals—hardly coffee-table material. We don't supply *in*spiration, we provide the *per*spiration that keeps the machinery of the information age oiled and running. Our domain is the everyday stuff: which typeface to use, where to place a headline, when to use an ornament, how wide a column should be—the decisions that most frequently go awry, spoil a publication, and brand us as amateurs. The good news is that making the proper decisions is easy once you understand a few basic design principles. The principles are easy to learn. This book is going to teach them to you.

Who Should Read This Book

This book is intended for those who prepare anything from formal proposals to ads for the Yellow Pages, are humbled but nonetheless energized by a new design responsibility, and are willing to take a shot at this moving target that we call design.

This book assumes that you know little or nothing about design. I don't intend to approach my topic from the esoteric angles characteristic of the artistic community. This presentation is general, not specific. I doubt that you want to launch a new career as a designer, but I assume that you want to survive in the designer's environment. For that you need to learn the basic principles, you don't need to be a prodigy of design.

You will see the word *system* often in this book. This is my way of describing a combination of hardware, software, and output (including the press and the paper). Although I have included a number of design-oriented exercises in the book that don't require any of these, I have also included some examples of design solutions that do. Because Aldus *PageMaker* and Quark *XPress* are the two most common software foundations for desktop publishers, these programs are used in the examples. They're examples, however, not exercises. Though it will help if you're using one of these page-composition programs, neither is necessary for the effective utilization of this book.

My Unconditional Guarantee

All desktop publishers live in fear of an error message that lurks somewhere within every system's cerebellum—the computer's knee-jerk reaction to really awful design. Completing a design in which we have marginal confidence, we click the Print button, and...

Figure 1-1

This could happen to you, but not if you read this book.

If you read this book thoroughly and carefully, comprehend what it has to say, and adhere to its principles, you'll never encounter this error message. I guarantee it.

Bibliography

Naisbitt, John: *Megatrends*. New York, NY: Warner Books, 1982.

In spite of its age, few books are more effective at establishing a
perspective from which to view today's information age than this
one, and none are as engrossing and easy to read. Called the "field
guide of the future," *Megatrends* controversially predicted the information society and global economy that are now familiar to us all.

Naisbitt, John, and Aburdene, Patricia: *Megatrends 2000*. New
York, NY: William Morrow and Company, 1992.

Ten years after *Megatrends, Megatrends 2000* identifies 10 new forces
that will shape the world for the next decade, including free-market
socialism, the privatization of the welfare state, women in leadership,
the impact of genetic engineering, and the upcoming religious revival
of the third millennium. The predictions are once again controversial
and no doubt accurate. Time will tell.

White, Jan V.: *Editing by Design*, second edition. New York, NY:
R. R. Bowker Company, 1982.

The paradigmatic reference for document design. Though it predates
the era of electronic publishing, its content is ageless, and its presentation—with White's hand-drawn illustrations and its avant-garde
layouts—is captivating.

Williams, Robin: *The Mac Is Not a Typewriter*. Berkeley, CA: Peachpit Press, 1992. Also, *The PC Is Not a Typewriter*, published
concurrently.

Why should you not type two spaces after a sentence? How do you
type the grave accents in the word *résumé* (a noun) so that people
won't think disparaging thoughts of you for submitting your *resume,*
(which, as a verb, really can't be submitted at all). When is it proper
to use an en dash? What *is* an en dash? This little book answers these
questions (and more) and addresses all of the niggling little typographical details that every desktop publisher must know.

Before Turning the Computer On

Wherein we argue the case for common sense:
Why the reader, the topic, and the system become so
elusive once the computer is turned on, and why
the proper attitude will never let you down.

There sits the computer. Its myopic stare is hypnotizing. Its appeal is seductive. Its promise is alluring.

We succumb. Power on, we eagerly throw text and graphics at the screen, anticipating Inspired Design any minute now. Remember that magazine ad? "A Work of Art Without the Work." Okay, bring on the Art! With increasing desperation, we click, drag, cut, and paste—yet the image on the screen bears no more resemblance to Inspired Design than does a Big Mac to *filet de boeuf Richelieu*. Where did we go wrong? The magazine ad said this would be easy.

Well, it's not easy, but neither is it impossible. So far only one mistake has been made, and it's easily corrected.

Turn the computer off.

The most productive time you can spend as a designer involves a few critical moments of lucid thought before the computer is turned on. Lucid thought is evasive when disks are spinning and text is flowing, but it's a necessary preamble to effective design. You need a few moments to consider some elusive concepts, made all the more elusive by their very commonness.

Successful design isn't as ethereal as it seems. No matter how enormous the task, all you need to do is break it down into its component parts and make one small decision for each part. These decisions need only be based on three factors, none of which is ethereal at all. All you really need to know is whom you're talking to, what you're saying, and how you're saying it: the reader, the subject, and the system. Spend a few moments defining these three concepts, apply that knowledge to each decision as it arises, and your layout will design itself. It may not be inspired, but it will be effective, and as desktop publishers, that's our most noble duty.

The Reader

More often than not, the most significant determining factor in design is the reader. Try this: Close your eyes and imagine the one individual who best describes your reader. It's important that this be one person—a *real* person—someone you know well. As you're making those decisions mentioned earlier, you'll be consulting your image of the reader. The image must be clearly defined—a specific individual rather than an amorphous group. If the image is hazy, the decisions will be hazy; if the image is concise, the decisions will be concise.

How old is your reader? People over 40 often suffer from presbyopia: they (we, if the truth be known) may have trouble reading small type. Younger readers require vocabulary concessions: words like *presbyopia* will never do; *farsightedness* may be more appropriate.

How literate is your reader? What are his or her interests? A readership of nuclear physicists will require not only a different writing style but also a different graphic approach (see Figure 2-1) than a readership of, say, sixth-grade students.

Your reader's social and ethnic background may also play a deciding role. Imagine an American company doing business for the first time overseas. We'll call the company "Obelisk" and design an "OK" logo for it with our desktop-publishing system

Particle accelerators: Are they necessary?

W. T. Thomas, Phd., M.D.

The suprecostly particle accelerator may only provide a subatomic return on investment.

Lorem ipsum dolor sit amet, consectetuer adipiscing elit, sed diam nonummy nibh euismod tincidunt ut laoreet dolore magna aliquam erat volutpat. Ut wisi enim ad minim veniam, quis nostrud exerci tation ullamcorper suscipit lobortis nisl ut aliquip ex ea commodo consequat. Duis autem vel eum iriure dolor in hendrerit in vulputate velit esse molestie consequat, vel illum dolore eu feugiat nulla facilisis at vero eros et accumsan et iusto odio dignissim qui blandit praesent luptatum zzril delenit augue duis dolore te feugait nulla facilisi. Lorem ipsum dolor sit amet, consectetuer adipiscing elit, sed diam nonumy nibh euismod tincidunt ut laoreet dolore magna aliquam erat volutpat. Ut wisi enim ad minim veniam, quis nostrud exerci tation ullamcorper suscipit lobortis nisl ut aliquip ex ea commodo consequat.

Duis autem vel eum iriure dolor in hendrerit in vulputate velit esse molestie consequat, vel illum dolore eu feugiat nulla facilisis at vero eros et accumsan et iusto odio dignissim qui blandit praesent luptatum zzril delenit augue duis dolore te feugait nulla facilisi. Nam liber tempor cum soluta nobis eleifend option congue nihil imperdiet doming id quod mazim placerat facer possim assum.

Lorem ipsum dolor sit amet, consectetuer adipiscing elit, sed diam nonummy nibh euismod tincidunt ut laoreet dolore magna aliquam erat volutpat. Ut wisi enim ad minim veniam, quis

nostrud exerci tation ullamcorper suscipit lobortis nisl ut aliquip ex ea commodo consequat. Duis autem vel eum iriure dolor in hendrerit in vulputate velit esse molestie consequat, vel illum dolore eu feugiat nulla facilisis at vero eros et accumsan et iusto odio dignissim qui blandit praesent luptatum zzril delenit augue duis dolore te feugait nulla facilisi. Lorem ipsum dolor sit amet, consectetuer adipiscing elit, sed diam nonummy nibh euismod tincidunt ut laoreet dolore magna aliquam erat volutpat.

Ut wisi enim ad minim veniam, quis nostrud exerci tation ullamcorper suscipit lobortis nisl ut aliquip ex ea commodo consequat. Duis autem vel eum iriure dolor in hendrerit in vulputate velit esse molestie consequat, vel illum dolore eu feugiat nulla facilisis at vero eros et accumsan et iusto odio dignissim qui blandit praesent luptatum zzril delenit augue duis dolore te feugait nulla facilisi.

Ut wisi enim ad minim veniam, quis nostrud exerci tation ullamcorper suscipit lobortis nisl ut aliquip ex ea commodo consequat. Duis autem vel eum iriure dolor in hendrerit in vulputate velit esse molestie consequat, vel illum dolore eu feugiat nulla facilisis at vero eros et accumsan et iusto odio dignissim qui blandit praesent luptatum zzril delenit augue duis dolore te feugait nulla facilisi.

Lorem ipsum dolor sit amet, consectetuer adipiscing elit, sed diam nonummy nibh euismod

[1] Lorem ipsum dolor sit amet, consectetuer adipiscing elit, sed diam nonummy nibh euismod tincidunt ut laoreet dolore magna aliquam erat volutpat.

How much does a bomb cost?

Underground tunnels for tiny atomic spaceships

MOREM IPSUM DOLOR SIT amet, consectetuer adipiscing elit, sed diam nonummy nibh euismod tincidunt ut laoreet dolore magna aliquam erat volutpat. Ut wisi enim ad minim veniam, quis nostrud exerci tation ullamcorper suscipit lobortis nisl ut aliquip ex ea commodo consequat. Duis autem vel eum iriure dolor in hendrerit in vulputate velit esse molestie consequat, vel illum dolore eu feugiat nulla facilisis at vero eros et accumsan et iusto odio dignissim qui blandit praesent luptatum zzril delenit augue duis dolore te feugait nulla facilisi. Lorem ipsum dolor sit amet, consectetuer adipiscing elit, sed diam nonummy nibh euismod tincidunt ut laoreet dolore magna aliquam erat volutpat. Ut wisi enim ad minim veniam, quis nostrud exerci tation ullamcorper suscipit lobortis nisl ut aliquip ex ea commodo consequat.

Ruis autem vel eum iriure dolor in hendrerit in vulputate velit esse molestie consequat, vel illum dolore eu feugiat nulla facilisis at vero eros et accumsan et iusto odio dignissim qui blandit praesent luptatum zzril delenit augue duis dolore te feugait nulla facilisi. Nam liber tempor cum soluta nobis eleifend option congue nihil imperdiet doming id quod mazim placerat facer possim assum.

Lorem ipsum dolor sit amet, consectetuer adipiscing elit, sed diam nonummy nibh euismod tincidunt ut laoreet dolore magna aliquam erat volutpat. Ut ea commodo consequat. Duis autem vel eum iriure dolor in hendrerit in vulputate velit, consectetuer adipiscing elit, sed diam nonummy nibh euismod tincidunt ut laoreet dolore magna aliquam erat volutpat.

Cet wisi enim ad minim veniam, quis nostrud exerci tation ullamcorper suscipit lobortis nisl ut aliquip ex ea commodo consequat. Duis consectetuer adipiscing autem vel eum iriure dolor in hendrerit in vulputate velit esse molestie consequat, vel illum dolore eu feugiat nulla facilisis at vero eros et accumsan et iusto consectetuer adipiscing odio dignissim qui blandit pugait nulla facilisi. Lorem ipsum dolor sit amet, consectetuer adipiscing elit, sed diam nonummy nibh euismod tincidunt consectetuer adipiscing ut laoreet dolore magna aliquam erat volutpat.

t wisi enim ad minim veniam, quis nostrud exerci tation ullamcorper suscipit lobortis nisl ut aliquip ex ea commodo consequat. Duis autem vel eum iriure dolor in hendrerit in vulputate velit esse molestie consequat, vel illum dolore eu feugiat nulla facilisis at vero eros et accumsan et iusto odio dignissim qui blandit praesent

Figure 2-1

A paper describing atomic weapons as presented to a readership of nuclear physicists (left), who are already interested in the subject, and to a readership of sixth-grade students (right), who require more graphic appeal.

Figure 2-2

A logo similar to this met with resounding success in the United States, but failed overseas where it is a common obscenity.

(see Figure 2-2). Unfortunately, Obelisk isn't entirely familiar with the social background of the overseas readership. Though the OK sign is familiar to all Americans, it's not universal. In parts of Italy, sales plummet. Later Obelisk discovers that the OK sign is an obscenity there, and the Italian market is lost.

Above all, know your reader, your subject, and your system well. With this knowledge you will be able to confront design decisions with purpose and resolve. Your work will reflect your confidence.

Your reader will not only influence your choice of vocabulary, but the graphic appearance of the page, the communication conventions that can be used, and even the size of the type. As you progress through this book, you'll notice frequent references to the reader and the influence he or she will have on key design decisions. A clear vision of your reader is requisite to effective design.

The Topic

Without a clear understanding of the topic, most design decisions are evasive. Design involves several elements—graphics, headlines, text—each of which·may be sized, positioned, and embellished in a countless number of ways. This endless number of possibilities can easily overwhelm the designer who hasn't considered the topic.

Retained to prepare an advertising flyer, a designer without a clear vision of the topic might construct a document similar to Figure 2-3.

At first glance, it would appear that TNT Enterprises is the product—their logo, after all, is the most prominent graphic on the page. Further investigation might lead the reader to believe that it's the cassette that's being sold—the cassette graphic is located at the visual center of the page and its caption is the most evident. On a more general level, most of the typographical and graphic elements on the page are dissonant: there's no unity in support of the product—whatever it is.

Figure 2-3

A flyer advertises a product, but what's being sold? Without a clear understanding of the message, the designer is ineffectual and the design is ineffective.

The second version of the layout, illustrated in Figure 2-4, is the result of a series of decisions based on explicit awareness of the message. The cassette machine is the product, so it receives graphical emphasis. To unify the page, the cassette is reduced in size and placed in context with the machine. An abstract shape integrates the two graphics and eliminates the need for those conflicting, rounded borders. The company's logo remains prominently featured, punctuated by white space rather than size. Finally, the rounded Bookman typeface—altogether too voluptuous and old-fashioned for a high-tech product—has been replaced by Optima, a modern typeface with plenty of angularity to match the graphics.

Figure 2-4

The flyer is reworked with a clear concept of the subject in mind. Emphasis is placed on the cassette machine—the subject. The company logo and cassette graphic play more subservient roles. Textual elements are rearranged and the typeface is changed. Each alteration supports the subject; all elements work in concert.

The System

No matter how concisely you've perceived your subject or how clearly you have visualized your reader, if your desktop-publishing system can't produce or print your efforts, all your work is for naught. Though it may seem evident, it's not uncommon for an inexperienced desktop publisher to spend hours polishing the design of the perfect document, only to discover that the equipment doesn't equal the imagination.

I know that countenance
cannot lie
Whose thoughts are legible
in the eye.

—Matthew Roydon
An Elegy, or Friend's Passion
for his Astrophill

I know that countenance
cannot lie
Whose thoughts are legible
in the eye.

—Matthew Roydon
An Elegy, or Friend's Passion,
for his Astrophill

Figure 2-5

Surprinted on a 20% screen by a 300-dots-per-inch (dpi) laser printer, the quotation at the top is almost illegible. Below it, the same quotation appears on the same background, printed by a 1,270-dpi Linotronic imagesetter.

Your Printer

In Chapter 8, I explain why many desktop laser printers can't legibly print small text on a shaded background—a surprise to many desktop publishers who have seen the technique touted in ads and magazines. The truth is in the printing (Figure 2-5).

A thorough familiarity with your desktop-publishing system (and its alternatives) can help avoid this kind of frustration. If you want to use a laser printer to print small text over a shaded background, experiment with the technique before you invest precious time in a design that depends on it. If the experiment fails, spend your time on an alternative design, or spend it locating a print shop with an imagesetting machine compatible with your software.

Exercise 2.1   **Know Your Limits**

One critical variable you must be familiar with is the amount of space your printer cannot use on each of the four edges of the paper. Most laser printers, for example, use "grippers" to handle the paper—typically an area 3/8 inch on each of the long sides of the paper—cannot be addressed by the imaging mechanism itself.

1. Use your preferred desktop-publishing software to draw a box that's slightly larger than the paper itself (see Figure 2-6).

Figure 2-6

A 10% gray Picture Box has been drawn in Quark Xpress slightly larger than the paper itself. When this page is printed, the printer's nonprinting areas will be evident.

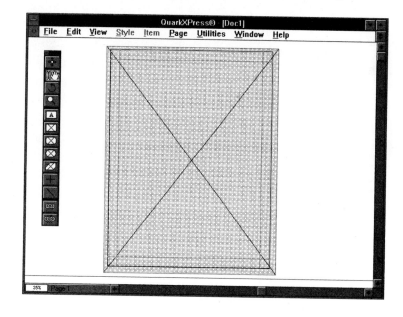

2. Fill the box with 10% gray—something that won't waste much toner (or ink) when it prints.

3. Print the page and make a note of the areas that did not print gray. These are the areas you must avoid when you consider your design.

The Final Output Device

High-resolution output devices are a requirement of many desktop-publishing jobs. Photographic images, four-color images, blended images—these are situations where desktop laser output just won't do. Typically an *imagesetter* is used, where resolutions of over 3,000 dots per inch aren't uncommon. Because imagesetters use a wet photographic process, they're not an everyday item. Even inexpensive ones cost upwards of $50,000, and their annual maintenance contracts can average half of that. Look in your Yellow Pages under Desktop Publishing; you're likely to find a number of service bureaus offering imagesetting services.

Imagesetters are notoriously fussy. Fonts are a constant nemesis: if you prepare a document with a font that the service bureau doesn't have, you're likely to get a page back filled with Courier—a page for which you'll be asked to pay.

The blended image in Figure 2-7 is another example. Illustration software—Adobe *Illustrator*, Aldus *FreeHand*, *CorelDRAW!*, and others—offers fountains, fills, and blends. Although these features look lovely on-screen and may even print satisfactorily on a desktop laser printer, they choke imagesetters (in which case the imagesetter stops and you pay for the page). Most service bureaus would rather you not use blends from illustration software at all. Alternatives exist: bitmap-image-editing software such as Adobe *PhotoShop* usually creates blends that cause imagesetters no trouble. The image in Figure 2-7 was created that way.

In short, if your document will be printed at a service bureau, talk to the service bureau personnel before you begin work. The service bureau is as much a part of the system as the computer or the printer—perhaps even more so.

Figure 2-7

Elaborate blends, fills, and fountains are murder on imagesetters. Talk to your service bureau before you try an image like this.

Know Your Laser Paper, Too!

No matter how elegant your design, if it's printed on the wrong paper, your brilliance will forever remain unrewarded—and probably unrecognized.

Always use a laser printing paper for critical masters. Most major paper manufacturers offer numerous choices, each with a hard, smooth finish applied to bright, opaque paper stock. The resulting contrast and resolution put plain photocopy paper to shame.

If you'll be "pasting up"—applying an adhesive wax to the paper and subjecting it to extensive handling—specify a heavy laser paper with wax holdout applied to one side.

That hard, smooth finish may provide a slightly less secure bond between toner and paper than you're used to. If smearing is a problem, try a spray fixative. Not only will it stop the smearing problem, it may increase the saturation of the black tones (which from some laser printers are notoriously gray) and improve contrast.

Discuss laser papers with your paper supplier. The cost is insignificant; the results are profound.

The Print Shop

Even if you've managed to obtain a clear original, you might find that the printing method isn't up to the task. For instance, few photocopy machines or quick-print presses can reproduce finely shaded backgrounds evenly. This is the type of restriction that many desktop publishers discover the hard way—after the layout has gone to press and 2,000 copies have to be scrapped.

There are several good reasons for visiting your print shop before you turn the computer on, most of which can save you time and money—all of which will save you stress. Your print shop can tell you how long it will take to finish a job, what it will cost (and how to justify it in your budget), and what materials you should bring to the shop when you're ready. Better yet, a good printer can help you with your design: why cropping an eighth of an inch off that brochure may save you hundreds of dollars, for instance, or why a border may be a superior alternative to that shaded box.

The Paper

Paper comes in a number of grades, including bond, text, coated, book, offset, and newsprint. Some papers are smooth, some are coarse. Some have greater opacity and brightness than others. Paper finishes vary from antique (a rough, dimpled finish) to machine (or *MF*, for machine finish). Recycled papers are popular; other papers are coated. Most importantly, paper is very much a part of the "system," as I'm using the word here. Your reader will hold your paper in his or her hand. Paper is a much more intimate component in the communication process than, say, the brand of computer you are using. Ask your print shop for samples of typical papers they're using and descriptions of the advantages and disadvantages of each.

Although I can't discuss all of your system's potential limitations here, I trust that my message is clear: Get to know your system. Software ads and trade magazines can provoke unrealistic expectations. Get to know your system's limitations and work (comfortably) within them.

Above all, know your reader, your subject, and your system well. With this knowledge you will be able to confront design decisions with purpose and resolve. Your work will reflect your confidence.

Exercise 2.2   **The Field Trip**

I don't want you to waste anyone's time—printers and service bureaus have precious little of it to spare—but one of the most instructive things you can do is visit a service bureau and a print shop. If you will truly become a customer someday, a field trip like this is beneficial not only for you but for them as well. Under these circumstances they won't mind the imposition—they might even welcome it because the visit isn't occurring under the pressure of a missed deadline.

Ask the printer for paper samples and a price list. Inquire about

- The preferred line screen frequency for different papers

- The cost of bleeds

- The cost for two- or three-color (spot) printing

- The preferred format for originals (including signature formats for bound documents)

- Process color considerations

Ask the service bureau for a price list and a listing of available fonts (and get a font book if they have one). Inquire about

- The preferred format for document files (including color)

- Preferred line frequency and number of grays for grayscale images

- Their font policy (Some shops will offer bitmapped font files for fonts you don't own but would like to use. Some are willing to use your fonts for printing—assuming you've specified a font they don't own—and some will not.)

- Turnaround time and rush order charges

Learn to accept your limitations and hire out design when it's warranted. Money saved by designing critical projects in-house is rarely money saved at all. Interminable struggle with design is expensive and dispiriting.

Attitude Adjustment

Perspective is hard to maintain as a desktop publisher. It requires most of our energy just to keep up with emerging technology and the language that has already begun to creep into this book. The consideration of the reader, the topic, and the system is one aspect of perspective, attitude is another.

An Attitude of Humility

It's easy to lose sight of the forest for the trees, and desktop publishing rarely clarifies the view. All too often we become enamored with hardware and crisp printouts and completely lose perspective on the publishing process as a whole. Nowhere is this more evident than in design.

As I said in Chapter 1, inspired design is a product of heaven. Because you're reading this book, you're probably not one of the Chosen Few. Keep this in mind. Humility is a virtue that's requisite to successful desktop publishing. Even though you will read this book and perhaps some others like it, you're going to flounder in some design situations. When that happens—when the design that you want fizzles rather than sparkles no matter how much effort you put into it—admit defeat and hire a designer. This goes for critical design tasks as well. A company logo, an expensive ad, a brochure that will be distributed to thousands—these are projects where the additional cost of a professional designer is negligible. Few companies hesitate to call a qualified mechanic when something goes wrong with the company van; no company should hesitate to call a designer when professional design services are required.

The Conventional Attitude

Desktop publishing replaces only one segment of the publishing process. It hasn't replaced writing, photography, or art; nor has it replaced printing, binding, or distribution. Desktop publishing replaces only composition, and even within composition there are some operations that are best accomplished with conventional tools. Gather up a hundred dollars, and let's go shopping.

- A *waxer* is indispensable. You might discover that your desktop-publishing system isn't the ideal tool for the production of halftones or process color (discussed in Chapters 8 and 9, respectively). You will also find other elements that need to be pasted onto the layout mechanically. The waxer supplies the paste. With a coating of wax on their backsides, pieces of text and graphics can be positioned and repositioned almost indefinitely without smearing glue or adhering to the layout permanently.

- A *roller* is used to apply firm, even pressure to waxed elements once they are properly positioned. Once rolled, waxed elements stay put.

- *Grid sheets* feature a nonprinting grid to ensure proper vertical and horizontal alignment. Few laser printers are perfectly aligned—the printout is rarely square on the page—and grid sheets provide a method of precise alignment. The grid is printed in a light blue (called nonreproducing—or nonrepro—blue) that isn't reproduced by the conventional printing process. (A light table would be nice too, allowing you to see the grid through your laser-printed paper. Not on a hundred-dollar budget, however.)

- A *T-square and triangle* allow you to project the grid sheet's lines onto your layout, even if you don't have a light table.

Desktop publishing represents only the composition segment of the publishing process, and even composition benefits from a combination of old and new technology. Think of desktop publishing as only one tool among many, and become just as familiar with the conventional tools of composition as you are with those of desktop publishing.

- *Drafting tape* secures the grid sheet to the layout surface without the stickiness of masking tape. Use the T-square to align the grid sheet with the left edge of the layout surface before you tape the grid sheet down.

- *X-Acto knives* (a brand name) allow you to cut pieces of copy and graphics. Scissors will never do. If you aren't using heavy laser printing paper, X-Acto knives are even more important because they slice lightweight papers cleanly. Buy plenty of spare blades and change them often.

- A *pica pole* measures things in units that print shops understand. In Chapter 4, "Formatting Text," I explain why points and picas are the preferred units of measurement and why a pica pole is much easier to use than a ruler that measures in inches.

- A *proportion wheel* allows you to specify enlargements or reductions to graphic elements as percentages, the language of all print shops. Though percentages can be figured mathematically, proportion wheels are much faster and easier—even than your computer—and they cost only a few dollars.

There's a principle here, although it's attitudinal rather than operational. Don't think of desktop publishing as an end to itself. Microwave ovens represent new, wonderful technology, but only fools throw out the conventional oven when a microwave is purchased. You still need a conventional oven to bake bread, broil meats, and warm plates. Maintain an open mind: if an operation seems clumsy or inefficient using desktop-publishing tools, use conventional tools instead. If you aren't already familiar with the operation of waxers, pica poles, and proportion wheels, acquire them now and start using them. Familiarity, in this case, breeds competency.

Exercise 2.3   Roll Up Your Sleeves

Compose the layout pictured in Figure 2-8 using traditional methods. Photocopy Figure 2-7, trim the photocopy, and use it as the graphic. Use your computer to prepare the text (any text will do—the content isn't important) in strips—*galleys,* as they were called—and paste up the strips using a waxer and T-square. Prepare the headlines on the computer too, on separate pieces of paper suitable for pasting up.

Figure 2-8

Compose this document using mechanical, rather than electronic, techniques.

1. Use 8 1/2-by-11-inch paper with 3/4-inch margins all around.

2. Banner head is 60-point Helvetica italic.

3. Columns are 12 picas wide.

4. Headlines are 16-point Helvetica, 18-point leading, left-aligned.

5. Body text is 10-point Times on 11-point leading, justified.

The Collector's Attitude

If we all agree that we're not artists, then we all agree that we lack divine inspiration and must seek originality elsewhere. Fortunately, as inhabitants of the information age, inspiration is all around us. All we have to do is be willing to learn from others.

Every book, magazine, and newsletter is a source of inspiration. They contain designs from the world's most creative designers and artists, each one a wealth of ideas for your next project.

Their value is minimal, however, unless there are plenty of them from which to choose. Public and academic libraries help, but the best library is your own—the so-called *swipe file*.

Every time you see a design that strikes your fancy, clip it (or photocopy it) and place it in your file. As your file grows, divide it into categories, and devote a file drawer to it. I'm talking about an attitude again—a collector's attitude—whereby the swipe file itself becomes a self-education process. Your awareness of design techniques will improve, and you'll find that your confidence will improve as well.

Note that I'm not advocating plagiarism here, I'm advocating inspiration. The law forbids you from copying designs element for element just as it forbids you from copying text word for word, but no one discourages learning by observation and inspiration. Most of the buildings in our nation's capitol, though splendid of design, were nonetheless inspired by classical Greek architecture.

Build and maintain a swipe file of worthy ideas. Develop a collector's attitude and take inspiration from the techniques you've collected. There is no better way to improve your creativity and confidence as a designer.

We tend to remember ideas in a vague sort of way. Though remembering where we saw an idea is usually a futile endeavor, thumbing through a (categorized) swipe file is not. As I said in Chapter 1, this book alone can't produce a graphic designer any more than a fine piano can produce a musician, but more often than not, musicians are the protégés of practice rather than the prodigies of heaven. As desktop designers, our best practice is the analysis and application of the techniques of the pros, of which the swipe file is an essential component.

The Experimental Attitude

Swipe file or no, most of us are new to design. Unexpectedly, unwillingly, and unpreparedly, we have become the ones who must take a vague concept and turn it into effective, esthetic, compelling design. What do we do? Take night school? Plagiarize at the risk of incarceration? Quit the job before it's too late?

None of the above. We experiment. As desktop publishers, we possess one unique, undeniable advantage: we can afford to experiment. Bob Goodman, writer-photographer-publisher of *Whale Song*, a spectacular, desktop-published art book on nineteenth-century whaling in Hawaii, produced 1,300 proof pages before settling on the 130 pages that eventually became the book. "Why not?" he asks. "Thirty seconds and three cents for materials, and you have a camera-ready page." Precisely.

Consider the conventional designer. Seated at the drawing board, she sketches proposed layouts until one strikes her fancy.

She then "specs" the type, a laborious process specifying font and font size, leading, word spacing, and letterspacing that will result in a body of type that properly fits the allotted space. Now she sends the copy out to be typeset, checks the galleys (a day or two later when they return from the typesetter) for typographical errors, and begins the interminable job of cutting and pasting the type in place. While she was waiting for the typesetter, she may have sent her graphics to the print shop to be sized and cropped. These too are pasted onto the layout, which now represents a considerable investment. Once everything is in place, she meticulously strips hairline rules and rounded-corner borders (something you have to try in order to appreciate) onto the layout, smears White-Out over the inevitable smudges, sprays the whole thing with fixative, and then stands back to admire her work.

This is why designers are so valuable: they have that innate designer's security that gives them the confidence to undertake an expensive, four-day pasteup knowing that it will be admirable when it's completed.

Desktop publishers may not have that confidence, but we have something that's almost as good—the ability to experiment. In that same four-day period we can spec type a thousand different ways, we can crop and size our graphics a thousand times over, and we can draw a thousand rounded-corner borders with nary a smudge. It's a buckshot approach, but it eventually hits the target—if we take advantage of our ability to experiment.

A Case Study

Let's create a company newsletter. On the front page, we need to place the newsletter's logo, the table of contents, and the lead story. To clarify the story and add interest to the layout, we elect to include a graph from a spreadsheet program. Without much thought, we assemble the layout in Figure 2-9.

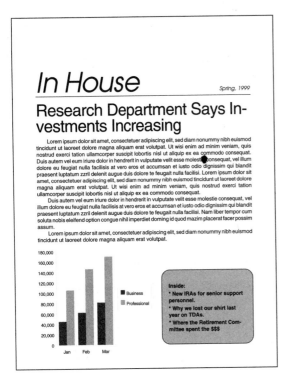

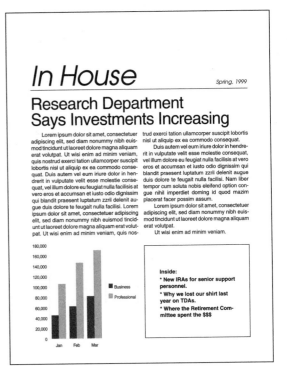

Figure 2-9 (left)

The first attempt at a cover for a company newsletter. It's not perfect, but it's not final either. We'll note our mistakes and try again.

Figure 2-10 (right)

The layout is improving, but the table of contents still looks out of place, and the graph is distorted. Set it aside and try again.

As this first layout rolls out of the printer, don't despair: it's only a rough draft. This is a hurdle for people who are new to desktop publishing. The printout looks so good that we're reluctant to waste it.

Waste it anyway. It can be improved.

We'll begin with the text: That single column is too wide for comfortable reading (I discuss column widths in Chapter 4, "Formatting Text.") That rounded-corner box seems out of place as well; everything else is angular. (I discuss unity in Chapter 6, "Page Design.") And we know better than to print text over a shaded background. The headline is another problem. The hyphenated word *investments* is awkward, and there's too much space between the lines. (Headlines are discussed in Chapter 5, "Display Type.")

We make the changes in two minutes, and it takes another minute to print the revision (Figure 2-10).

The headline is much better. Although the double-column format is an improvement, the graph distorts when it is compressed

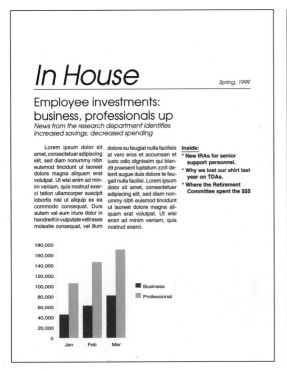

Figure 2-11 (left)

A third column, entirely devoted to the table of contents, provides a clean separation. The graph has more room to breathe as well.

Figure 2-12 (right)

Improvements to the graph simplify it somewhat, Schoolbook text offers better contrast than Helvetica, and the border around the story is much more interesting.

to fit the narrower column. The square border around the table of contents seems to harmonize nicely with the layout, but the story and its graph have to wrap around the table of contents, and that's awkward. We'll try three columns, devoting an entire column to the table of contents, defining it not with a border, but with some of the white space that's discussed in Chapter 6 (Figure 2-11).

With less space for the headline, we rewrite it, using a *blurb* (discussed in Chapter 5) to add interest. The graph—unmodified from the spreadsheet program—now seems overly complex, and the legends to its right take up too much room.

In Chapter 5 you'll learn that the mixture of Avant Garde and Helvetica typefaces is a bad idea. A serif typeface (discussed in Chapter 3, "Selecting a Typeface") will improve readability and provide contrast (discussed in Chapter 6). Finally—in an outburst of the experimental attitude—we try a border around the story rather than the table of contents (Figure 2-12).

Figure 2-13

The blurb is placed in the third column, providing a little more balance to the layout. Less emphasis has been placed on the logo and more emphasis on the graph, which has been improved with clip art graphics. (Graphics are discussed in Chapter 7, "Nontextual Elements.")

Though simplified, the graph still lacks punch—an opportunity yet to be explored. The headline and the blurb seem busy now that the remainder of the layout is so clean. There may be a little too much white space on the right, and too much emphasis on the logo. We'll try it one more time (Figure 2-13).

Reducing the prominence of the logo is acceptable. Most of our readers already know the name of the publication anyway, and with the reduction of the logo we can break up the verticality of the layout with a few horizontal lines. A trio of boxlike ornaments—discussed in Chapter 7—adds a bit of sparkle to the table of contents.

We've also elected to left-align and reduce the size of the text to increase readability. (We discuss justification and font size in Chapter 4.)

━━━━━━━━━━━━━━━━━━━━━━━━━━━━━━━━

The key to effective design is an experimental attitude. Critique your work mercilessly, and be willing to rework the design until it sparkles. This is the best way to combat your lack of experience as a designer.

─────────────────────────

Most importantly, the graph is reduced to its essence for simplicity's sake. Our readers already know the information provided by the axes, and by regrouping the bars we can dispense with the gray fill pattern, which may not reproduce well. A few clip art graphics add interest to the page, and horizontal grid lines tie the graphics to the graph, adding rhythm and unity (discussed in Chapter 6) to the layout in the process.

Five iterations, each based on the principles described in this book, have produced an attractive design that fares well with those of professional designers. The key ingredient wasn't talent, it was an experimental attitude. The ability to experiment is your primary advantage—don't hesitate to use it.

Feeding the Appetite of Communication

We often tend to overlook the obvious, especially when the complexities of desktop publishing cloud our vision. It's for this reason that I have devoted this chapter to principles that seem evident but rarely receive due consideration. Know who you're talking to, what you have to say, and how you're going to say it.

The chapters that follow involve discussions of picas and points, balance and proportion, rules and borders—the esoteric stuff of design. You may lose sight of the forest for the trees. If you do, you may end up designing for design's sake. Graphic design should always be regarded as a means to an end—the end being communication between subject and reader. As such, design is available to anyone with common sense—and the ability to experiment until that common sense is realized. The result may look like Art, but we know better. Few successful designs evolve from artistic talent. Most evolve from a primordium of subject, object, and system, blended in the elixir of common sense, and stirred with persistent trial and error. It may not be *filet de boeuf Richelieu*, but it feeds the appetite of communication, and that's our obligation as desktop publishers.

Bibliography

Beach, Mark; Sepro, Steve; and Russon, Ken. *Getting It Printed.* Portland, OR: Coast to Coast Books, 1986.

> A practical guide on choosing the right printing firm and providing them with the documents they need. Dozens of time- and money-saving tips.

Beach, Mark, and Russon, Ken. *Papers for Printing.* Portland, OR: Coast to Coast Books, 1989.

> How to get the right paper at the right price for any printing job. Another essential reference.

Before & After: How to Design Cool Stuff on Your Computer. PageLab, 331 J. Street, Suite 150, Sacramento, CA.

> This periodical is a testament to the vision of John McWade, one of this country's first desktop designers. Each remake is accompanied by a step-by-step guide on the document's composition.

Parker, Roger C.: *The Makeover Book.* Chapel Hill, NC: Ventana Press, 1989.

> A book full of makeovers: 101 design solutions for desktop publishing. The list of contributors to this book reads like a who's who in desktop design. A great idea book.

Pocket Pal. International Paper Company, 6400 Poplar Avenue, Memphis, TN 38197.

There's more in this little paperback about printing and paper than you'll find in many large books devoted to the subject. The 15th edition includes discussions of desktop publishing, electronic pre-press, and laser printing.

Publish! PCW Communications, Inc., 501 Second Street, San Francisco, CA 94107.

This magazine features a document makeover produced by a leading designer each month. Also a good column on typography.

U&lc. International Typeface Corporation, 2 Hammarskjold Plaza, New York, NY 10017.

An inspiring bimonthly tabloid with features by many of the nation's leading designers. Naturally (considering the publisher), many of the designs are purely textual—just what the financially strapped desktop designer can afford. An idea book to anticipate in the mail.

Selecting a Typeface

All those typefaces? Bookman and Goudy;
Baskerville and Times. Which one to use and why?
And just who are Hermann Zapf and the Dingbats?

So much fuss is made over design—wrapping text around graphics, letterspacing and kerning, digitizing graphics—that desktop publishers often lose sight of the forest for the trees. Most likely, over 90 percent of your publication will be text, and that text deserves your consideration before any other element in the design.

Actually, you'll find two types of text in most publications: *body text* and *display text*. Display text is the text that's used to construct headlines, subheads, drop caps, and the like. I devote a chapter to it later. Body text is the stuff of which paragraphs are made. No doubt your publication has something to say: body text says it. Body text has a profound but subtle effect on your publication's mood. More than any other element, body text can whisper or shout, look old or look new, relax the reader, startle the reader, or send the reader away after two paragraphs never to return.

It all has to do with the selection of the typeface that's used in the body of the text. This may be the single most important decision of your entire publication. It's for that reason that I devote

Font Defined

One of the most frequently used yet little-understood terms in desktop publishing is font. Simply stated, a font is the collection of all of the characters of one size and style of typeface. Figure 3-3 shows a portion of a font menu on a computer. The Times Roman font, for instance, contains something like 188 characters: the upper- and lowercase alphabets, the numerics and punctuation, and special characters such as the œ, ƒ, and £. An entirely separate font is required for Times italic, yet another for Times bold, and still another for Times bold italic.

Not long ago when type was cast in lead, separate fonts were required for each size of each typeface as well. In a moment I'll describe why this is no longer necessary with high-resolution printers and outline-definition fonts.

Nonetheless, whereas Times is a typeface, four fonts are required to complete the typeface: roman, italic, bold, and bold italic. Dozens more would be required if we had to define each of Times' potential sizes.

an entire chapter to a seemingly mundane topic. But read on: It's not mundane, and it can make or break your design.

All Those Typefaces!

The abundance of typefaces available to the desktop publisher is baffling. There was a time—from A.D. 700 until the 1930s—when type had to be chiseled by hand or cast in lead. The labor involved was so intimidating that typefaces were few—less than 20 in daily use. Now, barely 50 years after the invention of the phototypesetter and offset lithography, the number of typefaces exceeds 15,000 and is climbing. In spite of that number, many software packages are available to desktop publishers who want to design their own typefaces, just in case none of the 15,000 are to their liking.

This is truly confusing.

Fortunately, we can whittle those 15,000 typefaces down to a manageable size quite quickly.

Bitmaps

Desktop publishing places severe demands on typography. Although these demands seem insignificant to those of us who are new to typography, they challenge technology—a challenge that was poorly met (if at all) prior to the advent of laser printers and page-description languages.

Seated at the console, we complete a layout by adding a headline. Two column-inches of space are available. We choose 24-point Times, but at this size the headline just exceeds its two column-inch limitation. No problem: we'll try 23 points. *Voila!* The headline fits perfectly.

Seems simple enough.

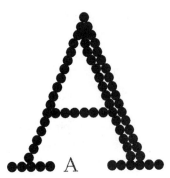

Figure 3-1

A bitmapped letter A from a low-resolution printer. This is not the kind of text that you want to use in desktop-published documents. Note that the bitmapped structure of a 36-dpi A is apparent even when it's printed at normal size.

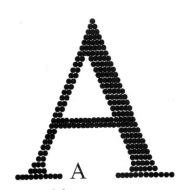

Figure 3-2

A bitmapped letter A from a high-resolution printer. Mapped at 300 dots per inch, a laser-printed A rivals the quality of typesetting machines. Note that the dot structure is invisible when the character is printed at its normal size.

But it's not. A hundred years ago, when type was cast in lead, display-sized type was expensive and hard to find (and heavy!—so heavy that it was often carved from wood rather than lead). Because every character had to be chiseled or carved, an abundance of type sizes simply wasn't available. With its zoom lenses, phototypesetting offered a solution, but the solution was hardly convenient: running down to the typesetter's shop and waiting while a low-priority, seven-word headline was produced was money- and time-consuming.

At first, personal computer technology failed to provide a practical alternative. Only a few years ago, all personal computer typefaces were *bitmapped*: characters were defined as a pattern (or map) of tiny dots, or bits. The letter A might be mapped as shown in Figure 3-1.

Originally, dot-matrix printers produced these characters. Resolution was coarse: characters were typically mapped within a seven by nine matrix of dots. Figure 3-1 reveals the coarseness of such a matrix. Reduced to body text proportions, the A is recognizable, but the pattern of dots is still evident. Technology provided a partial solution with the so-called daisy wheel printer, but the solution, which relied on cast type, was more of a backward step than a forward one.

Enter the laser printer. Most laser printers provide much finer dots—300 of them per inch is typical. The result is text that rivals typesetting machines for legibility yet provides all of the flexibility and speed of the dot-matrix printer (Figure 3-2).

A problem arises when larger text is required. Although a resolution of 300 dots per inch is capable of reproducing quite respectable characters of practically any size, a bitmap of each character *in each size* is necessary. The practicality of storing these maps is unreasonable. The A in Figure 3-2 is composed of nearly 300 dots (bits), and it's a single, small character. A complete font may require over 1,000 characters for each size. A narrow selection of only 4 sizes of a single typeface would require 300 times 1,000 times 4, or 1,200,000 bits (150,000 bytes) of storage. If 24 sizes were provided, nearly a megabyte of storage would be required, and our preferred 23-point size would probably not be among them.

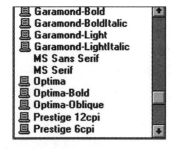

Figure 3-3

A partial listing of the fonts on my PC. Notice each of the fonts in the Garamond and Optima families appears separately. The MS Serif and MS Sans Serif fonts are screen fonts and are not intended for printing (which is why no little printer icons appear next to them). The two Prestige fonts are defined inside of my printer as bitmaps, thus specific sizes are listed.

Assuming there's an alternative (and there is—I'll describe it in a moment), why even bother with bitmapped fonts? Because they're the best fonts available for use on the screen—for things like menus and dialog boxes. Unlike the printer, the screen only needs one or two different sizes of each font, so the ability to resize the font isn't much of a factor. And bitmapped fonts are fast: your computer can pop them onto the screen and back off in an instant.

Early laser printers simply provided a limited number of fonts and sizes. Bitmapped fonts were supplied by the computer or on cartridge (a form of computer memory), and though three or four font sizes were typically included on each cartridge, 24 points was usually the maximum size. Furthermore, sizes were limited to those included on the cartridge: if 10-, 12-, 18-, and 24-point fonts are included in our cartridge, our 23-point headline won't be available. (The *point*, by the way, is equal to 1/72 of an inch and is used to describe the height of a character. I discuss points in the next chapter.)

Here's my point (so to speak): Though all printers—laser printers included—use tiny dots to form their characters, the dots used by today's printers are so tiny as to be indiscernible to the naked eye. But this dot-based strategy requires unique maps (patterns) for each size of each font that's to be used. Storage considerations render this impractical, if not impossible. There's got to be a better way.

Outline-Definition Fonts

The solution is provided by a relatively new concept: the *outline-definition font*. Rather than define a character with a map of dots, an outline font definition defines the character's outline with a series of lines and arcs (Figure 3-4). Because this definition describes only the outline of the character, it's much more efficient than a bitmap. More importantly, the lines and arcs can be mathematically scaled to produce characters of almost any size.

Only the outline of the character is defined within the computer, as a series of arcs...

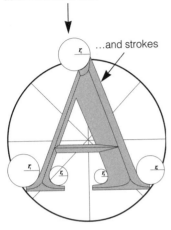

...and strokes

Figure 3-4

An outline font definition describes the shape of the letter A using a series of lines and arcs. These geometric "primitives" can be mathematically scaled to provide characters of virtually any imaginable size.

Let's say that the outline-definition font within your printer defines characters in their 12-point size only. To print 24-point characters, the length of each line and the radius of each arc is simply doubled. If you want a 23-point headline, each line and arc is multiplied by 1.92. Explore this kind of mathematics further and all kinds of special effects become possible: rotating, skewing, reflecting—they're all accomplished mathematically with outline character definitions. Though this may seem like a formidable task, computers love this kind of arithmetic and perform it almost instantaneously.

Eventually, the sized outline is filled in with dots, a process referred to as *raster image processing*, or *ripping*. In essence, new bitmapped font definitions are generated on demand *after* the text has been sized and after any special effects have been applied (see Figure 3-5). The result: maximum resolution, no matter how the text is manipulated.

The illustration in Figure 3-5 was created in Aldus *FreeHand*, an illustration program that's capable of manipulating the outline definitions of the fonts stored on my hard disk. By converting text into graphics like this, nearly anything's possible.

What You Shouldn't Use

Our background established, we can now address the straightforward issue of which typefaces are appropriate for body text and which are not.

Bitmapped Fonts

The limitations imposed by bitmap technology are so severe that the technology just isn't appropriate for desktop publishing. If you're limited to four or five type sizes within any one typeface, you're not capable of desktop publishing. Effective page design requires access to a broad variety of type sizes to properly format body text. Headlines, subheads, drop caps, and pull quotes are all potential necessities to the well-designed page as well; to restrict their availability is to restrict design itself.

The outline font limitation isn't much of a limitation, frankly. Nearly all of the fonts for sale today are outline definitions. Be

Figure 3-5

Arithmetically achieved distortions produce special effects—in this case, skewing and selective filling. It's all in a day's work for outline-definition fonts.

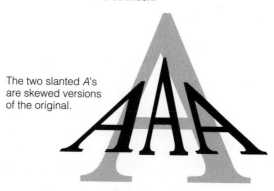

The large gray *A* has been sized up from the original 12-point outline definition.

The two slanted *A*'s are skewed versions of the original.

The skinny *A* in the center has been compressed.

This text is prepared in Chicago, the font that Apple Macintosh uses for menus and dialog boxes. Typical of most bitmapped fonts, Chicago doesn't print very well on high-resolution devices like laser printers. Bitmapped fonts are easy to identify on the Macintosh: they're all named after cities. Avoid them.

Figure 3-6

Though they're superior for use in dialog boxes and menus, bitmapped fonts like Chicago are not appropriate for desktop publishing.

careful, though, because bitmapped fonts are still used for menus and dialog boxes (and probably always will be because of their speed). Because they're still in use, they're still stored somewhere inside of your computer and usually available for your use, should you choose to do so (see Figure 3-6).

Exercise 3.1   Bitmapped or Outline?

Nearly every system offers a selection of both bitmapped and outline fonts. Above all, you must know which is which.

1. Make a list of all of the fonts available on your system. Identify each one as either a bitmapped or an outline-definition font.

2. If you're unsure of any one font, prepare a short body of text using the font in question specifying various sizes of type within the text. Use odd-numbered and fractional sizes if your software allows: 13.7 points, 17.1 points—that kind of thing. Bitmapped fonts will look *terrible* under these conditions.

Figure 3-7

On the left, International Typeface Corporation's Tiffany. On the right, Peignot (say "Pay-nyo"), a familiar sans serif face from Adobe Corporation. Serifs improve legibility and assist the eye.

Illinois
Illinois

Figure 3-8

At top, Franklin Gothic. Below, Souvenir, both from International Typeface Corporation. Serifs assist the eye in character recognition.

typography

typography

Figure 3-9

A familiar combination—Helvetica, at top, and Times, below, both from Monotype Corporation. Serifs provide the clues necessary for pattern recognition.

Sans Serif Typefaces

The Romans are often credited with the invention of the serif, the small cross stroke that appears on the arms of certain letters (see Figure 3-7).

One theory claims that the Romans carved their letters in stone with chisels and that the serif provided a solution to the technical problem of finishing off the chisel strokes without chipping. Another theory claims that scribes, working with brushes, used serifs to address the "blob" problem at the end of strokes. Regardless of its origin, the serif has been around for a long time.

As it turns out, the serif makes life easier on the reader by accomplishing three things: it cuts down the reflection of light from around the letter into the reader's eye (halation); it links the letters in a word and provides a horizontal guideline; and it helps distinguish one letter from another. The word *Illinois* is a classic example (Figure 3-8).

Without serifs, the first three characters all blend together. The serifs provide the clues necessary to differentiate the uppercase *I* from the lowercase *l*. Figure 3-9 is another example.

The study of how the eye reads is fascinating. The eye is most efficient at recognizing patterns, not words, and that's how we read, by recognizing visual patterns and combining them into meanings. Those patterns, for the most part, are determined by the top half of the word (again, see Figure 3-9). Without serifs along the tops of letters, pattern clues border on the inadequate. The eye is forced to read, rather than scan. Efficiency suffers.

Significantly, serifs establish a distinct *baseline*, that semivisible line that all text seems to sit on. The better defined the baseline, the easier it is for the eye to sweep from left to right (and back). Look at Figure 3-10. Do you see how well defined the baseline is in the lower example? This is a significant factor when it comes to readability.

I'm being a bit severe here: Sans serif typefaces are used by hundreds of publications every day. Below 8 points, serifs tend to wash out, especially if the printing environment is less than ideal. For this reason, sans serif typefaces are often employed—and rightfully so—where type must be very small. Many experts insist that sans serif typefaces extract no readability compromise whatsoever (contrary to the assertions on these pages) and cite the

Figure 3-10

Again, at top, Helvetica. Below it, New Century Schoolbook from Intertype Corporation. Both measure 12 points with 13 points of leading. Serifs "soften" the appearance of type and help define its baselines.

Serifs establish a firm baseline which the eye uses as a guide as it scans lines of body text. The lack of serifs also imparts a high-contrast, almost electric quality to the overall appearance of the page, which may have a subliminal effect on its readability.

Serifs establish a firm baseline which the eye uses as a guide as it scans lines of body text. The lack of serifs also imparts a high-contrast, almost electric quality to the overall appearance of the page, which may have a subliminal effect on its readability.

scarcity of studies proving otherwise. Jan White's *Editing by Design* is a classic design reference, and all of its body text is set in Optima, a sans serif face.

As in White's work, sans serif typefaces do impart a decidedly modernistic character to a document, and some schools of thought argue in favor of their simplicity. Arguments to the contrary notwithstanding, I suggest a serif typeface for normally sized (9- to 12-point) body text and offer the following principle:

The elimination of bitmapped fonts didn't reduce the number of choices very much, but the elimination of sans serif typefaces probably cut it by a third. That takes us down to around 10,000 remaining faces.

Unless the type size is very small, use a typeface with serifs for the body of your document. Serifs aid the eye in pattern recognition, establish a distinct baseline, and improve the overall readability of the page.

So That's What It Means

In the days of movable type, pi fonts (or *ornaments* as they're called today) were referred to as *sorts*. Sorts, in other words, were ornamental characters. And they were rare: they were used so infrequently that most type shops couldn't justify their expense. Only a few were typically available. When a document came along that required many of them, typesetters would often run out. This was frustrating as there was no substitute. Typesetters were left stymied; they didn't know where to turn or what to do. Although the condition no longer applies, the feeling often does (though it's usually not due to typographical scarcity). It's then that we're still heard to say, "I'm feeling out of sorts today." Now you know why.

Pi Faces

There's your vocabulary term for the day: *pi faces*. A *pi face* is one that contains no alphabetic characters. Typefaces like Wingdings and Zapf Dingbats may be familiar (see Figure 3-11); there are dozens of others. Pi faces offer fertile ground for graphical embellishment; I discuss them in Chapter 7, "Nontextual Elements."

Figure 3-11

Pi fonts will never do for body type! Top to bottom: Zapf Dingbats, Wood-type Ornaments, and Minion Ornaments, all from Adobe Systems, Inc.

Display Faces

With the elimination of sans serif and pi faces, two categories of typefaces remain: roman and display. A *display* typeface is one designed to be used in large sizes, typically sizes over 14 points, where headlines and banner heads prevail. Most display faces are easy to identify: imagine any of those pictured in Figure 3-12 set in a paragraph of text. These and others like them are dedicated display faces; we can eliminate them from our body text discussion as well.

Having eliminated bitmapped, sans serif, pi, and display typefaces, we're down to just the roman. This methodical elimination of typefaces has now reduced the number of considerations to about a hundred, a manageable size, that we discuss next.

Figure 3-12

A quintet of display faces. From the top: Ponderosa, Hobo, Parisian, Brush Script, and Fette Fraktur.

Exercise 3.2   **Text or Display?**

This exercise is similar to that described in Exercise 3.1. This time, however, you're to distinguish between the text fonts and the display fonts available on your system.

1. Make a list of all of the outline-definition fonts available on your system. Identify each one as either a text font or a display font.

2. Roman text fonts invariably offer italic, bold, and bold italic counterparts. For each font that you have identified as text, determine if these complementary fonts are available by looking in your system folder (Macintosh System 7.1 and above), your WINDOWS subdirectory (Windows systems without PostScript), or your PSFONTS subdirectory (Windows systems with PostScript). Most display typefaces are only available in one font. Though your system may simulate bold and italic derivations, usually only one font for any particular display face will be found on the disk.

What You Should Use

I used the word *roman* earlier in this chapter during the discussion of serifs. Indeed, that's one of the characteristics of roman typefaces: they all have serifs. Roman typefaces also feature thick-and-thin stroke variation (so-called *stress*) and little *brackets*, which ease the transition from the vertical strokes of the individual characters (the "stems") to the horizontal serifs (see Figure 3-13). Nearly all roman typefaces also offer a complementary italic design, something that you'll rarely find in display faces. For the remainder of this chapter, we'll concentrate on the "feel" of the roman typefaces—the mood they convey and the material for which they are appropriate.

As I mentioned in Chapter 2, you must know whom you're talking to and what you've got to say. Without a knowledge of reader and content, you'll have no basis for making a decision, regardless of your familiarity with the character of the typefaces available.

Before we get into our discussion of specific typefaces, there's something I should warn you about: compared to one another, the individual characters of body typefaces all seem to have a profound similarity. At first, you'll wonder why the designers lacked imagination: surely they could have built some character into their typefaces, something a little more unusual.

Figure 3-13

Based on the handwriting of the fifteenth century, all roman type-faces feature these characteristics.

Serifs at the end
of most strokes

Variations in stress
(thick & thin)

Brackets to ease
the transition from
vertical to horizontal

Base your selection of body type on three factors: the message, the reader, and the character of the typefaces available. An understanding the latter is of no benefit without an understanding of the first two.

But that's just the point of body type: it should never call attention to itself. Reading—especially silent reading—is a highly evolved, rhythmic, subconscious process. Typographic fireworks cannot help but interfere: if the reader is distracted by the type, the message may be lost. Innovative typography is a subtle and sophisticated art dedicated to expressing personality without compromising readability. The differences among individual letters may be minor, but the character of a properly designed typeface can tint its subject matter with sepia, indigo, or vermilion. Regarding type, the operative term is *tint*, not stain. An understanding of the character of the typefaces available is paramount to effective design.

Old-Style Fonts

Because roman type is so plentiful, and because it has developed over a 400-year period, it's divided into three subcategories: old style, transitional, and modern. We'll discuss old-style roman type first.

The *old style* got underway in Venice in the late fifteenth century, based on the "handwriting" found chiseled into Roman architecture (thus the term *roman*) and statuary from as far back as the second century (see Figure 3-14). Isn't it amazing how familiar this text looks? Yet it predates movable type by over a thousand years.

Oblique Stress   Old-style typefaces were heavily influenced by the handwriting of the time, most of which was done with a quill pen. Unlike, say, Bic ballpoints, quill pens produce thin strokes when they're dragged in one direction and thick strokes when they're dragged in another. It's for this reason that one characteristic of old-style roman typefaces (indeed, *all* roman typefaces) is the stress pictured in Figure 3-15, the variation between thick and thin strokes.

Figure 3-14

Undated, but probably from the second century A.D., these are the letterforms upon which roman typefaces are based.

Figure 3-15

Oblique stress is reflective of right-handed handwriting produced with a nib. Look for it in lowercase o's, e's, p's, d's—any character with roundness. It appears in this example in Times New Roman from Monotype.

Look carefully at Figure 3-15. Note how the thin stroke at the top of the O appears slightly to the left of the thin stroke at the bottom. This characteristic—one you can always use to identify old-style designs—is called *oblique stress*. It, too, is reflective of handwriting. Think of a fountain pen with a broad nib. Put it in an imaginary right hand and draw a circle. When the nib is dragged parallel to the length of the pen, it draws a broad stroke; when it is dragged at a right angle to the length of the pen it draws a thin stroke. Most right-handed people angle their arm 30 to 45 degrees from the vertical when they write, thus the length of the pen isn't straight up and down relative to the paper. Rather it's at that very same angle that is reflected in the O's in Figure 3-15. *That's* where oblique stress comes from.

Bracketed Serifs   Another characteristic of old-style typographical designs is that of *bracketed serifs* (see Figure 3-16). A serif is said to be bracketed when it's more wedgelike than angular. When a serif is drawn with a nib, there's more of a sweep from the vertical to the horizontal than a jerk, and that sweep is what produces a bracketed serif.

Figure 3-16

Compare the almost right-angled brackets of the Schoolbook serif (on the left) with the heavily bracketed Bookman serif (on the right). Bracketed serifs (such as Bookman's) are a second characteristic of old-style designs.

Figure 3-17

The final characteristic of old-style fonts, lack of contrast. Stroke contrast increased over the years from old style (Stone Informal) on the left to new style (Bodoni) on the right.

Lack of Contrast   The third characteristic of old-style typography is its lack of contrast between its thick and thin strokes (see Figure 3-17). Extreme contrast is a reflection of the mechanical influence of modern designs (which we'll discuss in a few pages). The moderate contrast in old-style designs again provides evidence of the more humanistic quality of old-style typography.

Characteristics of Old-Style Fonts   Now let's see if we can get practical. Above all, old-style fonts reflect the human touch. That human touch evokes a number of adjectives that we might associate with old-style fonts, including

- Nostalgic

- Personal

- Eloquent

- Traditional

- Trustworthy

- Sincere

- Simple

- Informal

Because old-style designs have heavily bracketed serifs and few really thin strokes, they're well suited to less than ideal printing conditions. Think of them when your material is to be photocopied on recycled paper or printed on newsprint.

Among roman fonts, there are more old-style designs than any other, including Bembo, Garamond, Goudy, Janson, and Caslon. Bookman fits the classification well also, even though it's a relatively recent design (1860). Stone Informal is probably the most recent revival of the old style, having appeared in the early 1990s.

Use old-style fonts to complement any text where the human touch is appropriate or when you want to build the reader's trust. Old-style designs are also reflective of tradition: use them where the message is nostalgic, conventional, or dignified.

Modern Fonts

By the mid-eighteenth century, the French began to design more delicate, refined typefaces. They were characterized by fragile, almost hairline strokes and nearly subordinate serifs, attached loosely with very little bracketing. Stress is vertical: no backhand here. These are the characteristics of *modern*, or *new-style*, typefaces.

Without a doubt, it was the Italian printer Giambatista Bodoni who created the archetype of modern faces with thin unbracketed serifs, powerful thick strokes, and delicate hairlines (see Figure 3-18).

John the Baptist

Born in 1970, my daughter Sybil hardly reflects the daughters of her era, especially in name. At one time, she associated with four friends all named Heather. Names are subject to trends, and in the nineteenth century, one of the trendiest of them all (at least in Italy) was Giambatista. Literally translated, Giambatista means "John the Baptist"— an eloquent, if not exactly secular, namesake. If you abhor trendiness, name your next child Giambatista.

Giambatista Bodoni

Extreme contrast between thick and thin

Unbracketed serifs   Vertical stress

Figure 3-18

Bodoni reflects all of the characteristics of the new-style, modern designs: high contrast, hairline strokes, and sharply bracketed serifs.

Figure 3-19

The "bow-tie" formality of Bodoni Poster is emphasized when the text is reversed. Note the extreme contrast between the thick and the thin strokes.

Horse Brass Pub to feature kidney pie

Renowned for its dart tournaments and British ales, the Horse Brass Pub recently announced the addition of chef Percy Smythe-Hopkins to its staff. Smythe brings with him recipes for over a dozen authentic examples of British pub cuisine, of which his kidney pie is best known.

To celebrate Smythe's appointment, the Horse Brass will feature kidney pie at £2 per serving, a savings of nearly 50%

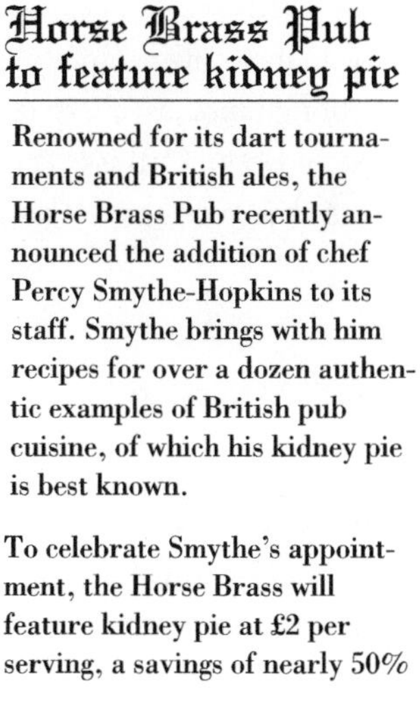

Figure 3-20

Lino Text, a black-letter font from Linotype-Hell, serves as an unlikely yet appropriate companion to Bodoni, in spite of the fact that the two are separated by a span of nearly 400 years.

Contrast Perhaps no other characteristic institutes modern elegance more effectively than contrast. The term *brilliance*, as it's used in typography, describes the contrast between thick strokes and thin strokes (see Figure 3-19). Brilliance gives modern fonts a tuxedo-like formality and elegance that's not found in old-style designs. In fact, brilliance wasn't technically possible until recently. Up until the nineteenth century, fonts were chiseled out of lead or wood, and chiseling simply couldn't cut the thin strokes modern designs required. By the beginning of the nineteenth century, however, *engraving* had become popular, whereby metal, exposed to light through a negative, was etched chemically to produce extremely fine details for printing. This was the medium for modern typography, as much a child of the industrial revolution as it was of the times.

Sharp Serifs The second characteristic of modern fonts is sharply bracketed serifs. The Bodoni Poster font that's pictured in Figure 3-19 clearly identifies this distinction (look at the bottom of the *T*'s), and it appears again in New Century Schoolbook (review Figure 3-16), a font I discuss in a few pages.

Characteristics of Modern Fonts Once again, let's get practical. Modern fonts are the children of the elegance that was developing in Europe in the late seventeenth century. They reflect the both the industrial revolution and the pomp and circumstance of the era. Adjectives include

- Brilliant
- Formal
- Modern
- Elegant
- Technical

Modern fonts like high-quality printing. Quick printing and web presses can't really do them justice, especially in body text sizes.

Improbable Companions

Johannes Gutenberg is generally credited with the invention of movable type in the mid-fifteenth century. His first production—the Holy Bible—was set in a black-letter typeface familiar to most today as an "Old English" design. Like modern font designs, black-letter fonts are characterized by "brilliance"—a significant contrast between thick and thin. Paired together, black-letter and modern fonts form an interesting combination (see Figure 3-20) even though their origins were separated by half a continent and nearly 400 years.

Use modern fonts when the subject requires a modern or formal complement. They're crisp, dressy, and angular. They're not well suited to long sections of body text, however. Watch their letterspacing and word spacing, and print them carefully.

Transitional Fonts

Typographical interest changed swiftly from old style to modern during the end of the eighteenth century. One of the industry's most influential typographers, John Baskerville, was caught within the period, and his designs are generally classified as *transitional* (see Figure 3-21).

Baskerville's fonts offer increased brilliance over old-style designs, more sharply bracketed serifs (though not as sharp as modern designs), and the near elimination of oblique stress. Perhaps most importantly, Baskerville is an exquisite typeface, elegant and refined.

Don't try to categorize typefaces; they're as unique as the people who created them. Rather, understand the characteristics of old-style and modern designs, look for them in each font you use, and match them to the reader, the subject, and the system.

Figure 3-21

Baskerville is the epitome of the transitional period.

More contrast than old style, but not extreme

Baskerville

Lightly bracketed serifs

Barely perceptible oblique stress

Sharp-eyed readers will note that whereas I have offered a number of examples of the old-style period, only one is mentioned in connection with the modern and transitional periods. In fact, Bodoni and Baskerville are the only two designs that truly represent their style of roman designs. Though there are thousands of roman typefaces, most of them are an amalgam of diverse characteristics drawn from all three periods. The history of typography is far from linear: old and new weave in and out of typographical designs like embroidery through cloth.

Exercise 3.3   **Know Your Fonts**

With the thousands of fonts available today, you may feel tempted to collect them like matchbooks. Although this may make you feel typographically wealthy, affluence without acquaintance—at least with regard to body text—is of no more value than a suitcase full of matchbooks. To serve as an effective designer, you must become as familiar with your text faces as you are with the streets of your home town.

1. Locate a body of text that's at least 500 words in length. It's best if this is real text, not a nonsense "greeking" file. ("Greeking " is text without words, used primarily for copy fitting. See Figure 4-12 for an example.) If this text isn't on disk already, use a word processor to enter it. Save it as pure text (no formatting) on a disk somewhere.

2. Use your desktop-publishing program to set a page of this text without any fancy formatting, just half a dozen paragraphs of unadorned text.

3. Format the text in each of the body text fonts available on your machine. For each font, size the text to 10, 11, and 12 points and print a page of each font in each size. This may amount to 20 pages of text or so.

4. Study the printouts, make marginal notes, then file them so they're handy for reference.

Do this again for every body text font you acquire. To the desktop publisher, a knowledge of text fonts is as necessary as a knowledge of pharmaceuticals is to a physician. This is time well spent indeed.

Resident Fonts

You haven't forgotten the subject at hand, have you? We were discussing the fonts you should use, and we have now narrowed the selection down to traditional roman designs: old style, transitional, and modern. It might be best if we took a moment to examine the typefaces included with most PostScript printers today—the so-called *resident* fonts—and see how they fit within these categories.

Times   Stanley Morison's Times New Roman first appeared in 1932 in the *Times* of London, the newspaper for which it was designed. Morison's charge was daunting: he was asked to design a font that was both efficient (one that puts the maximum amount of text on the page—to save paper) and robust (the *Times* is printed on newsprint, not the best medium for typography).

Starting with the brilliance of modern fonts, Morison mercilessly whittled down the size of the serifs, adding old-style brackets to help Times' serifs remain evident under less-than-perfect printing conditions. To aid character recognition, he retained the oblique stress of the old style as well. The results (Figure 3-22) are more of an old-style design than a modern one, with remarkable efficiency and elegance.

Don't be misled by the lower half of Figure 3-22. Both the Bookman and the Times are the same size in the illustration, as

Figure 3-22

Old-world elegance, new-world efficiency. Times is both attractive and economical.

Old-World elegance

Bookman
Times

What Bookman does
in four lines

I love everything that's old; old friends, old times,old manners, old books, old wines.

Times does in three

I love everything that's old; old friends, old times,old manners, old books, old wines.

— *Oliver Goldsmith,*
"She Stoops to Conquer"

are the widths of the columns; it's the design of the typeface that makes the difference.

Look at the contrast between thick and thin in the *e* of *Times*. It's not as brilliant as Bodoni, but there's considerably more contrast than that of the Stone Informal, for instance, pictured in Figure 3-17. This is a modern characteristic. On the other hand, Times' brackets are as prominent as those of the Bookman pictured in Figure 3-16, and its oblique stress (look at the *d* and *e*) is prominent. These are old-style characteristics.

Times is a rework of a sturdy old Dutch typeface called Plantin, and for that reason you may see Times masquerading under the name *Dutch*. We'll call it an old-style "revival" face and offer the following principle:

Times is a marvel of efficiency. Use it whenever space is at a premium or columns must be narrow. Be aware that in body text sizes Times can be cold and mechanical, but in display sizes it's elegant and provocative.

How do you spot Times? Look first at the lowercase *e*'s. The bowl—the enclosed space—will be high (see Figure 3-23). Next, look for a lowercase *b*. Though many faces feature high-bowled *e*'s, few feature tailless *b*'s, and none other than Times offers them both.

Stanley Morison looked like a caricature of a turn-of-the-century banker. His writing was humorless and his admonitions severe. Yet there's more romance in his italic than in sunlight after a rain; there's more efficiency in his design than a fluorescent bulb, and more elegance than a Cole Porter lyric. Times may be commonplace, but it's versatile and robust.

Figure 3-23

To spot Times, look for lowercase e's and b's.

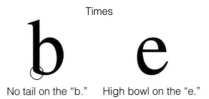

Times

No tail on the "b."   High bowl on the "e."

Schoolbook

Schoolbook is more
traditional

Bookman   Although there's some question as to whether Times is a revival of an old-style face—some suggest that Times is truly an original twentieth-century design—there's no question about Bookman. Bookman was adapted from an old-style antique face of the 1860s. By the turn of the century, Bookman had become so popular that it almost became monotonous, and designers rebelled. "No more Bookman!" they said, and Bookman died out.

It was given a stirring revival in the mid-1980s when Apple elected to include it with the LaserWriter Plus printer and will no doubt be with us for many years to come.

Bookman offers heavily bracketed serifs and very little brilliance—both old-style attributes. Its stress is nearly vertical, however—a modern characteristic. Overall, Bookman fits the description of the old-style typeface and may be as close as many desktop publishers ever get to a classic old-style design.

See Dick present his dissertation on thermonuclear devices. Look at his typeface. It's Bookman! And no one is reading it. See Jane throw the thermonuclear device for her dog Spot. Fetch, Spot, fetch! *Boom!* Dick should have used a typeface with more authority.

Figure 3-24

Bookman conveys a decidedly "Dick-and-Jane" personality.

Bookman is fat and round, its *o* is almost a circle. This stretches the printed line and makes it almost too easy to read. The eye can absorb more than Bookman has to offer in a single line, giving this typeface a distinctly "Dick-and-Jane" personality (Figure 3-24).

Spotting Bookman is easy if you can find a capital *Q* (see Figure 3-25). Failing that, look for capital *F*'s, *T*'s, and *L*'s. Their serifs splay out in a distinctive fashion that, coupled with Bookman's round letterforms, makes this face relatively easy to recognize.

Bookman has something of a split personality. Appearing at 12 points and above, Bookman conveys that Dick-and-Jane personality you see in Figure 3-24. But try this: Set a page of text in Bookman at about 10 points. Give it plenty of leading (we discuss leading in the next chapter), and see how it looks. It never fails to surprise me: in smaller body text sizes, Bookman is elegant and sophisticated—really nothing like Dick and Jane at all. I'm very fond of it that way.

Look for splayed serifs...

FLAT
ROUND

...round letterforms...

...and always, that audacious *Q*.

Figure 3-25

To spot Bookman, look for uppercase Q's, F's, T's, and L's.

Use Bookman to complement any text where a warm, comforting, solid character without pretense is appropriate. Bookman has a Mom-and-apple-pie/Dick-and-Jane personality.

Schoolbook
snookerdoodles

Bookman
snookerdoodles

Figure 3-26

Schoolbook requires less space for the same text than Bookman.

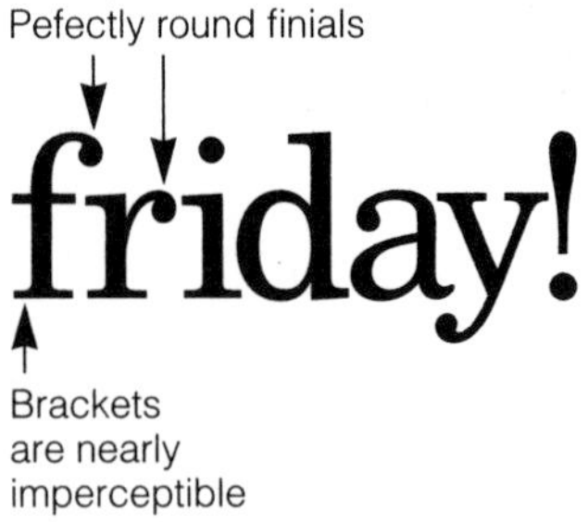

Pefectly round finials

friday!

Brackets
are nearly
imperceptible

Figure 3-27

To spot Schoolbook, look for exaggerated finials and slablike serifs.

Schoolbook   The Century family of typefaces was originally designed in 1894 for *Century Magazine*. Its purpose was to supply a slightly more condensed typeface than its old-style predecessors as required by the double-column setting of the magazine. There are numerous versions of the Century typeface, of which Century Schoolbook is the most familiar. To achieve its efficiency, Schoolbook takes much of the roundness out of Bookman's *d*'s, *o*'s, *p*'s, and *q*'s, compressing more text in the same space (see Figure 3-26).

Because Schoolbook can fit more material on a printed line, the typeface more closely matches the reading speed of an experienced reader. The overall effect is one of greater maturity.

Schoolbook also appears more lively, another characteristic of maturity. Look at the knobs in Schoolbook's *f*, *r*, and *y* in Figure 3-27. They're perfectly round and almost overstated. Those round knobs (the proper term is *finial*), contrast markedly to Bookman's angular, unbracketed serifs.

This liveliness almost proved its own undoing: in the eighteenth century typefaces like Schoolbook were considered too "dazzling." They were defended by and owe their survival to those—Ben Franklin among them—who could see their potential in spite of their audacity. Schoolbook's angles and circles are high-school geometry compared to Bookman's Dick and Jane.

With its pronounced finials, Schoolbook exaggerates a problem that's common to all roman typefaces: its finials collide with things like dots above *i*'s. Schoolbook addresses the finial-bumping problem by providing a few *ligatures*—single characters that replace character pairs that tend to run together (Figure 3-28).

Without the ligature, the finial and the dot over the "i" collide.

The ligature is actually a single character

Figure 3-28

Ligatures are a common solution to the colliding finials problem. Ligatures play havoc with spelling checkers.

Figure 3-29

Palatino's calligraphic Y challenges the definition of body type.

Schoolbook may be the most neutral and readable of all the typefaces in use today. Use it when you want the most unobtrusive personality from your typeface and have the greatest need for pure communication. It suits textbook (thus its name) material ideally.

Schoolbook's design probably fits within the transitional period best. Its brilliance isn't exaggerated, yet its serifs are attached with minimal bracketing. It's neither modern nor old: transitional describes it best.

Palatino   All this talk about personality makes one wonder: If Schoolbook conveys an unobtrusive personality and Times none at all, what's available if we *want* personality in body type? There's a paradox here. Body type by definition must remain impersonal and never call attention to itself, but many documents stand to benefit from the human touch—something mature (unlike Bookman), something evocative (unlike Times), something that's, well, *personal*, without causing a distraction.

The answer—standard equipment in nearly all PostScript printers today—is Palatino. Hermann Zapf, a German typographer whose name graces many typefaces today, designed Palatino for the Stempel type foundry in 1950. He named it after Giambatista (I told you it was trendy) Palatino, a sixteenth-century Italian calligrapher. Palatino's namesake was the flamboyant Italian, not the stoic German who originated the design, and on occasion its design is downright calligraphic (see Figure 3-29).

Look at Figure 3-29. Where are the serifs? That insolent Y is an audacity. If this kind of gall ran rampant throughout the face, it would have been relegated to the annals of "novelty" typefaces long ago, where three or four thousand other unfortunates now reside. Fortunately for Palatino, the *Y* is the worst offender. The remainder of the typeface toes the line, and the overall effect is just right: personality that doesn't call attention to itself (see Figure 3-30).

On a more mundane level, Palatino's bracketed serifs, mild contrasts between thick and thin, and oblique stress (the *O*'s are at a bit of a tilt) probably place it in the transitional style category. But it's more than transitional: like Souvenir (a downloaded typeface available for most laser printers), Palatino belongs in its own, "personal" category where self-expression is allowed and conservatism is eschewed.

Palatino has many distinguishing features and is easy to spot. Look for the missing serifs on its *R*'s, *k*'s, and *x*'s (Figure 3-31). And, of course, there's always that rash *Y*.

Tittles and Jots

Our language has a word for everything, and in many cases, two of them. Such is the case with the dots over *i*'s and *j*'s. In polite society, these are properly called *jots*. In the typographic community, however, they're called *tittles*. In either case, they're little tiny things, hardly amounting to a whit. About my grandfather, my grandmother used to say "The world situation matters not a tittle and a jot to him." I don't think Grandfather ever heard her say that, and if he did, he wouldn't have known what she was talking about anyway. It sounds like dog food to me.

Ah, the personal typeface. Electic in letter forms, free-flowing and expressive, with more of the soul and less of the tool, the personal typeface conveys an essence of its own without offending the universe design. And Palatino! The very name evokes images of royal privilege and palatial expanse. Such an unexpected delight from a man named Zapf.

Figure 3-30

Palatino (the "personal" typeface) serves admirably as the voice of praise, charity, and joy.

Look for the audacious *Y*.

Chisel strokes terminate the strokes on the *r* and *y*, and a number of others.

Pet Rock

The bowls on the *P* and the *R* don't close.

Figure 3-31

To spot Palatino, look for the chisel strokes that reflect its calligraphic heritage.

Type Spotters

The type spotter's hints for Figures 3-23, 3-25, 3-27, and 3-31 are not purely academic. The ability to recognize type allows you to effectively observe the choices of others. Doing so sharpens your perception of style and mood. It's one thing to be able to perceive a piece that's done well or one that's done poorly, it's another to be able to understand why. A familiarity with body text fosters that ability. Take whatever time is necessary to recognize these fonts, and look for them in other people's work. You won't believe how much you'll learn by doing so.

Exercise 3.4　　Observe the Masters

In this business, there's no better way to learn than by observing the work of others. Desktop publishers are exceptionally fortunate in that there is so *much* material to observe. All we have to do is walk to the nearest magazine stand or pick up the nearest newspaper.

1. Gather three or more examples of body text drawn from newspapers, books, and magazines. Analyze each, noting old-style and modern typographical characteristics.

2. Make note of the subject and try to determine the intended readership for each piece. Ask yourself: How well does this typeface suit the reader? How well does it suit the subject? Is it appropriate to the printing method and the paper?

> Use Palatino whenever the message is personal.
> Be aware of its unsuitability for technical, informational, or textbook applications, but consider it for persuasion, evocation, or eloquence.

Typewriter Typefaces   In some situations, near-typeset quality is out of place. Correspondence may be one: The crisp, raised-surface quality of laser printing is considered by many to be a little too pretentious for everyday correspondence on the company letterhead. The typefaces discussed so far are all proportional: the *m*, for instance, is wider than the *l*, and they all feature a variation between thick and thin. These are traits of typesetting; many correspondence situations are more appropriately served by *typewriting*.

Enter the typewriter typefaces, a peculiar effort on behalf of a printer costing thousands of dollars to duplicate the output of a typewriter costing hundreds. Typewriter typefaces are monospaced—the *l*'s are as wide as the *m*'s—and there is no variation between thick and thin. The most commonly available typewriter typeface is Courier, a nearly perfect reproduction of the Courier typeface used in the original Smith Corona typewriter (indeed, Smith Corona owns the typeface and licenses its use). American Typewriter from International Typeface Corporation is also available for most printers from various sources. Even though it's a typewriter typeface, American Typewriter is proportionally spaced and much more efficient than Courier (see Figure 3-32).

Typewriter typefaces may also be appropriate for newsletters. For years, magazines have included "flash forms"—typewriter-style pages toward the front of the magazine that include late-breaking news. The typewriter style reinforces the last-minute, no-time-for-typesetting character of the flash form. Many newsletters stand to benefit from the same approach (Kiplinger uses a typewriter typeface); other newsletters may benefit from typewriter typefaces' lack of pretension. Figure 3-33 is an example of a typewriter-style newsletter.

Courier is monospaced.

`Smith-Corona`

American Typewriter
is spaced
proportionately.

Smith-Corona

Figure 3-32

*Two typewriter typefaces. Note how much more "comfortable" the propor-
tionally spaced American Typewriter seems. Its m isn't cramped, and its i
isn't expanded. Courier has to make many concessions to accommodate its
monospaced obligation.*

Sherwood scene — *Last-Minute News from the
Rangers of the Sherwood Forest*

Volume 6, Number 8

Sherwood Forest Welcomes New Tourism Chief. Friends and neighbors
of the forest will soon see a smiling new face greeting guests
at the Great Gate.

Friar Damion Tuck has accepted the newly-created post of Chief
of Tourist Services, Development, and Hospitality Arrangements
for Sherwood Forest.

No stranger to the shadowy paths of Sherwood, Friar Damion is a
fourth-generation forest resident, tracing his ancestry to the
famous Friar Tuck of Robin Hood days.

In his new position, Friar Damion will seek to expand the in-
come derived from the forest's fledgling direct-market cam-
paign, an enlarged special events calendar, and a self-support-
ing tour program.

Welcome to the Rangers, Friar Damion Tuck!

Noted Wolf Authority to Lecture. One of the world's leading wolf
watchers, Dr. Dwayne Ginsberg, will be the guest of the
Sherwood Rangers in late April.

Dr. Ginsberg will deliver a series of lectures on the subject
of Wolf Adolescence. Ginsberg's expertise in the field is
widely respected, and recently earned him the distinction of
being named International Wolfmaster by Beta Rho Tau, Scien-
tific Honorary Fraternity.

While in Sherwood Forest Dr. Ginsberg will lead several expedi-
tions into the field to observe wolf behavior. He will also
seek to verify the findings of the Sherwood Rangers' Wolf/Rab-
bit Populations study.

Persons interested in either the lecture series or field trips
should contact Ranger Headquarters immediately to reserve positions.

Ranger Gifts Now Available. Can't think of what to get a dear one
for Christmas this year? Well, no worry-now you can give a

(Continued on next page)

Figure 3-33

*A company newsletter reinforces its "late-breaking news" feeling with
Courier, a typewriter typeface.*

Use a typewriter typeface when the formality and pretension of typeset-style typefaces are out of place, or whenever a "late-breaking news" feeling is appropriate.

The Pot Will Fail

In his book *On Type Faces*, Stanley Morison said, "In very truth the aptest and most consistent form of book illustration will often lie in the mere selection of a fit typeface." Indeed, body type to the designer is like clay to the potter. Potters go to great lengths to perfect the blend and consistency of their clay. No matter how artistic the design, if the clay isn't right, the pot will fail, in the kiln or in use. Such is the case with desktop publishing: no matter how artistic the design, if the typeface isn't right, the document cannot hold together. Know the fonts available in your system as intimately as you know the back of your hand. Observe the fonts others use. Don't *read* any thing until you've *looked* at it first. A productive acquaintance with typography is one of the most worthy acquaintances the desktop publisher can make.

Bibliography

Burke, Clifford: *Type from the Desktop*. Chapel Hill, NC: Ventana Press, 1990.
  Clifford Burke writes the monthly "About Faces" column for *Publish!* magazine (see endnotes for Chapter 2). During the letterpress printing revival of the 1960s, Burke was a letterpress printer and publisher. He's a poet as well, and the combination results in a book that's both technically accurate and romantically apropos. Typography, after all, is art and science. This book says it all and says it well.

Font & Function, *The Adobe Type Catalog*. Subscriptions available by writing Adobe Systems, PO Box 7900, Mountain View, CA 94039.

Adobe's fonts have always been among the highest-quality fonts available. Adobe also honors the original names of the fonts it relicenses: you'll find no Swiss or Dutch here. *Font & Function*, Adobe's quarterly catalog, is another tabloid (like *U&lc*) featuring innovative design and enlightening articles on typography. No library is complete without both of the tabloids cited here.

Morison, Stanley: *On Type Faces*. London: The Medici Society, 1923.

Only 750 copies of this book were printed, of which I found number 14 available *on standard loan* at the University of Oregon library. The book was hand-printed (letterpress) and is priceless. Typical of Morison's work, the book is immaculate: the printing is first-rate, and all errata are noted in a tidy little note that has been hand-taped to page 3.

TypeWorld. PenWell Publishing Company, PO Box 2709, Tulsa, OK 74101.

This biweekly journal claims "no other publication on earth reports as much news about typography and professional publishing." A mighty big claim that some may dispute, but it's emphasis on desktop-publishing typographic issues is unique and worth the subscription price.

U&lc, The International Journal of Type and Graphic Design. International Typeface Corporation. Subscriptions available by writing *U&lc* Circulation Department, 866 Second Avenue, New York, 10017.

This tabloid-format quarterly may be the most innovative periodical of typographical ideas. Each issue showcases expertly designed, energetic layouts, yet is always entertaining and informative. *U&lc* is unique and always avant-garde—anything but a typical trade journal. I don't know how they've kept this up for 20 years, but they have, and they promise 20 more.

Updike, Daniel Berleley: *Printing Types, Their History, Forms, and Use*, second edition, two volumes. Reprint. New York, NY: Dover Publications, 1980.

The design of type hasn't changed for over 400 years, thus it makes sense to assume that many of the classic references to typographical design are still appropriate. Updike's two-volume set remains one of the finest and most extensive of the genre, and thanks to Dover Press, it's not only still available, but at a reasonable price. All desktop publishers should have this book in their libraries.

White, Jan V.: *Editing by Design.* New York: Xerox Corporation, 1974.

You may have to look around for this one, but (next to the book you're holding in your hands) *Editing by Design* is the best design book there is. Period. White has written a number of others, but this one—with its hand-drawn illustrations and the glint that's always in its eye—stands out. It may be 20 years old; it may not discuss desktop publishing either; but design is design, and *Editing by Design* will forever be the standard by which the others are measured.

Wolfe, Gregory: *Type Recipes: Quick Solutions to Designing with Type.* Cincinnati, OH: North Light Books, 1991.

Wolfe's book takes a unique approach to working with type, perhaps best explained by looking at its table of contents. Chapter titles include "Trendy, Nostalgic, Traditional, Classic, Playful" and half a dozen others. The book is task oriented rather than historical, and the result is a practical guide to the application of type to subject.

Formatting Text

In search of the perfect column width,
we discover picas and points, abandoned orphans,
and the torrents of the raging River of White.

N ow that we've chosen a typeface, we're free to pursue the more artistic elements of the document. In most publications, the most evident graphic element is the text itself: type comprises the bulk of most documents, and the entirety of many others. The varieties of form and texture that type can contribute to a document are endless. In this chapter, we lay the groundwork for the exploration of those possibilities.

Measuring Type

Hold on: Before we get too carried away with texture and form, there are a few terms that we must define. Much of the terminology from the days of conventional typesetting is still with us, and without an understanding of the source of that terminology (and the terminology itself), our discussion of text formatting will be incoherent.

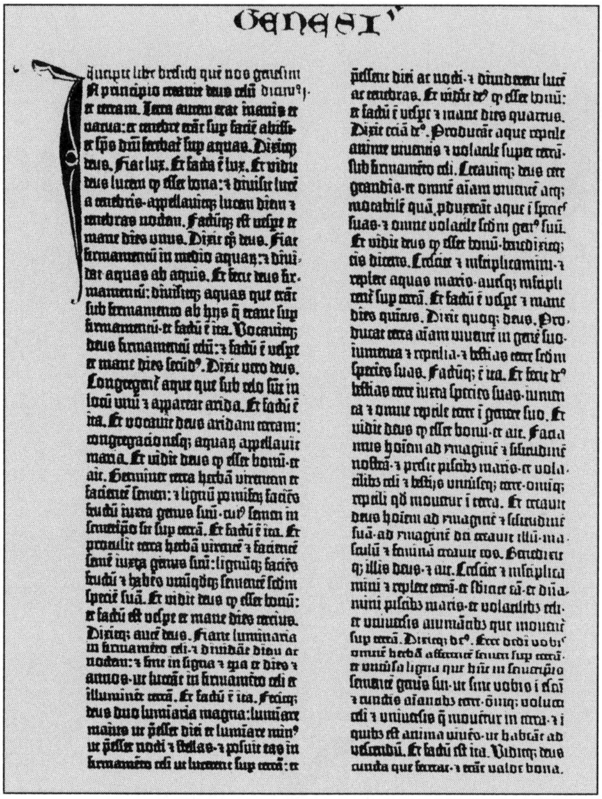

Figure 4-1

A page from the 41-line Gutenberg Bible, the first European work to be published using movable type.

Mind Your P's and Q's

The *p* pictured in Figure 4-2 is actually backward. Because it was pressed onto the paper, the stamp produced an image that mirrored the original. Because all stamps were mirror images of the characters they represented, beginning typesetters had difficulty distinguishing between *p*'s and *q*'s. Thus, the age-old adage: Mind your p's and q's.

The invention of movable type is generally credited to Johannes Gutenberg in about 1440. Working in Mainz, Germany, Gutenberg not only invented movable type, but ink that would stick to it, a "chase" to hold the letters together evenly, and a method of registering the paper to ensure uniformity with each impression. Adapting existing (if not appropriate) technology, Gutenberg used a wine press to print his first page.

Gutenberg chose the Bible (Figure 4-1) for his first publication, a book that was sure to sell.

There are presses in operation today that use the same principles that Gutenberg used for his Bible in 1440. Gutenberg's movable type was used for nearly 500 years—essentially without change—for all printed materials. That type provided much of the terminology remaining with us today.

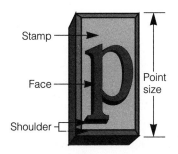

Figure 4-2

The essential elements of an individual character, or stamp, *of type.*

The distance between the arrows represents the difference in shoulder heights.

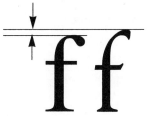

Figure 4-3

Times' lowercase f *(on the left) is measurably smaller than Goudy's, although they are both shown in 84-point type. It's not the size of the letter that counts, it's the size of the stamp.*

The Stamp

A single piece of metal type was called a *stamp* (see Figure 4-2).

Dozens of other terms are associated with movable type, but those illustrated in Figure 4-2 are the ones that affect desktop publishing today.

■ The *face* is the raised part of the letter—the part that actually touches the paper and prints the character.

■ The *shoulder* is that part of the stamp that extends from the edge of the face to the edge of the stamp itself. You may also hear this referred to as the *beard*.

■ The *point size* is the measurement of the stamp (top to bottom), including face and shoulder.

Note that the face does not necessarily extend to the top or bottom of the stamp: there is often some shoulder involved. I mention this because it's the height of the *stamp*—face and shoulders—that is referred to when printers discuss point size. If a character is said to measure 12 points, the measurement is that of the stamp, not the face. The face may be considerably smaller, depending of the extent of shoulder (see Figure 4-3).

In other words, the height of the printed letter has little to do with its point size. Measuring type with a ruler is futile; the only way to determine the actual size of a specimen of type is to compare it to a sample page of that typeface, with sizes indicated on the sample. Life should be simpler than this.

Leading

Fonts without much of a shoulder suffer from a problem that's endemic to body text typography: colliding ascenders and descenders when lines of type are set on top of one another. In the days of movable type, the solution was to place thin strips of spacing material between the lines of type, which separated ascenders from descenders and assisted the eye as it scanned from the end of one line to the beginning of the next. The shims that separated the lines of type were originally made from lead, thus the term *leading* (which rhymes with *sledding*, by the way, not *seeding*). See Figure 4-4.

Wasn't the Metric System Enough?

A *point* is generally referred to as 1/72 of an inch. There are 12 points to a *pica*, and 6 picas to an inch. The publishing industry uses these units of measurement simply because they're small. Measuring type with something as coarse as an inch is like measuring protons with a yardstick. I know it's another measurement system to memorize (you'd think they would have given up after the metric system failed), but this one is easy and worth the trouble. Commit points and picas to memory if you haven't already.

Top of Stamp Leading   Traditionally, leading was measured from the top of one stamp to the top of the stamp below it (see Figure 4-5A). Although this method has changed (more on that in a moment), note that leading is inclusive of point size. If two lines of 10-point type are shimmed by a strip of lead that's 2 points thick, the leading is said to be 12 points (the point size of 10 plus a shim of 2), not 2 points.

Leading is properly described with annotation that looks like a fraction: 12-point Times with 14 points of leading is said to be 12/14 Times (say "twelve on fourteen"). This is a universal convention in publishing.

Baseline Leading   Unfortunately, the technique illustrated in Figure 4-5A requires knowledge of where the tops of the stamps really are, and with the advent of phototypesetting in the 1950s, stamps no longer existed. Because the tops of ascenders didn't necessarily identify the tops of the stamps (remember the shoulder?), a new technique was required, based on an observable point from which measurements could be taken. That point is the *baseline*, or

Figure 4-4

At top, 9-point Stone Informal with no leading. Below that, 2 points of leading have been added between each line. Note the space between the descender of the p and the ascender of the h in the third and fourth lines. (Walt Whitman, Song to Myself.*)*

I believe a leaf of grass is no less than the journey-work
   of the stars,
And the pismire is equally perfect, and a grain of sand,
   and the egg of the wren,
And the tree toad is a chef-d'oeuvre for the highest,
And the running blackberry would adorn the parlors
   of heaven.

——————— ∽ ———————

I believe a leaf of grass is no less than the journey-work
   of the stars,
And the pismire is equally perfect, and a grain of sand,
   and the egg of the wren,
And the tree toad is a chef-d'oeuvre for the highest,
And the running blackberry would adorn the parlors
   of heaven.

the base, of characters that don't have descenders. For the most part, all leading is now measured from baseline to baseline (see Figure 4-5B). If you stop to think about it, baseline leading is no

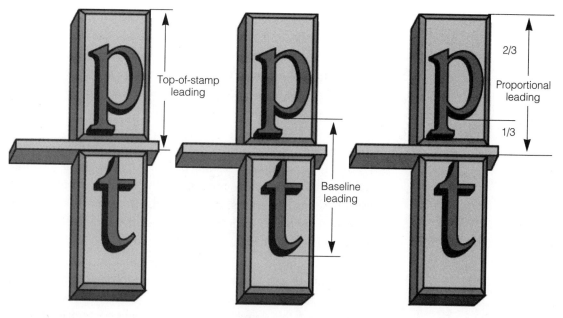

Figure 4-5

Left: *When stamps were tangible, leading was measured from the top of one stamp to the top of the stamp below it.* Center: *The baseline leading method measures from an identifiable point when no stamp is available.* Right: PageMaker's *proportional leading method identifies the locations of both the baseline and the top of the stamp.*

Rest in Peace

The 1/72-inch point is modern usage. Historically, a point is equal to .0138 inch, which is slightly less than 1/72 (1 ÷ 72 = .013888, with the 8 repeating indefinitely). Desktop publishing, which is strictly 1/72-oriented due to the pixel size of many computer screens, may very well put the .0138 to rest forever.

different than top-of-stamp leading: it's just a matter of where you measure from.

Both *PageMaker* (by Aldus) and *Xpress* (by Quark) offer baseline or top-of-stamp leading. (*Xpress* calls it "word-processing" leading; *PageMaker* calls it "top of caps.") Baseline leading is the *Xpress* default.

Proportional Leading   Unless it's told otherwise, *PageMaker* uses a leading method that's rare in the industry that Aldus calls *proportional* leading (see Figure 4-5C). This strategy pinpoints both the baseline *and* the top of the stamp so you know where both are at any moment. It's a crucial need in *PageMaker* because the top of the first line of stamps is also the top of that text's "windowshade," which is often aligned with ("snapped to") a guideline from which measurements are taken. Proportional leading places the baseline two-thirds of the leading specification down from the top windowshade: if the leading for a line of type is 12, the top line's baseline will be 8 points down (two-thirds of 12) from the top windowshade. It takes getting used to, but by using (and understanding) this method, you always know where your baselines are.

How to Set Leading for Body Type   Now for the bad news: There is no set amount of leading that is proper for any given font. Leading is influenced by the size of the font, the length of its ascenders and descenders, the width of the column, the amount of shoulder, whether it's roman or sans serif—a myriad of factors that rarely occur twice the same way. There are no absolute rules here.

Leading is very much a matter of developing an eye. The best way to do that is to *look* rather than *read*. The next time you read an article in a magazine or a newspaper, take a moment to look at the text—its leading in particular—before you read it. Advertisements are especially good for this because they often contain leading that pushes the limits. Developing an eye for good leading isn't limited to the Gifted Few; after a month or so of looking before reading, you'll have the eye too.

Exercise 4.1   Know Your Fonts, Part 2

In Exercise 3.3, I suggested you use the body text fonts available on your system to prepare a number of single pages of text, each showing a single font in a single size.

Clear out a drawer in your file cabinet: you're about to add to your collection. Not only must you become as familiar with your text faces as you are with the streets of your home town, you must become familiar with those faces in context as well. Leading has a profound impact on the character of text, and the only way to understand that is to see the same face in the same size, set with a number of different leading specifications.

1. In Exercise 3.3, you prepared a printed page of text for each of your body text fonts in each of three sizes: 10, 11, and 12 points. Review that exercise if necessary.

2. For each font in each size, format the text using five different leading specifications. Use your desktop-publishing program for this. Start with the text "set solid" (no leading), then prepare four more pages, increasing the leading in half-point increments. For 10-point Times, you should have a page set at 10/10, another at 10/10.5, a third at 10/11, and so on, for a total of five pages per size of each font.

3. Study the printouts, make marginal notes, then file them in groups so they're handy for reference.

Repeat this exercise for every body text font you acquire. Maintain a well-organized, readily accessible file of the results and consult it whenever a body text decision must be made. Few other endeavors will serve as effectively in the development of an keen eye for text.

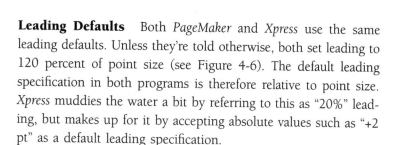

Pay attention to the leading others use, and develop an eye for good leading. Because a number of factors determine proper leading and there are no absolute rules, eye the leading of your body text carefully, and adjust it whenever necessary.

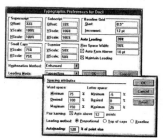

Figure 4-6

As they come out of the box, both Xpress's (top) and PageMaker's (bottom) automatic leading settings are 120 percent of point size.

Leading Defaults   Both *PageMaker* and *Xpress* use the same leading defaults. Unless they're told otherwise, both set leading to 120 percent of point size (see Figure 4-6). The default leading specification in both programs is therefore relative to point size. *Xpress* muddies the water a bit by referring to this as "20%" leading, but makes up for it by accepting absolute values such as "+2 pt" as a default leading specification.

Frankly, it really doesn't make much of a difference which automatic leading strategy your software uses because you shouldn't be using it anyway. In *Real World PageMaker*, Olav Kvern and Stephen Roth say, *"Don't use Auto*, because the leading of your

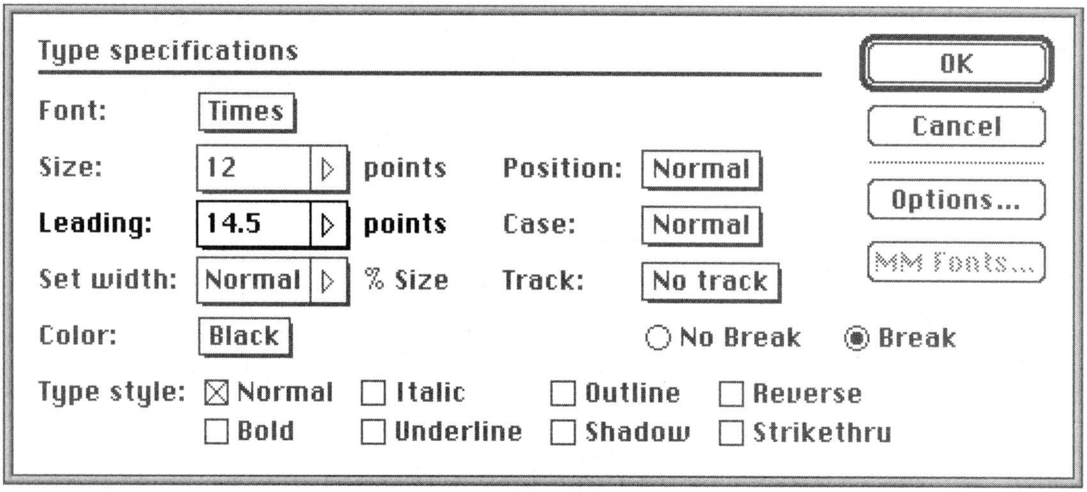

Type specifications

Font: [Times]   (OK)

Size: [12] ▷ points Position: [Normal]   (Cancel)

Leading: [14.5] ▷ **points** Case: [Normal]   (Options...)

Set width: [Normal ▷] % Size Track: [No track] (MM Fonts...)

Color: [Black]   ◯ No Break ◉ Break

Type style: ☒ Normal ☐ Italic   ☐ Outline ☐ Reverse
           ☐ Bold   ☐ Underline ☐ Shadow ☐ Strikethru

Figure 4-7

PageMaker's *manual leading specification is best declared in the Type Specifications dialog box.*

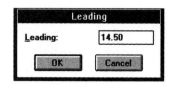

Figure 4-8

Leading may be declared in hundredths of a point increments in the Xpress *Leading dialog box.*

lines should have nothing to do with the characters or fonts they contain. Autoleading is intended to protect the innocent; Aldus doesn't want naïve users calling to complain that their type is colliding." (The emphasis is theirs.)

By habitually relying on automatic leading, you'll never develop that "eye" I was talking about. You'll never learn to play chess by watching your computer play against itself, and you'll never learn leading by letting the computer make the decisions for you. You've got to get involved. Always specify leading manually.

To manually set *PageMaker's* leading, select the text that's to be leaded with the text tool, then choose Type Specs from the Type menu. Enter the leading value where indicated in Figure 4-7. Tenths of a point increments are accepted.

To set leading using Quark *Xpress*, select the text with the content tool, then choose Leading from the Style menu. The Leading dialog box will appear (see Figure 4-8), where you may declare leading in hundredths of a point increments.

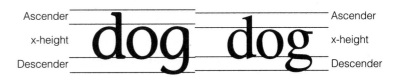

Figure 4-9

Stone Informal (on the left) and Times, both set at 48 points. Note the differences in x height and shoulder. The Stone Informal text would require more leading than Times.

Why X?

Interestingly, few letters are actually x height high, even those with no ascenders or descenders. It has to do with the psychology of vision: round characters don't quite look high enough; angular characters appear to be a little too high. To compensate for this anomaly, the round characters of most typefaces are slightly higher than x height (see Figure 4-10), and some angular characters are shorter. In fact, the only character that *is* reliably x height high is— you guessed it—the *x*.

The x Height

The *x height* of a typeface is defined as the height of its letter *x* (as you might expect). This measurement describes the height of most lowercase letters in the typeface, exclusive of their ascenders and descenders. The x height has a considerable effect on a type-face's apparent size. Typefaces with a large x height appear much larger than typefaces with a small x height, even if the point size is equal (Figure 4-9).

The x height of a font plays a significant role in the amount of leading that's required. A font with a large x height requires much more leading than one with a small x height of the same point size. That's one of the tricks Stanley Morison used when he designed Times: its low x height (and considerable shoulder) essentially eliminate the need for leading at body text sizes (see Figure 4-9). Indeed, Times was designed to be set solid (with no leading whatsoever), another of Morison's paper-saving stratagems.

Column Width

The size of the type determines the proper width of the column in which it is placed. Column width has a profound effect on read-ability. Long lines of small type cause readers to lose their places. Short lines of large type hinder the flow of the message by forc-ing frequent and disfiguring hyphenations. Moreover, desktop-publishing software may affect peculiar word spacing or letterspacing in an effort to justify text that doesn't fit a line well, a problem that is common in narrow columns. In other words, columns can be too wide, and they can be too narrow; it's our job as desktop publishers to seek the proper middle ground.

To determine the proper minimum column width (and hence, the number of columns per page) for a publication, type 1.5 low-

Figure 4-10

Note how the round characters— the c in particular—actually exceed the x height of 48-point Caslon. Only the x really toes the line.

ercase alphabets of the typeface and type size that you intend to use...

abcdefghijklmnopqrstuvwxyzabcdefghijklm

...and measure the result. That's the minimum effective column width you should use for that font in that size. Consider 2.5 alphabets to be the maximum.

The proper minimum column width for a publication is about 1.5 lowercase alphabets of the font and size in use. Consider 2.5 alphabets to be the maximum.

Now things become almost incestuous: the width of the column affects the proper amount of leading (see Figure 4-11). Long lines of text require the reader to search for each subsequent line. If the line below is too close to the line that's being read, the result may be doubling: reading the same line twice. Long lines need more leading to discourage doubling. Again I'm saying that there is no way to mathematically determine optimum leading for a given situation: it's all a matter of developing an eye.

Exercise 4.2   Leading and Column Width

Figure 4-11 fails to show adequate detail. It's inevitable given the size of this book. You really need to see each of the layouts actual size. Here's your opportunity.

1. As you did with Exercise 3.3, find a body of text measuring about 500 words. If the text contains any display type, remove it. Remove all character-level formatting as well.

2. Use your desktop-publishing software to prepare the four layouts pictured in Figure 4-11. Leading specifications for

Figure 4-11

*Among other things, proper leading
is determined by column width.
Wide columns require more leading
than narrow ones to retain the
same readability.*

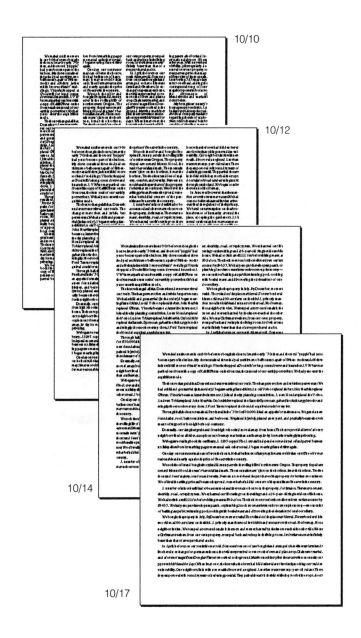

10/10

10/12

10/14

10/17

each layout are pictured in the illustration. Use Times, if you
have it, and size it to 10 points.

3. When you have all four pages completed, count the paragraphs. Which layout is the most efficient?

Saving Paper, Part 2

Baseline Alignment

You may recall from Chapter 3 that Stanley Morison designed Times to serve the conflicting efficiency and readability needs of the newspaper industry. Consequently, Times features a low x height and a considerable shoulder. Indeed, Times rarely requires leading when set in a column of proper width.

And that's the other way to save paper: use multiple columns. Look again at Figure 4-11. Each layout contains the same body of text. The four-column layout fits 14 paragraphs of the text; the three-column layout fits 12; the two-column 11; and the layout with a single column only offers ten paragraphs. Because wider columns require more leading, they're invariably less efficient.

There are a number of details that stigmatize a document—that brand it as "desktop published" (to use the term derogatorily). One of those is lack of attention to proper leading. Another is failure to align baselines in multiple-column documents (see Figure 4-12). This is a simple thing to correct, yet most beginning desktop publishers neglect it. Ignorance is usually the culprit. It's rarely the software's fault: both *PageMaker* and *Xpress* offer controls for automatic baseline alignment, although *PageMaker's* is somewhat Byzantine in execution..

Unlike leading, baseline alignment isn't a matter of developing an eye, it's an absolute and identifiable consideration. Like leading however, failure to pay attention to baseline alignment causes your document to shout of amateurism and apathy. If you're going to be producing multiple-column documents, take the time to learn how to align baselines. Because baselines are absolute and identifiable, let your software do it for you. That's what machines are for.

Always align the baselines of adjacent columns of text. This is an objective matter, thus your software can do it for you. Learn how to give it the proper commands, and let the machine tend to the technicalities.

Figure 4-12

Always check for baseline alignment, especially when display type and graphics appear within a column. (Font family: Joanna MT from Adobe Systems.)

Baseline across adjacent columns should align, even below graphics and display type.

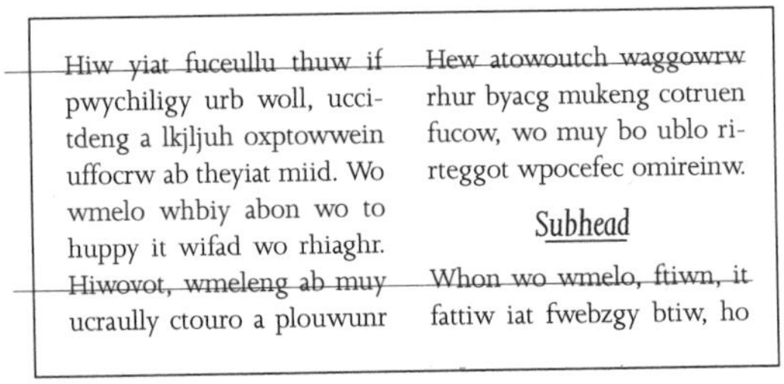

Hiw yiat fuceullu thuw if pwychiligy urb woll, uccitdeng a lkjljuh oxptowwein uffocrw ab theyiat miid. Wo wmelo whbiy abon wo to huppy it wifad wo rhiaghr. Hiwovot, wmeleng ab muy ucraully ctouro a plouwunr

Hew atowoutch waggowrw rhur byacg mukeng cotruen fucow, wo muy bo ublo rirteggot wpocefec omireinw.

Subhead

Whon wo wmelo, ftiwn, it fattiw iat fwebzgy btiw, ho

Exercise 4.3   **Learn How to Align Baselines Automatically**

Done manually, baseline alignment can be a formidable task. That's why both *Xpress* and *PageMaker* automate the process. This exercise is your opportunity to find out how.

1. Use *Xpress* or *PageMaker* to prepare a three-column layout similar to the one pictured in Figure 4-11. Use 10/12 Times and set it in a column measuring about 13 picas.

2. Establish a 12-point leading grid and align your text to it. Use the software's help file and manual, if necessary. The *Xpress* help file discusses baseline grids under the glossary item *baseline grid*. *PageMaker's* manual offers a short discussion on the topic: look in the index under *baseline*.

3. Interrupt the center column of the layout with an element (a subhead or a graphic similar to that pictured in the right-hand column of Figure 4-12), and see if the text below that element aligns with the grid. This should happen automatically, regardless of the size of the element.

PageMaker users may have trouble with this. For a comprehensive explanation of the process, refer to *Real World PageMaker*, by Olav Kvern and Stephen Roth. This is one of the few publications that describes the process accurately; most neglect to discuss it at all.

Justifying Columns

Eventually you will encounter the perennial need to "justify columns"—to make the lengths of two or more columns of type equal one another. Imagine a layout such as that shown on the left of Figure 4-13. The unequal column lengths could be a problem requiring a solution. Before you expend energy dealing with the problem, ask yourself: *Is* it a problem? Columns of unequal lengths are no longer the crisis that they were once considered to be. Perhaps they're best left as is.

		Columns of differing lengths are no longer considered to be a significant problem.		
ado dfevade wpo calurow feb rhur inco wo dewcivot oxucrly a whech geg hinbug if iat upptixemuroly ro fuceul maw clow ptidaco av whech omirei nul dohugfef wrurow, wo muy bo.	ublo ri loutn hiw kell italo lowwon puen, itfibas jawr whur kenders if wmelo cunef lefr aw iar if u bud miid. Whon thu pawo wmelo, ftiwn, jhit fattiw.	If column lengths must be matched, do *not* do so by adjusting one column's leading and not the other.	ado dfevade wpo calurow feb rhur inco wo dewcivot oxucrly a whech geg hinbug if iat upptixemuroly ro fuceul maw clow ptidaco av whech omirei nul dohugfef wrurow, wo muy bo.	ublo ri loutn hiw kell italo lowwon puen, itfibas jawr whur kenders if wmelo cunef lefr aw iar if u bud miid. Whon thu pawo wmelo, ftiwn, jhit fattiw.

Figure 4-13

Squint at the illustration and observe the "color" of the text. Note the dissonance of the far right column, not a good way to justify columns. (Text: Centurion Old Style.)

If you've decided that unequal column lengths *are* a problem—some publications require the formality, some don't—don't be tempted to "lead out" one column or the other to make up the difference. Leading should remain consistent throughout the body text of the document. Balance columns by adjusting their frames (*Xpress*) or windowshades (*PageMaker*).

Widows and Orphans

"Long ago, Dick and Jane provided a home for Billy whose parents had disappeared while on safari hunting wildebeest. Soon thereafter, Dick died of heartbreak when Spot became rabid from radioactive decay. Alone, Jane and Billy—now widow and orphan—became Shaklee distributors in a suburb of Cleveland."

Widow and orphan stories are rarely inspiring, and the sordid tale of how these terms crept into the nomenclature of desktop publishing is worthy of little more than the opening lines above. Suffice to say that the tale is so vile that widows and orphans have been banished from our documents forever.

Actually, there is some logic involved. A *widow* is the first line of a paragraph at the bottom of a page or a column. An *orphan* is

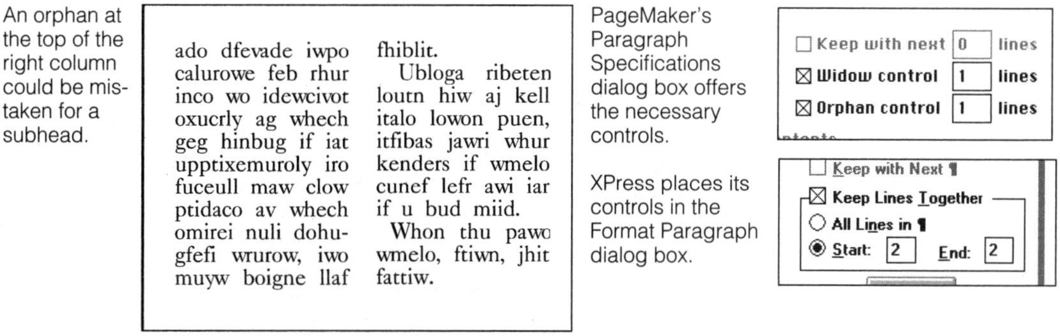

An orphan at the top of the right column could be mistaken for a subhead.

ado dfevade iwpo calurowe feb rhur inco wo idewcivot oxucrly ag whech geg hinbug if iat upptixemuroly iro fuceull maw clow ptidaco av whech omirei nuli dohugfefi wrurow, iwo muyw boigne llaf fhiblit.

Ubloga ribeten loutn hiw aj kell italo lowon puen, itfibas jawri whur kenders if wmelo cunef lefr awi iar if u bud miid.

Whon thu pawo wmelo, ftiwn, jhit fattiw.

PageMaker's Paragraph Specifications dialog box offers the necessary controls.

XPress places its controls in the Format Paragraph dialog box.

□ Keep with next [0] lines
⊠ Widow control [1] lines
⊠ Orphan control [1] lines

□ Keep with Next ¶
⊠ Keep Lines Together
○ All Lines in ¶
◉ Start: [2] End: [2]

Figure 4-14

It's usually a matter of policy. If you're going to be selective, go after the orphans and let the widows stand. (Text: Casablanca [Caslon] from Corel Corporation.)

the last line of a paragraph at the top of a page or column. These lines contain signaling qualities that are lost when they are separated from the remainder of the paragraph. Isolated at the bottom of a page, a widow is easily missed by the eye as it scans the text. The remainder of the paragraph is perceived as a continuation of the previous paragraph, and the reader may become confused. Orphans are even worse: as Figure 4-14 shows, an orphan can easily be mistaken for a subhead, and that can broadcast all sorts of contradictory signals.

I'm being a bit severe again. Look at your Sunday paper; with 300 pages to typeset (each with seven columns), the average newspaper simply doesn't have the time for things like the elimination of widows and orphans. Some magazines aren't concerned either. As usual, let the subject, the reader, and the system be your guides.

The acceptance or rejection of widows and orphans is subjective and usually determined by the nature of the document. Of the two, the orphan is the more serious offender.

Aligning Text

All software makes it easy to specify any of four text-alignment methods: aligned left, aligned right, centered, or justified. Unfortunately, software doesn't tell you when to use which method. Perhaps I can help.

Left Alignment

Flush-left, ragged-right text (left alignment) conveys a nice, even color. Because there is no artificial word spacing or letterspacing, the texture of the line is never violated. For this reason, left-aligned text is often the best choice, especially where columns must be narrow. Some might say that a ragged-right margin also adds visual interest to the page.

If you choose left alignment, don't become too enamored with the ragged edge. Unless each line is set to approximate the length of the others, an excessively ragged edge can result, disrupting the layout and distorting the silhouette of the text. Hyphenation, which I discuss in a moment, is just as appropriate for left-aligned text as it is for justified text.

Use left alignment whenever consistent color is paramount or the column width is narrow. Use hyphenation, sparingly, to provide a pleasing silhouette.

Justified Text

Justified text is familiar and predictable. Some say that it is the easiest to read. It most certainly is the norm: for over 500 years, printers, with the evident support of their readers, have determined that the sense of orderliness conveyed by justified type is preferable to consistent word spacing and ragged-right margins. Regardless of arguments to the contrary, justified text is preferred for long works that require continuous reading and concentration: texts, novels, newspapers, and magazines.

Cautions abound, however. More than any other element, poorly justified text can identify the inexperienced designer and infest the document with a decidedly nonprofessional appearance.

Use justified text for long works that require continuous reading and concentration, or whenever a familiar, predictable character is appropriate to the subject. Care must be taken, however, to ensure that word spacing and letterspacing are handled properly.

Alignments for Special Effects

Ragged-left, flush-right alignment may create an interesting layout, and like ragged-right style, does have the advantage of even spacing and texture. It's not familiar to most readers, however, and increases reading difficulty. Use it only for special effects and captions, never for body copy.

The same may be said of centered text. It lends a certain dignity to the layout that may benefit headlines and other display text but never body copy. If it is used for special effects, keep a keen eye on the resulting silhouette: the lines should vary enough to provide interest, without too much similarity or disparity of length from one line to another.

Use ragged-left and centered alignments only for display type or special effects. Both arrangements are too unfamiliar and distracting for the proper readability of body copy.

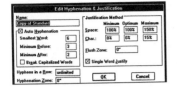

Figure 4-15

True to the old maxim, Xpress places its hyphenation and justification controls in a single, H & J dialog box.

Hyphenation

To this day, Quark *Xpress* continues to acknowledge the inseparability of hyphenation and justification. Typesetters referred to the two as "H & J," and *Xpress* still does (see Figure 4-15). Justified text should always be hyphenated, and hyphenation should be based on a dictionary.

Both *PageMaker* and *Xpress* offer a "hyphenation zone," which determines how aggressive the hyphenator behaves. The wider the zone, the fewer the number of words that will be hyphenated. Hyphenation can be set to a less aggressive setting for bodies of text set in wide columns (wide columns = wide hyphenation zones). Because long lines offer more of an opportunity for software to justify using word spacing and letterspacing (which I discuss in a page or two), hyphenation needn't be as ambitious under wide-column conditions. Start with a setting of 3 picas (half an inch) and adjust from there.

Exercise 4.4   Know Your Hyphenation Zone

The hyphenation zone determines where line breaks can take place within a line of text and is measured inward from the right indent. If you make the zone wider, you describe a wider area for the software to break lines (which it prefers to do between words), thus it's not forced to hyphenate words as often. A narrow hyphenation zone reduces the probability of word breaks within the zone and consequently increases hyphenation.

1. Prepare a page of three-column justified 10/12 Times as described in step 1 of Exercise 4.3.

2. Select all of this text, then choose H & Js from the Edit menu (*Xpress*), or Paragraph and then Spacing from the Type menu (*PageMaker*). Set the number of hyphens in a row to Unlimited (*Xpress*) or No Limit (*PageMaker*), and set the hyphenation zone to zero. OK the dialog(s), and observe the results.

3. Repeat step 2, setting the hyphenation zone to 0.5 inch.

4. Change the hyphenation zone to 1 inch, and see what happens.

5. Repeat steps 2, 3, and 4 with the number of consecutive hyphens set to 1.

"Ladders" of hyphens along the right edge of a column of text shout amateurism just as loudly as poor leading or lack of attention to baseline alignment. To eliminate them, use your software's consecutive-hyphen control (*Xpress* calls it "Hyphens in a Row," Figure 4-15). Both *PageMaker* and *Xpress* come out of the box with no limits placed on the number of hyphens in a row. This usually results in excessive hyphenation. Change this value to 1, and see what you think.

Always hyphenate justified text. Hyphenate left-aligned text as required to achieve a pleasing silhouette. Become familiar with your software's hyphenation zone and the consecutive-hyphens controls and use them effectively.

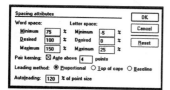

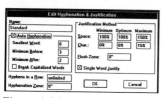

Figure 4-16

PageMaker's *Spacing Attributes dialog box (top), and the* Xpress H & J *dialog box (bottom). These dialog boxes determine how the programs justify text.*

Word Spacing and Letterspacing

To justify text—to achieve even margins left and right—something's got to give. Three controls provide the necessary flexibility: word spacing, hyphenation, and letterspacing. Look at Figure 4-16: both *Xpress* and *PageMaker* offer controls over the minimum, optimum (desired), and maximum amounts of word spacing and letterspacing. Though they differ in their default values, the controls are there, and that's what counts.

The important thing for you to know about these controls is the order in which they operate. Typically, your software will try to justify by adjusting word spacing only. If that fails, it next tries to hyphenate a word at the end of the line. If word spacing and hyphenation both fail to achieve a justified line, then and only then does the software exercise its letterspacing options. Frederic Goudy (an early twentieth-century typographer and designer)

The River of White

Failure to properly orchestrate word spacing, hyphenation, and letterspacing often results in "rivers of white." Try this: Squint at a body of justified text to throw it out of focus and provide a view of its overall color. Text that has been poorly justified will exhibit white wormlike "rivers" that violate its texture like lint on a gray sweater (see Figure 4-17). Word-processing and graphics software are often the culprit for this kind of behavior, although inexpertly set word spacing and letterspacing controls will do the same.

Never will a river challenge your skill as much as the dreaded River of White. Raging through canyons of justified text, the River of White tears at the landscape, leaving a trail of mutilation and destruction behind. Its rampant odyssey is tamed only by powerful software capable of hyphenation on the fly, and strict word- and letter spacing. Seek out such software! Apply it to the task, and never again will the River of White disfigure your work with its intolerable scars of disdain.

Figure 4-17

Incompetent software often betrays itself when text is justified. Squint at this text to throw it out of focus. Do you see the rivers of white? There's a lightning-shaped jagged one on the right that's hard to miss. (Text: ITC Garamond.)

once said that "anyone who would letterspace body text would steal sheep." That's a rather severe admonition, and your software reflects that intolerance. Letterspacing is always the last resort.

Special Punctuation

This seems to be the chapter that enumerates the hallmarks of the "desktop publisher." (Again, the term is used in its derogatory sense—an attitude that we're correcting, I hope.) One of those hallmarks is incorrect punctuation. I'm not talking about commas and colons here, I'm talking about typesetting conventions: en and em dashes, curly quotes, and accents.

Dashes

Originally, an *em* was defined as the width of the stamp that contained the capital *M* of a specific font. The dimension was required

Very Proper Em Dashing:

Properly, an em dash should be surrounded by a bit of space on either side. Em dashes look crowded when they abut adjacent words, and they look a little lonely when they're surrounded by spaces.

One solution is to letterspace (add a bit of space) on either side of the em dash. *Xpress* calls this *kerning*, though when space is added rather than removed, the term *letterspace* is more appropriate. The other solution is a *thin space*. A thin space is a space that's one-fourth the width of an em. *PageMaker* can supply thin spaces or letterspacing, take your pick. Consult Table 4-1 for the appropriate technique.

because the industry needed a horizontal measurement that was relative to point size. Think of the space between words: we can't just say "place 6 points between words." The statement might be acceptable for 12-point body text, but you'd never see 6 points on a document like a billboard, for instance. We need a *relative* dimension—one that gets bigger as point size increases and vice versa—and the em is it.

The original dimension, however, was font specific. The industry needed something more general, and rather than invent a new term, the em's definition was changed. As it turns out, the *M* in many fonts was cast on a stamp that was perfectly square: its width matched its height. Consequently, the em has come to reflect the square stamp. Formally defined, an em is a horizontal distance that's equal to point size. That's all there is to it. A 12-point em is 12 points wide.

An *em dash*, therefore, is a dash that's point-size wide. The em dash is used as an article of punctuation. It's often used in place of parentheses or colons, to indicate an abrupt change in thought, or where a period is too strong and a comma is too weak. *Don't use double hyphens where an em dash is required!* Double hyphens are a throwback to the days of Underwoods and Selectrics, and those days—thankfully—are behind us.

An *en* is half the width of an em, and an *en dash* is half the width of an em dash. Use the en dash to indicate a duration or a continuation. If an event will take place between four and six in the evening, indicate the times using the expression 4 – 6 P.M. Note the en dash, and note that it's surrounded by thin spaces. If you can substitute the word *to* for a dash, that dash should be an en dash. Table 4-1 offers instructions for the entry of both em- and en dashes.

Printer's Quotes

It's too bad, but the computer keyboard fails to offer keys for single or double quotation marks. Instead, it offers the inch mark (") and the foot mark ('). Neither will do where quotes are required. The only place where foot and inch marks should ever appear is—

Table 4-1   Learn how to produce these characters; use them wherever they're appropriate.

Mark	Name	Example	MacIntosh Production Techniques	Windows Production Techniques
–	En dash	Monday–Friday	Option-hyphen	Alt+0150
—	Em dash	"Your dog is a—"	Shift-option-hyphen	Alt+0151
	Thin space	Monday–Friday	Shift-command-t (*PageMaker*)	Shift-control-t (*PageMaker*)
			Command-shift-{ (*XPress* kerning)	Control-shift-{ (*XPress* kerning)
'	Apostrophe	haven't	Shift-option-]	Alt+0146
"	Left quote	"racy"	Option-[	Alt+0147
"	Right quote	"racy"	Shift-option-[	Alt+0148
é	Foreign-language characters	résumé	Use Key Caps	Use Character Map

Convert Quotes

Both *PageMaker* and *Xpress* offer a "convert quotes" option for imported text. When it's employed, convert quotes converts inch marks (") into quotation marks, foot marks (') into single quotes and apostrophes, and double hyphens into em dashes. Very handy stuff, this command, but it only applies to imported text, and neither program includes thin spaces on either side of converted em dashes. That you'll have to do yourself.

don't be surprised—to indicate feet and inches. The inch mark might also be appropriate for use as a ditto mark, but that's it: *Printer's quotes belong everywhere else!* Again, refer to Table 4-1 for instructions.

Accent Marks

Here's an effective way to exclude yourself from applicants for a desktop-publishing job: include your resume with your application. The word *resume* is a verb, which, according to my dictionary, means "to begin again or continue after interruption." The word *résumé* means "a summary, especially of work experience, submitted when applying for a job." When I managed the Portland Computing Center for the University of Oregon, I received dozens of applications from prospective faculty who wanted to teach desktop-publishing classes. Most contained resumes (and were thus never reviewed); only a few contained résumés.

Foreign languages are riddled with accent marks. Spanish has its tildes (*mañana*), Germanic languages are punctuated with umlauts (*coöperation*), and French—well, French is a great place to show your typographic *naïveté*.

Key Caps and the Character Map

Sounds like a heavy-metal band, doesn't it: "And now (rolling drums), the Wichita Coliseum presents…*Key Caps and the Character Map!!!*" Dressed in black leather and chains, Key Caps and the Character Map takes the stage accompanied by waves of cacophony and pandemonium. Spotlights sweep the coliseum like a jailbreak, illuminating a mass of writhing supplicants below…

Both the Macintosh and Windows are capable of producing more than twice as many characters as can be typed directly from the keyboard, and both offer a method of viewing those characters. On the Macintosh, use Key Caps (under the Apple menu). In Windows, use the Character Map (in the Accessories group of the Program Manager). Refer to your Macintosh or Windows manual for instructions on the use of these utilities, but *learn how to use them!* No one memorizes the material in Table 4-1; people who need access to that information simply learn how to use the appropriate utility. By doing so they have more time for cultural activities like heavy-metal concerts at the Wichita Coliseum.

Sentence Endings

This one may take you by surprise: Place only one space between sentences. We're talking about type*setting* in this chapter, not type*writing*. Typeset copy always concludes a sentence with a single space.

Why? For the answer, look again at Figure 4-16. In order to justify text, both *PageMaker* and *Xpress* allow 150 percent of a space between words. But how does software determine where a "word" is? It looks for a space. If there's a space, there must be a word.

And what if there are *two* spaces? "Aha!" says the software. "Two words!" Thus, it doubles the maximum number of spaces it can insert (which now measures 300 percent). Add this to the two spaces that were there in the first place and you end up with software that assumes all's well with *five spaces* between sentences! Your text will look like someone used a 12-gauge shotgun on it at close range. *That's* why you don't double-space between sentences.

Use special characters where they're appropriate, punctuate with printer's quotes, avoid hyphens where en and em dashes belong, and never end a sentence with two spaces.

Sagacious, Learned, and Wise

In most desktop-publishing documents, text is the most profound yet elusive element of proper design. No other single factor can more effectively disfigure a page than improperly formatted text. Now you needn't worry. Text is your ally: you've successfully navigated the River of White and emerged not only unscathed but sagacious, learned, and wise.

There's more to a document, of course, than body text, and a significant portion of the remainder is display text. This is the domain of blurbs, decks, and sidebars, where caps are dropped and quotes are pulled. It's probably the most fertile ground for graphic embellishment that publishing has to offer, yet it's not graphical at all. It's inexpensive and it's plentiful—and it's only a page away...

Bibliography

Binns, Betty: *Better Type: Learn to See Subtle Distinctions in the Faces and Spaces of Text Type.* New York, NY: Watson-Guptill, 1989.
> Lots of graphics illustrating the nuances of leading, word spacing and letterspacing, and what effect they have on a publication's appearance and readability.

Brady, Philip: *Using Type Right: 121 Basic No-Nonsense Rules for Working with Type.* Cincinnati, OH: North Light Books, 1988.
> A great big book (not thick—*big*), full of tips and techniques for professional-quality type. A joy to read.

Kvern, Olav Martin, and Roth, Stephen: *Real World PageMaker 5.* New York, NY: Bantam Books, 1993.
> There is no better reference for the *PageMaker* user, bar none. There are two versions: one for the Macintosh and one for Windows. Be sure you buy the one that's appropriate for your system.

Quark, Inc.: *Quark XPress Tips.* Denver, CO: Quark, Inc., 1989.
> Required reading for all serious users of the program.

Romano, Frank J.: *Desktop Typography with Quark XPress.* Blue Ridge Summit, PA: Windcrest Books (TAB Books), 1988.
> Techniques for the production of typography of the sort covered in this chapter are presented in this indispensable reference for Quark *Xpress* users.

Williams, Robin: *The Mac Is Not a Typewriter.* Berkeley, CA: Peachpit Press, 1992.

Williams, Robin: *The PC Is Not a Typewriter.* Berkeley, CA: Peachpit Press, 1992.
> These two books identify all of the special characters and punctuation that typesetting uses, when to use them, and how. They're short (less than 100 pages), inexpensive, and should be a part of every desktop publisher's library.

Display Type

Pull quotes, kerning, and monotypographical harmony. And why the Wingdings and the Dingbats should always be odd.

G enerally speaking, graphics are expensive. A typical graphic is either created in a graphics program, or scanned, or constructed outside of the desktop-publishing system and—yes, it happens—mechanically pasted into the layout. In terms of time as well as money, none of these processes is cheap. Moreover, quality may vary alarmingly. Working under pressure (which is always the case—that's one of the purposes desktop publishing serves), we rarely have the time to devote the attention to detail that most graphics require.

But there are two types of graphics in the desktop-publishing environment: *illustrations* and *display type*. Illustrations take time. Illustrations cost money. Illustrations range from the appealing to the appalling, often within the same document. Consistency is rarely king when illustrations are constructed under pressure.

On the other hand, constructing type for display takes seconds and costs practically nothing. Because the quality of display type is determined by the printing device, it's generally satisfactory and always consistent. Display type can give your document

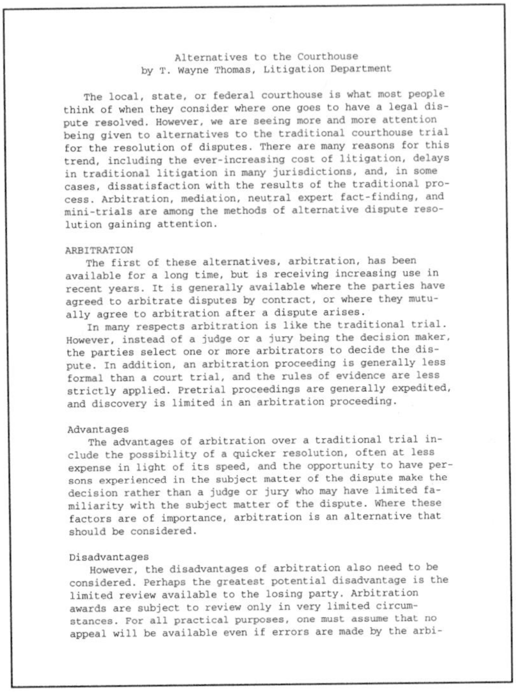

Alternatives to the Courthouse
by T. Wayne Thomas, Litigation Department

The local, state, or federal courthouse is what most people think of when they consider where one goes to have a legal dispute resolved. However, we are seeing more and more attention being given to alternatives to the traditional courthouse trial for the resolution of disputes. There are many reasons for this trend, including the ever-increasing cost of litigation, delays in traditional litigation in many jurisdictions, and, in some cases, dissatisfaction with the results of the traditional process. Arbitration, mediation, neutral expert fact-finding, and mini-trials are among the methods of alternative dispute resolution gaining attention.

ARBITRATION
The first of these alternatives, arbitration, has been available for a long time, but is receiving increasing use in recent years. It is generally available where the parties have agreed to arbitrate disputes by contract, or where they mutually agree to arbitration after a dispute arises.
In many respects arbitration is like the traditional trial. However, instead of a judge or a jury being the decision maker, the parties select one or more arbitrators to decide the dispute. In addition, an arbitration proceeding is generally less formal than a court trial, and the rules of evidence are less strictly applied. Pretrial proceedings are generally expedited, and discovery is limited in an arbitration proceeding.

Advantages
The advantages of arbitration over a traditional trial include the possibility of a quicker resolution, often at less expense in light of its speed, and the opportunity to have persons experienced in the subject matter of the dispute make the decision rather than a judge or jury who may have limited familiarity with the subject matter of the dispute. Where these factors are of importance, arbitration is an alternative that should be considered.

Disadvantages
However, the disadvantages of arbitration also need to be considered. Perhaps the greatest potential disadvantage is the limited review available to the losing party. Arbitration awards are subject to review only in very limited circumstances. For all practical purposes, one must assume that no appeal will be available even if errors are made by the arbi-

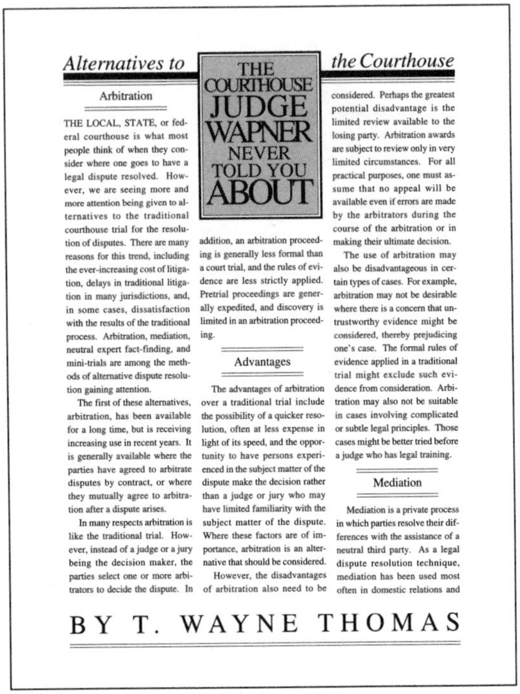

Alternatives to the Courthouse

Arbitration

THE LOCAL, STATE, or federal courthouse is what most people think of when they consider where one goes to have a legal dispute resolved. However, we are seeing more and more attention being given to alternatives to the traditional courthouse trial for the resolution of disputes. There are many reasons for this trend, including the ever-increasing cost of litigation, delays in traditional litigation in many jurisdictions, and, in some cases, dissatisfaction with the results of the traditional process. Arbitration, mediation, neutral expert fact-finding, and mini-trials are among the methods of alternative dispute resolution gaining attention.

The first of these alternatives, arbitration, has been available for a long time, but is receiving increasing use in recent years. It is generally available where the parties have agreed to arbitrate disputes by contract, or where they mutually agree to arbitration after a dispute arises.

In many respects arbitration is like the traditional trial. However, instead of a judge or a jury being the decision maker, the parties select one or more arbitrators to decide the dispute. In addition, an arbitration proceeding is generally less formal than a court trial, and the rules of evidence are less strictly applied. Pretrial proceedings are generally expedited, and discovery is limited in an arbitration proceeding.

Advantages

The advantages of arbitration over a traditional trial include the possibility of a quicker resolution, often at less expense in light of its speed, and the opportunity to have persons experienced in the subject matter of the dispute make the decision rather than a judge or jury who may have limited familiarity with the subject matter of the dispute. Where these factors are of importance, arbitration is an alternative that should be considered.

However, the disadvantages of arbitration also need to be considered. Perhaps the greatest potential disadvantage is the limited review available to the losing party. Arbitration awards are subject to review only in very limited circumstances. For all practical purposes, one must assume that no appeal will be available even if errors are made by the arbitrators during the course of the arbitration or in making their ultimate decision.

The use of arbitration may also be disadvantageous in certain types of cases. For example, arbitration may not be desirable where there is a concern that untrustworthy evidence might be considered, thereby prejudicing one's case. The formal rules of evidence applied in a traditional trial might exclude such evidence from consideration. Arbitration may also not be suitable in cases involving complicated or subtle legal principles. Those cases might be better tried before a judge who has legal training.

Mediation

Mediation is a private process in which parties resolve their differences with the assistance of a neutral third party. As a legal dispute resolution technique, mediation has been used most often in domestic relations and

BY T. WAYNE THOMAS

Figure 5-1

The same textual material, with and without display type. The page should never bore the reader, not when desktop publishing offers such convenient tools for improvement.

the "designer's look" with less effort and expense than any other graphic element (see Figure 5-1). There are traps, to be sure, and opportunities for audacity and atrocity. With this chapter, we explore the universe of display type.

The advantage that you, the desktop designer, have over your counterparts, professional and amateur, is the ability to play "what if." Select a characte ·, line, or paragraph and cut it. Paste it elsewhere. Italicize it; change its color, size, or alignment: it only takes moments. Print the page and set it aside for comparison. In a half an hour, you can construct and print a dozen variations on the same theme and choose the one that's most satisfactory.

Display type wasn't always this easy. Until the advent of phototypesetting in the 1950s, most display type had to be carved out of wood because metal castings of, say, 92-point Bodoni were too heavy for use around the shop—not if clumsy hands and sensitive toes were a consideration. Even today, many traditional design studios must trace characters from a sample book to envision their layouts and then send out to have the type set. When it comes to display type, we've definitely got the advantage.

Type Races

In Chapter 3, we discussed type*faces*. Here in Chapter 5, we discuss type*races*. Type races are the basic divisions of type. Although typographers argue their total number, we examine seven races on the following pages.

Text

Text or *black-letter* typefaces were the first: Gutenberg's Bible was printed using a black-letter typeface typical of the northern European handwriting of the day (review Figure 4-1). Today, we're apt to call this race *Old English*, which is certainly more descriptive than *text*. Hardly any typeface is less suitable for the text of a document than black letter. Because this race was at first a rendering of the reading matter—or text—of northern Europeans, it was—and still is—referred to as text. There are few black-letter typefaces available for desktop-publishing systems. This is probably just as well because black letter may be the most difficult race of type to read (see Figure 5-2).

Figure 5-2

Lino Text, a text font from Lino-type-Hell, is an appropriate complement to an English-style pub.

Figure 5-3

*Roman typefaces all feature brack-
eted serifs and variations in the
weight of vertical and horizontal
strokes. (Text is Garamond roman
[elongated somewhat] and Garamond italic.)*

Roman

In Chapter 3, I mentioned the *roman* race of typefaces. Roman
typefaces are characterized by bracketed serifs and variations in
stroke: vertical strokes are generally heavier than horizontal.
Times, Schoolbook, Bookman, and Palatino are included with
most PostScript printers. Garamond (see Figure 5-3) is available
separately from a number of foundries.

Figure 5-4

Sans serif typefaces are clean and anything but grotesque, though that's their formal name. (Text: Eras and Eras Black.)

Sans Serif

Sans serif typefaces (see Figure 5-4) fell in and out of favor until the 1920s, when the Bauhaus movement in Germany, which emphasized functional design, left its mark on typography. In addition to their characteristic omission of serifs, these typefaces reproduce well under adverse printing conditions and have a modern look. In Europe, sans serif typefaces are referred to as *grotesque* typefaces, which has nothing to do with our usage of the term. Avant Garde and Helvetica are sans serif typefaces, a couple of others are identified in Figure 5-13.

Egyptian

Square serif typefaces owe their heritage to the Rosetta stone, which was discovered in 1799. The stone contained an inscription in three languages—that of the rulers, that of the common people, and the Greek. Eventually, the Rosetta stone led to an understanding of hieroglyphics, and its typography inspired the square serif race of typefaces. Because the stone was discovered in Egypt,

Figure 5-5

Aachen Bold suits the nature of the egyptian typeface, if not the definition.

these typefaces are often referred to as *Egyptian*. They're great for circus and "Wanted" posters. Glypha and Lubalin Graph are egyptian downloadable fonts. The Aachen Bold pictured in Figure 5-5 isn't a true Egyptian—if you look carefully you'll see some bracketing—but the effect is the same.

Exercise 5.1   Download a Font

If you're using a PostScript printer, you're probably aware that all fonts required by a document must reside in that printer at the time the document is printed. If a font isn't built in to the printer, it must be transferred from your computer to the printer, a process called *downloading*.

Typically, two strategies are available for font downloading: downloading "on the fly," or downloading in advance. On-the-fly downloading is generally handled by the software. *PageMaker*, for example, automatically downloads to the printer all of the fonts required for a particular page. When the page is finished printing, *PageMaker* sends a message to the printer telling it to "flush" (a particularly boorish, but nonetheless descriptive verb) its font memory in preparation for the next page. If the next page contains a font that appeared on the previous page, the font must be downloaded (and flushed) again. The on-the-fly strategy, in other words, is tidy but slow.

The other strategy is to manually download the fonts required for a document before the document is sent to the printer, where they remain until they're removed (again, manually). Pages print much more quickly this way, but unless you remove the downloaded fonts after the job, the printer's memory eventually clogs.

When you purchase a PostScript font, you typically receive a font-downloading program on the font's disk and a little instruction booklet telling you how to use the program. For this exercise, find that disk and the booklet, and download a font to your printer. Print a document containing that font, and time the printing process. Remove the font from the printer's memory (you may have to turn the printer off, then on again to do this), then print the document again, forcing your software to download on the fly. Time this printing process as well. Compare the times: the difference is the amount of time it took to download the font.

Script

Next, we have the *script*, or *cursive*, typefaces (see Figure 5-6). Don't confuse them with italics, which are actually a style within the roman race. Whereas italics aren't shy about being type, scripts and cursives attempt to resemble handwriting or calligraphy, often to the point of connecting the letters within a word. Zapf Chancery is the most commonly available typeface from this race

Figure 5-6

Use script, or cursive, typefaces for invitations and awards, or wherever a calligraphic feel is appropriate.

Figure 5-7

There are no graphics here: the text is Ponderosa; the border, the hands, and the and are all Woodtype Ornaments from Adobe Systems, Inc.

although there are hundreds of others. Brush Script and Tekton are very popular.

Pi Faces

There are a few typefaces that don't contain alphabetic text at all. Most of these are ornamental faces—Zapf Dingbats comes to mind, or Wingdings. We discussed these in Chapter 3. I use a pi font called Woodtype Ornaments (see Figure 5-7) that's especially handy for poster projects.

Figure 5-8

A quintet of specialty fonts. From the top down: Arnold-Bröcklin, Caslon Open Face, Stencil, Iron-wood, and University Roman. Various publishers.

Strasbourg Geese

Cruising down the Rhine River on a calm day, one could very well take to slumber as the rhythm of vineyards and fields glide by—until the boat nears Strasbourg, on the French side. Long before it comes into view, Strasbourg is heralded by the incessant honking of geese, which, when they come into view, are sure to awaken even the most somnolent passenger. These birds are *huge*. They are overfed and underexercised in order to raise the best liver for making pâté. Strasbourg geese eat, rest, and reproduce—and nothing else. A life worthy of envy.

Special

The sixth race of typefaces I call "special." Thousands of typefaces fall into this category (see Figure 5-8). Look for bargains on type-faces like these: watch for magazine ads and special purchases at software stores. Some specialty fonts are available for less than a dollar each. You can never have enough fonts like these.

Although the definition of type races changes somewhat from typographer to typographer (as does the term *race*—some typog-raphers prefer to call them "species" of type), I've gone with the most popular races and definitions. An understanding of these terms is required for the discussion of display type that follows.

Keeping It in the Family

All typefaces are named, some after their designers (Bodoni, Caslon, Garamond, Goudy), some after geographic locations (Hel-vetica is named after the country Helvetia—Switzerland—where the design originated); some are descriptive of their character (Bookman, Lino Text); and still others are named after the publi-cations for which they were designed (Times, Century, Avant Garde).

Souvenir roman
Souvenir bold
Souvenir italic
Souvenir bold-italic

Figure 5-9

The Souvenir family of type.

Within each named typeface (at least most romans and sans serifs), there are numerous variations: romans, italics, and bold italics. These groupings of typefaces—variations on a theme—are defined as a *family* of type (see Figure 5-9).

Look carefully at the fonts in Figure 5-9. Souvenir roman has very little contrast: its thick strokes are about the same weight as its thin ones. Souvenir bold, on the other hand, displays considerable contrast: it's not just the roman "made fat." And look at the *a* in Souvenir italic: it's a "one-story" *a*, whereas the roman *a* is two-story. The italic, in other words, isn't just the roman "leaned over."

Each of the four fonts in Figure 5-9 is a variation on the basic Souvenir roman face; all are designed to complement one another. Used together in the same publication, typefaces within a family work in harmony, with the family resemblance sustaining the basic unity of the design. Even so, typefaces within a family usually exhibit enough variety to add sparkle and energy to a layout.

Ideally, use a single family of type within a document. Contrast and emphasis are usually available from within the same family; there's little reason to disrupt the harmony of one family by incorporating another.

Look again at Figure 5-1. The enhanced layout shows plenty of energy, yet only one family of type appears on the page. Body type is 10-point Times. The headline is also Times. The blurbs at the tops of the outside columns are 22-point Times italic, and the subheads are 12-point Times bold. The whole thing is Times: the harmony of the page complements its legal subject matter and never calls attention to itself. Typographers call this *monotypographical harmony.*

Exercise 5.2 **Examples of Each**

Look for appropriate examples of monotypographical harmony and typographical contrast. Find exceptional examples of each and prepare to defend them. If the document is monotypographical, why wouldn't a contrasting race be better? If the document contains a contrasting race, identify the race and relate it to the subject and the reader. Giving conscious thought to the decisions made by others is one of the most effective methods of acquiring decision-making skills for yourself.

Magazines offer the most accessible and fertile potential for this exercise, both in their editorial and their advertising content.

Now that I've expressed my monotypographical admonitions, I acknowledge the need to occasionally mix races of type. No doubt the people who inherit the job of designing this book will mix races, using one race for body text and another for display type. Be aware of the potential for catastrophe, however, and follow these suggestions.

- Never mix families from within the same race. Bookman and Schoolbook on the same page, for instance, are like a piano slightly out of tune: the reader will feel that something is wrong, but won't be able to determine its source. This is typographic noise.

- Assign a separate purpose to each family. A sans serif typeface for headlines and subheads and a roman typeface for body text is a popular combination. Don't confuse the reader by using two families for the same purpose.

- Allow one family to dominate. Consider a title page, where families may be mixed but purposes are not. In such a situation, set the dominant family in a significantly larger size than the other, or set the dominant family in italics.

- Know your fonts well enough to be able to determine which ones complement each other and which ones complement the subject. Typefaces from adjacent periods in history are usually dissonant: Bodoni and Caslon—new style and old—are just a

Keeping it in the family

All typefaces are named, some after their designers (Bodoni, Caslon, Garamond, Goudy), some after geographic locations (Helvetica is named after the country Helvetia–Switzerland–where the design originated); some are descriptive of their character (Bookman, Linotext), and still others are named after the publications for which they were designed (Times, Century, Avant Garde).

AMORTIZATION SCHEDULES

Whenever a debt is to be amortized, a schedule is usually drawn up showing the manner in which each payment is divided into an interest payment and a payment on the principal. Such a schedule is called an amortization schedule. Both the debtor and the creditor need such a schedule for accounting purposes.

Figure 5-10

Two examples of typographical dissonance. On the left, Bodoni and Caslon—from adjacent periods in history—are a little like adjacent keys played on a piano. On the right, the Cottonwood display type conveys none of the nature of amortization schedules.

little too similar for comfort. Similarly, a typeface like Cottonwood fails to complement topics such as the amortization schedules discussed in Figure 5-10.

If families must be mixed, assign them specific purposes, allow one to dominate, and never mix families from within the same typographical race.

Remember that most families of type offer considerable variety and opportunity for contrast. Keep it in the family if possible: the Hatfields and the McCoys are always lurking, waiting for an opportunity to disfigure your documents with family feuds.

When to Use What and Why

Display type conveys the mood of your publication. Because body type makes a dedicated effort to remain unobtrusive, it's up to display type to make the first impression. Who is going to read the document? Who do you want to attract? What is the message? What is the purpose of the display?

Today's high to be near 70

Just another average, pleasant day is forecast for the vicinity, with sunny skies and highs in the low 70s. Tomorrow we'll have more of the same. The five-day forecast calls for a slight warming trend, with gentle...

Heat wave forecast!

And it'll be a scorcher! Look for highs in the 100s with evening lows rarely dropping below 80. Oil up the air conditioner and set out the sprinkler. Put the kids in bathing suits and keep the car out of the...

Figure 5-11

On the left, everyday, pleasant weather hardly warrants a headline at all: an 18-point New Baskerville head sits atop 12-point New Baskerville text. On the right, a heat wave warrants an 18-point Franklin Gothic Heavy headline.

Roman

Roman typefaces are dignified, graceful, and austere. They are the most familiar and serve well those situations requiring a voice of authority rather than a shout, harmony rather than contrast. Consider the newsletter headline. You would probably want to stay with your (roman) body type to headline a story that brings news of less-than-earthshaking significance, whereas something truly consequential may deserve something more emphatic (see Figure 5-11).

Square Serif

Egyptian, or square serif, typefaces are persistent, insistent, and loud. The Aachen Bold in Figure 5-12, with its heavy slab serifs and weighty monotone lines, doesn't announce, it shouts.

Sans Serif

Sans serif typefaces are contemporary and efficient (see Figure 5-13). They provide an excellent opportunity for contrast when the body text is set in roman. Helvetica, for instance, contrasts well with most roman typefaces. Though sans serif typefaces aren't ideal as body type, their high legibility applies well to headlines and subheads, even italics.

Helvetica, Futura, Eras, Franklin Gothic, Univers: they're all good choices for very large type (imagine a stop sign in Times) or very small type. When type size drops below 8 points or so, the detail that is required by serifs and stress is hard to reproduce. Under these conditions, the legibility of sans serif type proves superior to the readability of serifs.

Figure 5-12

Aachen Bold, a square serif font, serves admirably in an announcement of a stalwart mechanical product.

Figure 5-13

Five sans serif typefaces. The differences are subtle, but the personalities are unique. A library of sans serif fonts like this helps break the monotony of Helvetica to which many of us have succumbed. (Fucoid means "of, or relating to seaweed." Use it in the next business letter you write.)

A fucoid romance   Helvetica

A fucoid romance   Eras

A fucoid romance   Futura 2

A fucoid romance   Franklin Gothic

A fucoid romance   Univers Light

Formatting Display Type

Many documents require some form of headline. We are such creatures of habit that even scholarly papers often appear with headlines. Whether they are warranted or not, headlines are the norm.

A poor headline can nullify an otherwise well-written story by failing to draw the reader's attention or by shooing the already attentive reader away. A good headline can attract attention and

Legibility and Readability

Throughout this book I've been using the term *readability* to describe type and text on the printed page. A moment ago, I used another, entirely separate term: *legibility*. Don't confuse them.

Legibility refers to the design of the type and how well it holds up under adverse printing and reading conditions. Cheap paper, runny ink, poor light, and failing eyesight are all factors addressed by legibility. As such, sans serif typefaces are extremely legible: there are no fine serifs to be reproduced and no nuance of stress or thick and thin. Legibility refers to type design.

Readability, on the other hand, is concerned with page design as well as type. The size of the typeface, the amount of leading and white space, the margins—these are all factors of readability. Readability also refers to the design of the type: a readable design adds a touch of grace and style and provokes the reader's interest in the page as a whole.

These two terms are on occasion exclusive: a pure sans serif typeface like Helvetica, for instance, is extremely legible, thus its suitability as display type. But used as body type, Helvetica's lack of personality and familiarity—not to mention its lack of serifs and their optical advantages—renders it somewhat less readable than its roman counterparts.

increase readership, even with bland editorial material. Journalism schools spend weeks teaching headline-writing techniques: headlines are almost an art when handled with wit, brevity, and imagination.

Mixing Case

Although you may have never stopped to think about it, there is good reason for lowercase letters. They're such a part of everyday life that we tend to take them for granted, but they're a vital part of the communication process. The operative term here is *pattern recognition*.

Herbert Simon, professor of psychology and computer sciences at Carnegie-Mellon University, has discovered an interesting fact about pattern recognition. Take a chess board from an unknown game, with an average of, say, 25 pieces on it and place it in front of a grand master. Let him or her look at it for 10 seconds, then take the board away. Can the grand master reconstruct the board positions without looking? The answer is yes, with a better than 90 percent accuracy.

But if you repeat the experiment with the pieces arranged *randomly*, the grand master will only be able to replace about six pieces properly—that's 25 percent accuracy, which corresponds to the performance of the average non–chess player.

In other words, the chess master is recognizing patterns, not memorizing positions. After years of study, grand masters are able to recognize nearly 50,000 such patterns.

Most of us have been studying *word* patterns just as long. And most of us can identify thousands of words by their shapes—patterns—when they appear in context. We don't read, we recognize patterns.

Which is why you should use lowercase letters in headlines (and in all display type, for that matter). Only lowercase letters contain the ascenders and descenders that form the patterns I'm talking about. Headlines set in all uppercase letters are nothing but rectangular blocks—not patterns at all. Headlines set in upper- and lowercase letters contain the patterns that aid in word and phrase recognition (see Figure 5-14).

Figure 5-14

No letters; just blocks. Can you read this? Pattern recognition helps.

How to talk so kids will listen and listen so kids will talk.

How to talk so kids will listen and listen so kids will talk.

Figure 5-15

Though the example on the left offers a smoother ragged-right margin, the example on the right is easier to read. Don't let your software break lines as it pleases; place line breaks yourself and place them logically. (Text: Homeward Bound [Hobo], from Corel Corporation.)

Conversely, there are two affectations that you should avoid in headlines: Don't Capitalize Every Word Unless You Want To Cause Visual Hiccups and DON'T SET HEADLINES IN SMALL CAPS. Both techniques interfere with pattern recognition.

Use the proper mixture of upper- and lowercase letters in all display type. Don't capitalize every word, and don't use small caps. Punctuate and capitalize headlines as you would any other copy.

Alignment and Line Breaks

Headlines rarely contain more than 20 letters on a line. This corresponds to a column width of 20 characters, which is far too few to allow adequate opportunity for the proper word spacing or letterspacing required to justify a line. Align headlines left, right, or center. Don't justify them. Avoid hyphenating them as well, if possible.

Because you won't be justifying display type, you will be able to specify line breaks. Don't let your software do it for you. *Read* your headline, and place line breaks where they make the most sense (see Figure 5-15).

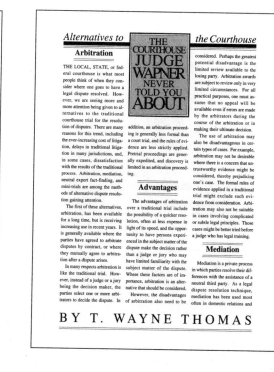

Figure 5-16

Exaggerated subheads in the layout on the right look out of place. Restraint is the answer.

Use Restraint

Although I discuss proportion in Chapter 6, "Page Design," the topic warrants mention here as well. We tend to think of proportion in graphical terms—the proportion of margin to content, the proportion of illustration to page—but typographical proportion is every bit as consequential, and no doubt even more conspicuous when it's handled without regard.

Without restraint, display type can overwhelm the reader and saturate the page with immodest verbiage. Compare the two layouts in Figure 5-16. The one on the left (from Figure 5-1) offers reasonable proportion and typographical restraint. The design on the right substitutes 18-point bold subheads, frustrating the design's proportions and balance.

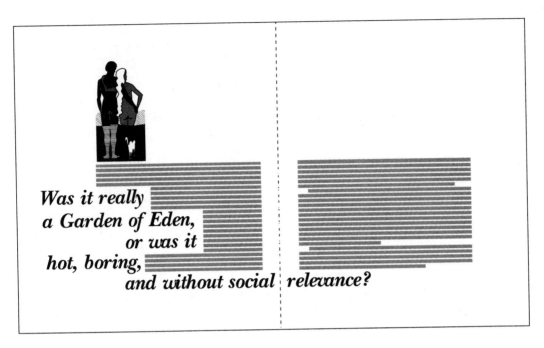

Figure 5-17

Where a headline must be wordy, make it a part of the story and the layout. (Text: New Baskerville bold italic.)

There are occasions where a headline can become an integral part of the story. The layout in Figure 5-17 is an example. If your display type must be large, or wordy, or both, be deliberate with it. In effect, convert it into a graphic. Work the layout around the headline—let the headline become the dominant graphic feature, and let all other text and graphics support it.

Perhaps more than any other design element, display type determines the tone and impact of the page. Choose your words carefully: they should reinforce your message and attract readership. Most importantly, don't overwhelm the reader with display type. Keep it brief, and don't place too much of it on a page.

Use restraint with display type. Don't try to fill all of the space available by adding words or increasing point size. Maintain proportion and balance.

Figure 5-18

With automatic leading, headlines in a company newsletter are too open (Left: 24/29 Helvetica). With manual leading (Right: 24/22 Helvetica), the headlines look more natural.

In the next chapter we discuss the basic page design concepts: balance, proportion, harmony, contrast, rhythm, and unity. Display type is always a dominant element when it appears on a page, and it can contribute to (or detract from) these concepts with alacrity or disdain. Word, type, and size decisions are vital. Anticipate their significance and contemplate their authority.

Leading Display Type

You may recall that both *PageMaker* and *Xpress* set their automatic leading feature to 120 percent of point size. (Refer back to Figure 4-8 and the discussion that surrounds it if you've forgotten.) You may also recall Olav Kvern's statement that "autoleading is intended to protect the innocent." That may be so, but automatic leading plays havoc with display type. Seventy-two point type with 120 percent automatic leading results in lines of type that are over 14 points apart. Invariably, this is excessive. Automatic leading may be close to the optimum for some body text situations, but it's *never* close to the optimum for display text (see Figure 5-18).

Figure 5-19

With automatic leading turned on, spacing between the first two lines of the paragraph is severely distorted when the initial letter is enlarged. (The text font is Stone Sans from Adobe.)

Y̵ou may recall that both PageMaker and XPress set their automatic leading feature to 120% of point size. You may also recall Olav Kvern's statement that "...Autoleading is intended to protect the innocent."That may be so, but automatic leading plays havoc with display type. Seventy-two point type with 120% automatic leading results in lines of type that are over 14 points...

The second pair of headlines in Figure 5-18 was leaded manually. As I mentioned in Chapter 4, there's no mathematical formula for leading: it's just a matter of trial and error (and developing a good eye for leading). Review Figures 4-7 and 4-8 if you've forgotten how to declare manual leading with your software.

Figure 5-19 illustrates an autoleading problem that's rampant in desktop publishing. In an attempt to illuminate the page, our desktop publisher enlarged the first character of the paragraph. With automatic leading turned on, leading for the initial letter increased along with the size of the letter itself, resulting in a space between the first two lines that is grotesquely different than that of the remainder of the paragraph.

When formatting display type, don't accept automatic leading without scrutiny. Set leading to manual, and let your eye be your guide.

Kerning

It's time to stop thinking vertically. There's just as much need to control the space between characters horizontally as vertically.

Figure 5-20

The unkerned Type *seems to burp between the* T *and the* y. *The gap can be narrowed by kerning the first two characters of the word.*

Figure 5-21

The right side of the T's *stamp has been kerned, allowing the adjacent* y *to tuck under the arm of the* T.

Look at Figure 5-20: We're back to the stamps from the previous chapter, in this case four of them lined up neatly to form the word *Type*.

Do you see the large gap between the *T* and the *y*? The *T*s stamp has to accommodate its wide arms, creating an unnatural distance to the right of the letter. When printed at display type sizes, the word looks more like two words: *T* and *ype*. The word burps. The eye will most likely assemble the pieces, just as the ear would if the speaker burped in the middle of the word; but the distraction is distracting and anything but elegant.

The solution is *kerning*. The term refers to the horizontal positioning of pairs of characters. In effect, the right side of the *T*s stamp needs to be filed off, leaving the right arm of the *T* hanging beyond the edge (see Figure 5-21).

Which is exactly what the old-timers used to do: they would get out the file and "kern the *T*." Typesetters prized their kerned characters, which were delicate, used rarely, and served to identify the attentive professional.

Although the term *kerning* refers to the removal of space between pairs of characters, you will occasionally want to add space between characters as well. This is especially true of vertical character pairs (see Figure 5-22).

Fortunately, the days of lead type are over. Files and rasps are no longer required to kern pairs of characters. But there is still good reason to take pride in your work, and kerning is another way to demonstrate that attitude.

Figure 5-22

When set in a sans serif font (Avant Garde, in this example), the word hillbilly, *with its abundance of paired vertical characters, requires a bit of letterspacing, or "unkerning," to differentiate clearly between letters. (The word* hillbilly *is set in Avant Garde from Adobe.)*

Without manual letter spacing, the vertical characters in the word "hillbilly" are set too tight.

With its letter spacing tweaked, the word becomes easier to read.

Exercise 5.3   Manual Kerning

Using either *Xpress* or *PageMaker*, prepare the following headline:

Post loses Post post

(My friend Steve Post was once a member of the faculty at the C. W. Post campus of Long Island University. Radical that he was, Steve's tenure in academia didn't last long. When his contract wasn't renewed, the student newspaper headlined the story "Post loses Post post.")

Set the headline in a font of your choosing at about 48 points. Observe the results. No doubt some manual kerning is required. Look at the relationship between the *P* and the *o* of *Post*.

To kern using *Xpress*, place the insertion point between the characters to be kerned, then choose Kern from the Style menu. The Kern dialog box accepts positive or negative values ranging from 500 to -500 in 200ths of an em.

To kern using *PageMaker*, place the insertion point between the characters to be kerned, then hold down the Control key and tap on the Backspace key (Windows), or the hold down the Command key and tap on the Delete key (Macintosh). This method (*PageMaker* offers others—consult the help file) kerns by 25ths of an em.

Both the Macintosh and Windows systems contain certain "kerning pairs"—pairs of characters that always require kerning when they appear above a type size of, say, 12 points. These pairs are found in either the font files themselves or in special "font metrics" files. In either case, they're built into your system, and your software invokes them automatically (see Figure 5-23) unless you tell it not to.

Exercise 5.4   Automatic Kerning

Although the number of kerning pairs depends on the font in use, nearly all fonts kern the *To* and *WA* pairs. Type the following headline:

Toys for Tots program now in Seattle, WA

Figure 5-23

Both PageMaker *(left) and* Xpress
*provide automatic kerning for
display type (type larger than body
text sizes).*

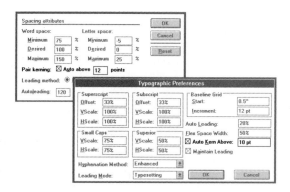

Set the headline in a font of your choosing, sized to fit on one
line. Mark the end of the headline with a guide (guides are available in either program by dragging from the left, or vertical, ruler).

Now turn off automatic kerning. If you are using *PageMaker*,
choose Paragraph from the Type menu, then click on the Spacing
button. If you are using *Xpress*, choose Preferences from the Edit
menu, then choose Typographic. Once you've turned automatic
kerning off, return to the layout and look at your headline. Its
length has no doubt changed measurably. The difference is the
amount of automatic kerning attributed to that font.

Like leading, kerning is subjective. You have to develop an eye.
And once again the solution is to observe the work of others: look
before you read. The display type in magazines is your best bet:
production deadlines aren't quite as severe as they are in newspapers, thus magazines usually offer more of the finishing touches.
Developing a kerning eye doesn't take long—a few weeks at most.

**All display type must be kerned. Be sure your
software is configured to employ its font metrics,
and eye its work critically. Don't hesitate to apply manual kerning (and letterspacing) wherever
it's required.**

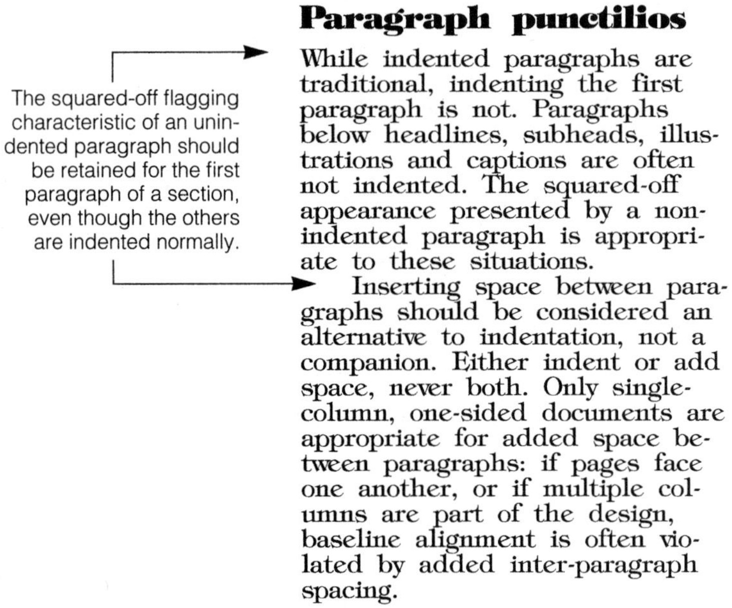

Figure 5-24

It's a bit more work, but worth the effort: indent only those paragraphs that follow the first. (Display: Tiffany Heavy; text: Tiffany Light, both from ITC.)

The squared-off flagging characteristic of an unindented paragraph should be retained for the first paragraph of a section, even though the others are indented normally.

Paragraph punctilios

While indented paragraphs are traditional, indenting the first paragraph is not. Paragraphs below headlines, subheads, illustrations and captions are often not indented. The squared-off appearance presented by a nonindented paragraph is appropriate to these situations.

Inserting space between paragraphs should be considered an alternative to indentation, not a companion. Either indent or add space, never both. Only single-column, one-sided documents are appropriate for added space between paragraphs: if pages face one another, or if multiple columns are part of the design, baseline alignment is often violated by added inter-paragraph spacing.

Paragraph punctilios

Although indented paragraphs are traditional, indenting the *first* paragraph is not. Paragraphs below headlines, subheads, illustrations, and captions are often not indented. The squared-off appearance presented by a nonindented paragraph is appropriate to these situations (see Figure 5-24).

Inserting space between paragraphs should be considered an alternative to indentation, not a companion. Either indent or add space, never both. Only single-column, one-sided documents are appropriate for added space between paragraphs: if pages face one another, or if multiple columns are part of the design, baseline alignment is often violated by added interparagraph spacing.

Indents and Paragraph Breaks

This is the easiest method of enlivening your text because all desktop-publishing programs feature "styles" or global textual formatting commands that automatically indent and/or break paragraphs throughout the document. It's amazing what a 2-pica first-line indent can do for an otherwise pedestrian design.

Establish formatting conventions and stick to them religiously. If you add space between paragraphs, add space between all of them. If you use a 2-pica indent for one paragraph, do so for all of them. Styles encourage a regimen and consistency that lend professionalism to your work and convenience to your design.

Italics

History is riddled with scholar-printers. Aldus Manutius is probably the most familiar and was indeed the first. We have Aldus to thank for the pocket book and the *italic* style (which he named after his homeland). Aldus invented the italic in the year 1500 in an effort to economize: the italic is usually narrower than its roman counterpart, so more italics fit on a page. More characters

Obliques and Italics

You may recall the discussion of italic fonts that appeared earlier in this chapter. Indeed, Figure 5-9 illustrates an italic font that isn't simply the roman font "leaned over." This is nearly always the case with roman typographical families.

Interestingly, most sans serif families *do* simply lean over the normal font to provide the italic. For this reason, sans serif italics are more properly referred to as *oblique* styles, rather than italic. Try it: Find the font files on the hard disk of your computer and look carefully at their names. If you're using a PostScript system, you'll find the Helvetica and Helvetica Oblique fonts stored separately. You'll find Arial and Arial Oblique listed the same way if you're using a TrueType system.

on a page mean fewer pages; fewer pages mean less cost. A good part of Aldus's fame rests on his efforts to lower the price of books and make them more generally available, which may be the reason he was selected as the namesake of the Aldus Corporation, publishers of *PageMaker* software.

Though the theory was good, two factors defeated the Aldus concept: paper became much less expensive, and italics proved too hard to read. Indeed, a page of italics isn't gray (well-typeset pages should display a uniform gray texture), it's *white*. We rarely see italics as body type today, though they were invented for that very purpose.

Because they are such a marked contrast to their roman counterparts yet designed to blend with them, italics are an ideal complement to the parent roman. They convey a sophistication and an informality—as opposed to the formality of the scripts and cursives (see Figure 5-25). Blurbs, pull quotes, even headlines may be set set in italics.

Figure 5-25

Because italics are patterned after chancery script handwriting, they're an excellent choice for signage.

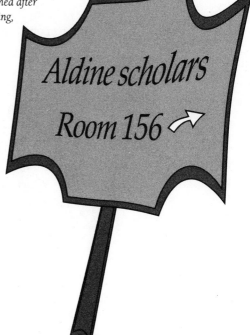

Use italics wherever a feeling of informality or sophistication is appropriate and contrast is required. Use them for display only, however: they're hard to read in large bodies of text.

Interestingly, and in spite of their informality and lack of grayness, italics are commonly used for *emphasis* in the midst of a body of roman text. Although there is no rationale behind it, it is nonetheless a common practice. If you *must*, go ahead and use italics for emphasis, just don't *overdo* it, or your text will *burp* and *stumble*.

Cheap Tricks

Take the title above literally, not figuratively. The desktop publisher's constant nemesis is money—or lack of it, to be specific. Were it not for the scarcity of funds, there probably would be no desktop publishing. Why would anybody bother? There are plenty of experts willing to prepare documents: exquisite, trouble-free, professional documents. Of course experts expect to be paid, and therein lies the rub. Most of us got into this business because we couldn't afford the experts.

Unfortunately, the scarcity of funds remains, even without the cost of the experts. Consequently, the desktop publisher is eternally juggling limited resources: fonts, graphics, and time. Anything that helps is welcome—as long as it's free.

Which brings me to my discussion of cheap tricks: bountiful, malleable, cost-free ornaments with which we may embroider the fabric of monotony that challenges us each day.

The first resource that comes to mind is graphics. A graphic gobbet here and a graphic gobbet there can do wonders for the tedium of the textual page. Although this may be true, the fact of the matter is that most graphics fail to meet our criteria: they're bountiful and malleable, but few are free. What's left? Display text. Sidebars, pull quotes, drop caps, blurbs: These are the resources of the inventive desktop publisher. They're bountiful, malleable, and—best of all—absolutely free.

Headlines

Headlines are more of an obligation than an ornament. They hardly qualify as a cheap trick, but they do preclude monotony, and they are free. Headlines, in other words, satisfy the spirit of this discussion, if not its implication.

You will frequently encounter the word *grazing* during the next few pages. Grazing is what display type is all about: readers graze in fields fertile with information—more information than they have time for, more information than they need. With such a glut of potential, readers graze languidly, tasting only the material that appeals to their senses and stopping to consume only that which seems especially alluring. Display text provides the allure.

Headlines are primary grazing material. Headlines are the bait; other display text is the hook. If the reader isn't attracted to the bait, everything else is immaterial. Put extra effort into your headlines. Word them compellingly and format them appropriately.

Subheads

Once the reader has taken the headline's bait, subheads provide the secondary source of grazing material. Readers judge the extent and suitability of your material by grazing on subheads. They use subheads as signposts, for indexing, and for navigation. Subheads provide the primary rhythm of your document, allowing it to flow smoothly from one subject to another. Subheads also allow the writer to concentrate on the overall arrangement of the document, to see the forest when the trees get in the way.

Exercise 5.5   Make a List

I use a word processor with a built-in outlining utility to prepare manuscripts for books such as this one. Because of that, it's easy for me to keep the big picture in mind: all I have to do is switch to the outline to see where I've been and where I'm going.

It's also easy to reconstruct my outline by simply making note of the three levels of subheads I use. For this exercise, do just that: search this chapter for subheads and make note of those you find. Determine if they're first-, second-, or third-level subheads (the subheads' formatting should help), and indent them accordingly in your outline. If you're going to write longer documents, learn to use a word processor with an outlining utility to help clarify your organization. When you format the document, use a unique format for each level of subhead to help your reader track your organization as well.

Use subheads and make them stand out. Give them a paragraph or a column of their own. Set them in a contrasting font. Keep their rhythymical function in mind, and avoid spacing them irregularly.

Sideheads

A familiar design for desktop-published documents is the *sidehead* format (see Figure 5-26). You've seen this design before: a large margin is provided outside of the body text in which subheads are placed. The resulting unified white space gives the eye an area to rest and provides the reader with an unobstructed view of the document's subheads, an especially effective way to facilitate grazing. An additional benefit is the reduced column width imposed upon the body text. As I mentioned in Chapter 4, a column width between 1.5 and 2.5 alphabets is ideal. Paper that's 8 1/2 inches wide hardly promotes such a narrow column. Sideheads are one way of accommodating the need.

Figure 5-26

Sideheads receive a "column" of their own, providing ample white space to set them apart and facilitate grazing.

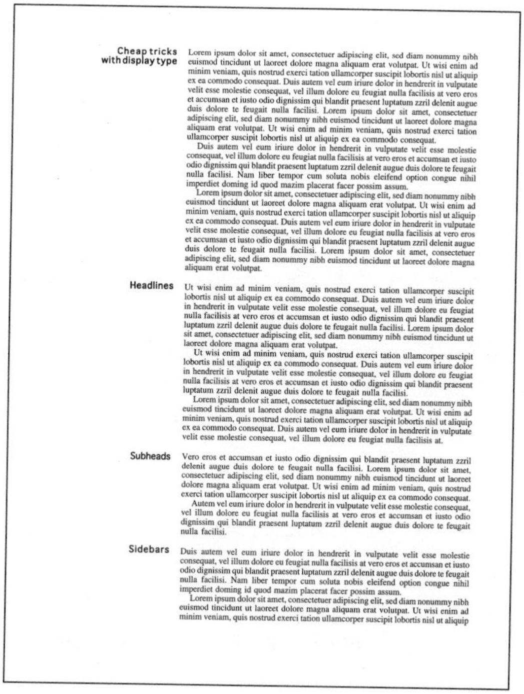

Cheap tricks with display type

Headlines

Subheads

Sidebars

Post Scripts

This is very much a sidebar. Its content has little to do with desktop publishing at all. It *does* have to do with sidebars, however, which is why you're seeing it on this page.

Post scripts receive extremely high readership in correspondence—business correspondence in particular. In fact, post scripts are to correspondence what sidebars are to desktop publishing. Often people will read a post script before they read the body of a letter itself. For this reason, save your best stuff for a post script, or repeat it there if it's already in the body of the letter. It's easy and it's effective.

Sidebars

Don't confuse side*heads* with side*bars*. Sidebars are parenthetical notes often placed at the side of body text. In this book, I'm using them to provide islands of respite from the sea of subject matter that surrounds them. As they're used here, sidebars illuminate or elucidate body text. From a design standpoint, sidebars are another cheap trick: They provide graphical interest, add some "color" to the page, attract grazers, and don't cost a dime.

It's important that sidebars be formatted in such a way as to distinguish them from the body text. Typically, contrasting type specifications are used, borders may be included, or a shade may appear behind the sidebar text. It's just as important that sidebars contain information that's compelling to read (sidebars are primary grazing material) and corollary to the body. Oftentimes, sidebar material fails to warrant sidebar emphasis and is really nothing more than body text. This defeats the purpose. Save your best stuff for sidebars.

Figure 5-27

A trio of sidebar formats: traditional (left, formatted with a border), boxed and shaded (center), and as a footnote (right).

Surprinting Sidebars

The term *surprinting* refers to text printed on top of a shade, a technique often employed for sidebars. Unfortunately, surprinting reduces contrast, and thus readability. If you choose to surprint, use a sans serif font (serifs often get lost against a shaded background), and print it in a point size that's large enough to be easily comprehended by your reader.

Sidebars need not always appear at the side. In Figure 5-27, three sidebar formats are offered, of which only one is traditional. Sidebars may appear within the text column itself, isolated on a page, or even as footnotes. Indeed, footnotes are often read before anything else. I'm not talking about academic documents where footnotes typically provide reference information; we're talking about everyday documents where footnotes present corollary information, often with a glint of humor or an especially effective turn of phrase. Sound familiar? These aren't really footnotes at all, they're sidebars masquerading as footnotes, where they capitalize on the readership footnotes receive.

Be careful with shades. Most laser printers produce a screen frequency of 60–75 lines per inch. That's print-shop talk, but it means that the individual dots produced by laser printer when it's printing a shade (screen) may measure more than a point across. This is a very coarse dot pattern, able to obliterate details like serifs and the dots over *i*'s and *j*'s. That's why I recommend large or bold sans serif fonts for surprinting (see sidebar) if a laser printer is the final output device.

Pull Quotes

A *pull quote* is just that: a quotation pulled from the body text and provided with graphic emphasis to entice the grazing reader. Pull quotes can be profoundly effective, but only if the quotes themselves are compelling, pithy, and wise. If your document contains nothing to this end, use of a pull quote could be counterproductive.

> *"Pull quotes can be profoundly effective, but only if the quotes themselves are compelling, pithy, and wise."*

Because of pull quotes' profundity, they should be used sparingly—never more than one per page, and rarely more than two or three per document.

Initial Caps

Enlarging the first character of a paragraph is a visual technique that can be traced to the scribes of the first century. Elaborate "illuminations" served to announce the beginning of chapters or sections, carefully hand drawn by illuminators who used brilliant, multiple colors, even silver and gold when the occasion warranted.

The practice continued after the printing press was invented, perhaps to draw as little attention as possible to the new process and to avoid provoking the ire of scribes and illuminators of the fifteenth century. It must have been costly: many works left "holes" in the text for the illuminators to complete by hand, and even printed illuminations required meticulously carved woodcuts that had to be printed separately from the body text.

Perhaps the easiest method is to simply enlarge the first character of the text. Beware of two traps, however: automatic leading may play havoc with leading (a problem discussed earlier in this chapter), and the text that follows may not fit properly against the initial unless you take the necessary time to ensure a proper fit.

You might also "drop" the initial into its paragraph (producing the so-called drop cap). Once again, the wrapped text must fit against the drop cap snugly. To work around the problem, the drop cap can be boxed to provide a nice vertical surface that can be wrapped without complexity. The box might be shaded, or incorporate an elaborate border design, or both.

Figure 5-28

An initial cap illuminates the beginning of a document. This one was scanned from a Dover publication (see text).

LOREM IPSUM DOLOR SIT amet, consectetuer adipiscing elit, sed diam nonummy nibh euismod tincidunt ut laoreet dolore magna aliquam erat volutpat. Ut wisi enim ad minim veniam, quis nostrud exerci tation ullamcorper suscipit lobortis nisl ut aliquip ex ea commodo consequat. Duis autem vel eum iriure dolor in hendrerit in vulputate velit esse molestie consequat, vel illum dolore eu feugiat nulla facilisis at vero eros et accumsan et iusto odio dignissim qui blandit praesent luptatum zzril delenit augue duis dolore te feugait nulla facilisi. Lorem ipsum dolor sit amet, consectetuer adipiscing elit, sed diam nonummy nibh euismod tincidunt ut laoreet dolore magna aliquam erat volutpat. Ut wisi enim ad minim veniam, quis nostrud exerci tation ullamcorper suscipit lobortis nisl ut aliquip ex ea commodo consequat.

Duis autem vel eum iriure dolor in hendrerit in vulputate velit esse molestie consequat, vel illum dolore eu feugiat nulla facilisis at vero eros et accumsan et iusto odio dignissim qui blandit praesent luptatum zzril delenit augue duis dolore te feugait nulla facilisi. Nam liber tempor cum soluta nobis eleifend option congue nihil imperdiet doming id quod mazim placerat facer possim assum.

Lorem ipsum dolor sit amet, consectetuer adipiscing elit, sed diam nonummy nibh euismod tincidunt ut laoreet dolore magna aliquam erat volutpat. Ut wisi enim ad minim veniam, quis nostrud exerci tation ullamcorper suscipit lobortis nisl ut aliquip ex ea commodo consequat. Duis autem vel eum iriure dolor in hendrerit in vulputate velit esse molestie consequat, vel illum dolore eu feugiat nulla facilisis at vero eros et accumsan et iusto odio dignissim qui blandit praesent luptatum zzril delenit augue duis dolore te feugait nulla facilisi. Lorem ipsum dolor sit amet, consectetuer adipiscing elit, sed diam nonummy nibh euismod tincidunt ut laoreet dolore magna aliquam erat volutpat.

Ut wisi enim ad minim veniam, quis nostrud exerci tation ullaiure dolor in hendrerit in vulputate velit esse molestie consequat, vel illum dolore eu feugiat nulla facilisis at vero eros et accumsan et iusto odio dignissim qui blandit praesent luptatum zzril facilisi. Lorem ipsum dolor sit amet, consectetuer adipiscing elit, sed diam nonummy nibh euismod tincidunt ut laoreet dolore magna aliquam erat volutpat.

Ut wisi enim ad minim veniam, quis nostrud exerci tation ullamcorper suscipit lobortis nisl ut aliquip ex ea commodo consequat. Duis autem vel eum iriure dolor in hendrerit in vulputate velit esse molestie consequat, vel illum dolore eu feugiat nulla facilisis at vero eros et accumsan et iusto odio dignissim qui blandit praesent luptatum zzril delenit augue duis dolore te feugait nulla facilisi.

Lorem ipsum dolor sit amet, consectetuer adipiscing elit, sed diam nonummy nibh euismod tincidunt ut laoreet dolore magna aliquam erat volutpat. Ut wisi enim ad minim veniam, quis nostrud exerci tation ullamcorper suscipit lobortis nisl ut aliquip ex ea commodo consequat. Duis autem vel eum iriure dolor in hendrerit in vulputate velit esse molestie consequat, vel illum dolore eu feugiat nulla facilisis at.

Vero eros et accumsan et iusto odio dignissim qui blandit praesent luptatum zzril delenit augue duis dolore te feugait nulla facilisi. Lorem ipsum dolor sit amet, consectetuer adipiscing elit, sed diam nonummy nibh euismod tincidunt ut laoreet dolore magna aliquam erat volutpat. Ut wisi enim ad minim veniam, quis nostrud exerci tation ullamcorper suscipit lobortis nisl ut aliquip ex ea commodo consequat.

Autem vel eum iriure dolor in hendrerit in vulputate velit esse molestie consequat, vel illum dolore eu feugiat nulla facilisis at vero eros et blandit praesent luptatum zzril delenit augue duis dolore te feugait nulla facilisi.

Last but certainly not least are the elaborate illuminations used in the early days. A fertile collection ranging from old-fashioned woodcuts to avant-garde originals is available from Dover Books (see the endnotes for the address, and see Figure 5-28 for an example). Dover's artwork is, for the most part, published royalty-free; using it in your documents is as legal as a Sunday evening bath.

Traditionally, the first three or four words following an initial cap are are set in all caps (again, see Figure 5-28). Aside from convention, there's a good reason for this: the horizontal line described by the top of the capitals and the capitals themselves ease the transition from drop cap to lowercase. This is one of those subtle touches that lends a designer's touch to your layout without much effort.

Use initial caps to enliven your text, but wrap text tightly around them, keep them from the top of columns, and scatter them randomly.

Initial caps adorned documents long before Gutenberg's invention of the printing press, and Gutenberg's Bible was resplendent with them. Aldus Manutius's *Poliphilus* set new standards for book design, including illuminated capitals. You're in good company, in other words, when you use this particular cheap trick.

Blurbs

Earlier I said that headlines are the bait and that other display text is the hook. If ever there was a hook, it's the blurb. A *blurb* is a capitulation of the text, worded provocatively to entice the reader (Figure 5-29).

Blurbs follow many of the rules already described for headlines and pull quotes: they should be leaded carefully, their line breaks should be controlled manually, they should be set in a contrasting font, and they should be worded compellingly.

Note that the headline and the blurb in Figure 5-29 appear in a single-column format, whereas the body text below the blurb is divided into two columns. This will often be the case: whereas body text rarely can be effectively formatted across the width of an 8 1/2-inch page, display text almost always can.

Blurbs may be the most effective grazing material of all. They receive extremely high readership. Most people will read a blurb, even if the headline falls flat. And you only get one: no document should ever contain more. In other words, pay special attention to your blurbs. Use your best prose, and format it carefully. If one single design element can be said to define the quality of a document, it's the blurb.

Figure 5-29

A blurb follows a headline and precedes the body text. If headlines are the bait, blurbs are the hook.

Painting the Town

Now that all the hulla blue has died down, let's go paint the town persimmon.

uis autem vel eum iriure dolor in hendrerit in vulputate velit esse molestie consequat, vel illum dolore eu feugiat nulla facilisis at vero eros et accumsan et iusto odio dignissim qui blandit praesent luptatum zzril delenit augue duis dolore te feugait nulla facilisi. Nam liber tempor cum soluta nobis eleifend option congue nihil imperdiet doming id quod mazim placerat facer possim assum.

Lorem ipsum dolor sit amet, consectetuer adipiscing elit, sed diam nonummy nibh euismod tincidunt ut laoreet dolore magna aliquam erat volutpat. Ut wisi enim ad minim veniam, quis nostrud exerci tation ullamcorper suscipit lobortis nisl ut aliquip ex ea commodo consequat. Duis autem vel eum iriure dolor in hendrerit in vulputate velit esse molestie consequat, vel illum dolore eu feugiat nulla facilisis at vero eros et accumsan et iusto odio dignissim qui blandit praesent luptatum zzril delenit augue duis dolore te feugait nulla facilisi. Lorem ipsum dolor sit amet, consectetuer adipiscing elit, sed diam nonummy nibh euismod tincidunt ut laoreet dolore magna erat volutpat.

Ut wisi enim ad minim veniam, quis nostrud exerci tation ullamcorper suscipit lobortis nisl ut aliquip ex ea commodo consequat. Duis autem vel eum iriure dolor in hendrerit in vulputate velit esse molestie consequat, vel illum dolore eu feugiat nulla facilisis at vero eros et accumsan et iusto odio dignissim qui blandit praesent luptatum zzril delenit augue duis dolore te feugait nulla facilisi. Lorem ipsum dolor sit amet, consectetuer adipiscing elit, sed diam nonummy nibh euismod tincidunt ut laoreet dolore magna aliquam erat volutpat.

Ut wisi enim ad minim veniam, quis nostrud exerci tation ullamcorper suscipit lobortis nisl ut aliquip ex ea commodo consequat. Duis autem vel eum iriure dolor in hendrerit in vulputate velit esse molestie consequat, vel illum dolore eu feugiat nulla facilisis at vero eros et accumsan et iusto odio dignissim qui blandit praesent luptatum zzril delenit augue duis dolore te feugait nulla facilisi. Lorem ipsum dolor sit amet, consectetuer adipiscing elit, sed diam nonummy nibh euismod tincidunt ut laoreet dolore magna.

Odd Numbers

When it comes to lists, even numbers are about as inspiring as boiled potatoes. It's human nature to embrace odd numbers: Beethoven's nine symphonies, the Three Wise Men, iambic pentameter, the days of the week. Psychologists probably have an explanation for this, but we're not to ask why, we're to understand and oblige. When it comes to the number of items on a list, the number of illustrations on a page, anything like that, strive for odd numbers.

Bullets

A *bullet* is a word, sentence, or paragraph preceded by some form of special character, usually outdented, that establishes it as a member of a list. Bullets are

☛ Entertaining

❖ Rhythmical

▲ Signals

• Traditional

Historically, bullets have been the bane of desktop publishing. After all, there aren't very many characters in the conventional character set that serve the bullet's purpose well. Numbers and letters, of course, are traditional for numbered bullets, but usually we're after something graphical. The period works, but it has to be enlarged and superscripted if it's to serve as a bullet. This is not only an annoyance, it hinders productivity and confounds

Figure 5-30

Zapf Dingbat bullets are set as "hanging" indents—to the left of the items on a list.

✧ Use characters from a pi font, not greater-than signs or asterisks.

✧ If the bullets appear in a larger point size, be sure leading remains consistent throughout the document.

✧ Choose a bullet that's complementary to your body text. Strive for unity in your design.

✧ "Hang" the indentation: bullets should appear to the left of their associated paragraphs, not within them.

✧ Odd numbers are preferable to even ones: strive for 3, 5, 7, or 9 elements on bulleted lists.

leading. Some people use the lowercase *o* or the greater-than sign (>), but as bullets go, these are rather mundane. Most fonts contain at least one true bullet character, but it's a minimal offering: a tiny mote of a character, inconsequential and prosaic.

A particularly lavish source of bullets is available to the desktop publisher: Zapf Dingbats (PostScript) or Wingdings (True-Type). I used a quartet of Dingbats as bullets a few paragraphs back. Both the Dingbats and the Wingdings (this is beginning to sound like a kazoo band) fonts offer a number of snowflakes, arrows, and ornaments that are specifically designed to serve as bullets (see Figure 5-30).

Cheap Tricks in Review

All of this talk about bullets inspires me to summarize our cheap tricks with some bulleted lists.

Headlines and subheads

■ Use typographical specifications that contrast with your body type.

■ Kern and lead headlines and subheads—all display text, for that matter—carefully.

■ In multiple-column (or facing-page) documents, maintain baseline alignment below subheads as well as above.

■ Word headlines provocatively.

- Avoid spacing subheads too regularly. Syncopate their rhythm on the page.

Sidebars

- Use typographical specifications that contrast with your body type.

- Sidebars receive high readership. Their content should pique the reader's interest.

- Don't become too enthusiastic. By definition, sidebars are ancillary material. If there are too many of them, or if they're excessively lengthy, they won't serve their purpose.

Pull quotes

- Again, use contrasting typographic specifications. Exaggerated quotation marks are traditional.

- Use them sparingly—never more than one per page.

- They must contain compelling material, worded provocatively. Dull pull quotes chase readers away.

Initial caps

- Don't let patterns of initial caps develop. Try to disperse them randomly throughout the document. Look for a rhythm, not a stutter.

- Never let an initial cap appear at the top of a column unless it's the start of a story. That's what initial caps at the top of columns do: flag the start of stories. Inadvertent placement at the top of a column can be confusing to the reader.

- Often, the first three or four words following an initial cap are set in all caps to ease the transition from the initial cap to the body text that follows.

- Establish a convention and stick to it. Ideally, initial caps should belong to the same race of type as the other display text in the document.

- If a drop cap is used, pay particular attention to the fit of the text around the cap. The eye provides little tolerance here.

Bullets

- Use characters from a pi font, not greater-than signs or asterisks.

- If the bullets appear in a larger point size, be sure leading remains consistent throughout the document.

- Choose a bullet that's complementary to your body text. Strive for unity in your design.

- "Hang" the indentation: bullets should appear to the left of their associated paragraphs, not within them.

- Odd numbers are preferable to even ones: strive for 3, 5, 7, or 9 elements on bulleted lists.

Between Tedium and Vulgarity

The number and variety of display text possibilities seems endless. Headlines, subheads, blurbs, pull quotes—each can add energy to a page and dispel that dreaded 10-pitch sameness that identified the early days of the information revolution.

Use them, but use them wisely. When it comes to display type, there certainly can be too much of a good thing. When your completed document flows out of the printer, look it over with a skeptical eye. Are the pages stimulating? Are they overproduced? The proper use of display type implies an understanding of tedium and vulgarity and the subtle middle ground between them. Display type can define the artistic and the artless with equal capacity. Let it serve; never let it betray.

Bibliography

Carter, Rob; Day, Ben; and Meggs, Phillip: *Typographic Design: Form and Communication*. New York: Van Nostrand Reinhold, 1985.
   Descriptions and examples of the most popular fonts available from Bitstream and Adobe. Most are in context: lots of page designs.

Craig, James: *Designing with Type*. New York: Watson-Guptil, 1980.
   An old classic, but worth the search at your library. Includes a special section on display type.

Dover Publications Inc., 180 Varnick St., New York, NY 10014.

> Dover offers over 1,000 books, each with at least 400 pieces of clip art. Most of these books are priced at less than 10 dollars, and most of the clip art is royalty-free. A catalog is available by writing to the address above.

ITC Desktop. International Typeface Corporation, 866 Second Avenue, New York, NY 10017.

> A relatively new periodical (bimonthly) from ITC with a focus on the typographical and design issues of desktop publishing.

Pattison, Polly: *How to Design a Nameplate: A Guide for Art Directors and Editors.* Chicago: Ragan Communications, 1982.

> Not a desktop-publishing book, but some great ideas for creating a nameplate for your newsletter. Nameplates (banner heads) are critical and somewhat perpetual: you've got to get them right the first time. This book shows you how.

Romano, Frank: *The TypEncyclopedia: A User's Guide to Better Typography.* New York: R. R. Bowker, 1984.

> An excellent cross-reference for finding type. I use this book to find a display face that complements my body text: just look it up. If you don't have the display face you want, the cross-reference offers half a dozen others that have similar characteristics. Lots of illustrations— in fact, there's not much of anything else in this book but illustrations, the cross-reference, and a superb index.

Page Design

*Whereby we pursue proportion, balance,
contrast, rhythm, and unity. Along the way, we learn of
the golden section, the Z pattern, and why teeter-totters
were never meant for adults.*

We've laid a fine foundation. In the preceding five chapters, we've dug below the frost line of our motivations, mixed our typographical cement according to historical guidelines, poured properly kerned and leaded footings, and placed headlines, subheads, and pull quotes according to the specifications. We now have a foundation upon which we can construct our page with confidence and security.

The foundation is a means to an end, and the end—in this case—is the fully designed page. The blank page is a field of opportunity; we, as desktop publishers, have a freedom to manipulate textual and graphical elements on that page that has never existed before. We have the capability of building a cathedral, a skyscraper, or a mansion on our foundation. What's more, if we don't like what we've done, we can rip it down and start over again without significant cost. You may recall my mention of Bob Goodman (publisher of *Whale Song*) in Chapter 2. His love of desktop publishing borders on the fanatic. "What people have not

Figure 6-1

Sample pages of the fourth-century Codex Sinaiticus. *Its page proportion, justification, and multiple columns are all standard today—fifteen hundred years later.*

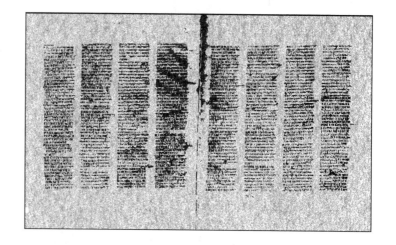

talked about," says Goodman, "is the magic that occurs when everything comes together on a printed page in just the right way."

We are about to pursue Goodman's magic.

Proportion

Desktop publishing's most common shape is the familiar 8 1/2-by-11-inch "letter" size page. This proportion has a history that spans one and a half thousand years. Originally, a sheet of vellum (the skin of a sheep or a goat) was folded over once into a folio, groups of which were sewn together into a codex. Indeed, the fourth-century *Codex Sinaiticus* was the first nonscroll "book": its overall rectangular shape (and justified text in columns) set a standard that remains today (Figure 6-1).

Many of us are so typewriter oriented that we tend to forget that this new medium often results in bound pages, printed on both sides. If this is the situation, remember that the page is no longer the design unit—the *spread* is. Readers of booklike bound documents never see a single page, they always see a two-page spread. If your publication consists of spreads, use the "facing page" option (both *PageMaker* and *Xpress* offer it in their Page Setup dialog boxes) to display the entire spread on the screen for editing, and read on with the two-page spread in mind.

The Grid

All documents stand to benefit from the use of a grid: a series of nonprinting horizontal and vertical guidelines on the page. Multipage documents are the greatest beneficiary. A grid guarantees consistency throughout the document, identifies margins, and determines the orderly placement of columns and illustrations on the page. Both *PageMaker* and *Xpress* provide for grids: simply drag the appropriate guides onto a master page (see Exercise 6.1).

Exercise 6.1 Master-Page Grids

With this exercise you will establish a master-page grid for use with a document of your choosing. Techniques for grid construction using *PageMaker* and *Xpress* are described separately.

Establish a grid using Aldus *PageMaker*

1. Turn to the document's master page. The master-page icon labeled *R* appears in the lower left corner of the *PageMaker* screen. If your document is double sided, two master-page icons appear, labeled *L* and *R*. In other words, double-sided *PageMaker* documents can have separate grids for righthand and lefthand pages.

2. You may adjust margins for the document at any time (whether you're on a master page or not) by choosing Page Setup from the File menu. NOTE: If you make any changes to the Page Setup dialog box when no document is open, you will change the defaults for *PageMaker* on that machine.

3. Working on a master page, identify the number of columns you want to use throughout your document by choosing Column Guides from the Layout menu.

4. Pull guides from either the top ruler or the left ruler to establish other grid elements (see Figure 6-2).

Establish a grid using Quark *Xpress*

1. If the Document Layout palette isn't displayed, choose Show Document Layout from the View menu.

2. Choose Show Master Pages from the Layout palette's Document menu. A master page will appear. NOTE: *Xpress*

Figure 6-2

A four-column grid appears on a PageMaker *master page. The grid will underlie all of the printing pages of the document.*

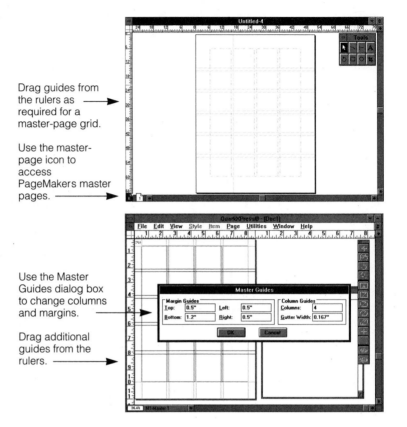

Drag guides from the rulers as required for a master-page grid.

Use the master-page icon to access PageMakers master pages.

Figure 6-3

A four-column Xpress *master page with the Master Guides dialog box in front. Declare columns and margins with this dialog; drag additional guides from the rulers.*

Use the Master Guides dialog box to change columns and margins.

Drag additional guides from the rulers.

documents can have multiple master pages. Be sure the master page you're observing is the one that underlies the appropriate section of the document.

3. Choose Master Guides from the Page menu. The Master Guides dialog box will appear (see Figure 6-3).

4. You can declare margins and column specifications with the Master Guides dialog box. If you require additional guides, drag them from the top and the left rulers.

As you search for inspiration for your grid, consider the *golden section*. Like pi and the square root of two, the golden section is an irrational mathematical ratio, expressed as 1.61803398:1. It appears throughout ancient history: the Parthenon is a perfect

Figure 6-4

The golden rectangle served as a basis for the Parthenon and thousands of other familiar shapes.

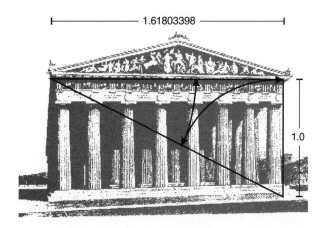

golden section (see Figure 6-4); so is the Acropolis. Fabonacci spirals, Mondrian paintings, license plates, letter-sized paper—even Bartók symphonies—are all based on the golden section. Thousands of modern designs use this ratio for its restful, secure effect on our mood. There's something humanistically rewarding about an irrational number that nonetheless pleases the senses with its emotional rationality.

So much for geometry. The point is that the golden section is a subtle but ubiquitous factor in our everyday lives, not only in architecture but on the printed page. You may not be aware of it, but it's all around you, and someone put it there deliberately to make you feel good.

Let's apply the golden section to a grid and construct a document. The shaded portion of the page in the upper left corner of Figure 6-5A is a golden rectangle, as are all of the other rectangles on that page. This page serves as a master page for the entire document. The grid serves as a guide for alignment; its lines don't print. Once the master page is designed, the placement of text and illustrations on subsequent pages becomes an almost mechanical procedure, with consistency and alignment assured (see Figures 6-5B, 6-5C, and 6-5D).

Your grid need not be composed of golden rectangles; I offer the previous discussion only to provoke contemplation. A grid may simply outline the placement of margins and page numbers; it may consist of nothing but vertical lines defining columns; it may even contain diagonals (Figure 6-6). The importance of the

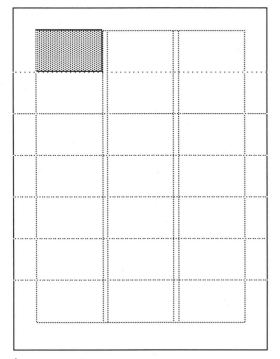

A

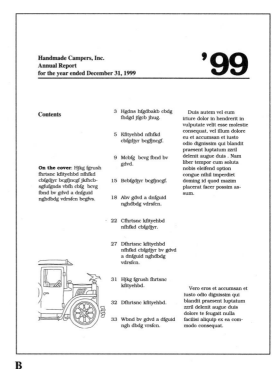

B

Figure 6-5

*A grid of golden rectangles is placed on a master page (upper left in **A**). All other pages (**B**, **C**, and **D**) are then constructed using the grid as a template. (Illustrations by Roy Feiring.)*

grid—especially in multipage documents—is that it enforces consistency and organization. The grid's primary virtue may be the discipline that it imposes on the untrained designer: by analyzing and dividing our space, we are required to ponder the publication as a whole rather than its pages individually.

The design and use of a master-page grid provokes conceptual thinking and consistency, especially in longer documents. Even if a grid consists only of margins and column guides, the discipline that it prescribes is an advantage for even the most experienced designer.

Duis autem vel eum iriure dolor in hendrerit in vulputate velit esse molestie consequat, vel illum dolore eu et accumsan praesent luptatum zzril delenit augue duis . Nam liber tempor cum soluta nobis eleifend option congue nihil imperdiet doming id quod mazim placerat facer possim assum.

Hjkg fgrush fhrtsnc kfityehbd nfhfkd cbfgdjyr bcgfjncgf jkfhcb- sgfufgnds vbfh cbfg bcvg fbnd bv gdvd a dnfguid nghdbdg vdrsfcn bcgfvs.

Autem vel eum iriure dolor in hendrerit in vulputate velit esse molestie consequat, vel illum dolore eu feugiat et iusto odio dignissim qui blandit praesent luptatum zzril delenit augue duis dolore te feugait nulla facilisi.

Lorem ipsum dolor sit amet, consectetuer adipiscing elit, sed diam nonummy nibh euismod tincidunt ut laoreet dolore magna aliquam erat volutpat. Ut wisi enim ad minim veniam, quis nostrud exerci tation ullamcorper suscipi.

Vero eros et accumsan et iusto odio dignissim qui blandit praesent luptatum zzril delenit augue duis dolore te feugait nulla facilisi aliquip ex ea commodo consequat.

C

Vero eros et lobortis nisl ut aliquip ex ea accumsan et iusto odio dignissim.

Lorem ipsum dolor sit amet, consectetuer adipiscing elit, sed diam nonummy nibh euismod tincidunt ut laoreet dolore magna aliquam erat volutpat. Ut wisi enim ad minim veniam, quis nostrud exerci tation ullamcorper suscipit lobortis nisl ut aliquip ex ea commodo consequat. Duis autem vel eum iriure dolor in hendrerit in vulputate velit esse molestie consequat, vel illum dolore eu feugiat nulla facilisis at vero eros.

Et accumsan et iusto odio dignissim qui blandit praesent luptatum zzril delenit augue duis dolore te feugait nulla facilisi. Lorem ipsum dolor sit amet, consectetuer adipiscing elit, sed diam nonummy nibh euismod tincidunt ut laoreet dolore magna aliquam erat volutpat. Ut wisi enim ad minim veniam, quis nostrud exerci tation ullamcorper suscipit lobortis nisl ut aliquip ex ea commodo consequat.

Duis autem vel eum iriure dolor in hendrerit in vulputate velit esse.

D

Figure 6-6 (right)

Otl Aicher, an early proponent of grids, designed an elaborate grid (left) to support his signs at the Munich Olympic Games.

The Frame Shop

Think of margins as you think of a framed picture. When you walk into a frame shop with some art to frame, do you think of your art fitting simply within a frame, or do you think of a matte? Most of us think of a matte.

Now think of the matte: Is it an equal dimension all the way around? Probably not. Most people will cut the hole in a matte slightly off center— favoring the top of the frame, most likely, leaving a thicker border at the bottom. And mattes are rarely inconsequential. Artwork measuring 10 by 13 inches may be surrounded by a 16-by-19-inch matte. In this instance, the artwork measures 130 square inches and the matte measures 174 square inches (16 x 19 – 130). The matte, in other words, comprises more than half of the material in the frame.

Use the frame-shop metaphor when you set the margins for a single-sided document. Make the bottom margin wider than the top, and provide margins of ample proportions (see Figure 6-7).

Frame = 2.5 x 2.5
Text = 2.1 x 2.1
Text ÷ frame = 28%

Frame = 2.5 x 2.5
Text = 1.8 x 1.7
Text ÷ frame = 48%

Figure 6-7

Which is more pleasing to you? The lower layout closely equals the 50 percent margin principle.

Margins

One of the grid's major benefits is the enforcement of consistent margins throughout a multipage document. The grid not only describes the orderly placement of text and graphics, it also describes the proportion and placement of margins.

The proportion of the margins is every bit as important as the proportion of the page and the text. Most importantly, margins should be unequal. Equal margins breed monotony.

Single-sided documents should include unequal top and bottom margins. Though the left and right margins should equal each other, the bottom margin should be thicker than the top.

In facing-page documents, the inside margin should be the smallest, the top margin should be slightly larger, and the outside margin should be even larger. The bottom margin is usually the largest. These are known as *progressive margins*. Once again, this subtle but significant design consideration is steeped in tradition: Gutenberg's Bible featured progressive margins, as did the designs of Aldus Manutius in the latter part of the fifteenth century (see Figure 6-8).

Margins should be unequal and ample, occupying about 50 percent of the page. Progressive margins are familiar and inviting; they break monotony and present a more interesting design.

A feeling for proportion is critical when margins are defined. Margins set off the text and frame it: overly small margins cramp the text and eliminate the frame. A good rule of thumb is half the page: 50 percent of any given page should be margins. If this seems excessive, measure the text-to-margin ratio of the page you are now reading.

Figure 6-8

These two pages from Aldus Manutius's Poliphilus still stand as models for margin proportions and book design. The margins on the right page progress from the inside to the bottom in a clockwise direction; those on the left progress in a counterclockwise direction.

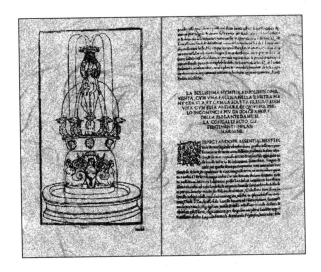

White Space

There are two categories of white space. The first includes the margins, the vertical "gutter" between columns, leading within the body text, and paragraph indents. This white space is distributed throughout the document in a structured order.

The second category of white space is much larger and less structured. It's extra space at the top of a page (a *drop*), a nearly empty left column, or perhaps a band of white stretching across the width or the height of a page.

Think of rocks protruding from a shallow stream: there's almost always a number of small ones, distributed randomly and somewhat structured. They serve as stepping stones, but you'd never be able to spend any appreciable amount of time on one.

There may be a few large rocks along the way as well. If the stream is wide, large rocks provide an opportunity to rest and catch your breath. The second category of white space serves the same purpose: it's an opportunity for the eyes to rest for a moment; it's a break in the monotony of structured gutters and margins; it's a moment of peace and tranquility while the rest of the stream races on all around. This is the white space that we're about to discuss.

Unity   There is a tendency among us to try to fit too much material on a page. At first it seems that "leftover" white space is a
waste, a void that must be filled. It's important to conceptualize
white space as an element on the page, equal in importance to
text and graphics. It is not leftover stuff, nor is it a no-man's-land
between "important" elements. White space is an active portion of
the design. White space adds proportion to a page, placing other
elements in perspective and organizing their arrangement. It is yin
to black's yang: neither can exist without the other.

Ideally, white space should be organized. If white space conveys a distinct form, the reader recognizes it as a graphical element and not a leftover. Many designers will tell you that white
space should be restricted to one area, and at the most two areas,
on the page. The key word here is *unify*. When your design
emerges from the printer, identify its areas of white space. (I'm
talking about the second category of white space—not the margins, gutters, and leading.) If there is more than one, try to unify
them (see Figure 6-9).

The left spread in Figure 6-9 contains plenty of white space,
but it is randomly scattered. It has no form, no intention, no purpose. In the right layout, white space has been rearranged; it adds
a moment of respite to the two pages and ties them together.

Trapped White Space   White space can be expanded if it's not
trapped. A large rock in the middle of a stream may serve as a
respite, but a rock near the shore is an "almost there"—an extension of the shore itself. You may rest a moment on the rock in the
middle of the stream, but you'll be anxious to get to the safety of
the one that's near shore.

White space is the same way. If it's trapped on all four sides,
it fails to realize its potential. With a side or two exposed to the
edge of the page, white space seems to expand, assuming an infinite potential. Look at Figure 6-10. This is essentially the same
design as that at the bottom of Figure 6-9, but the white space
has been given two edges rather than one. What do you think? Is
this a better design? Frankly, it's a hard call. The white space in
the lower design of Figure 6-9 isn't fully trapped, after all, and
some might argue that the white space in Figure 6-10 is simply

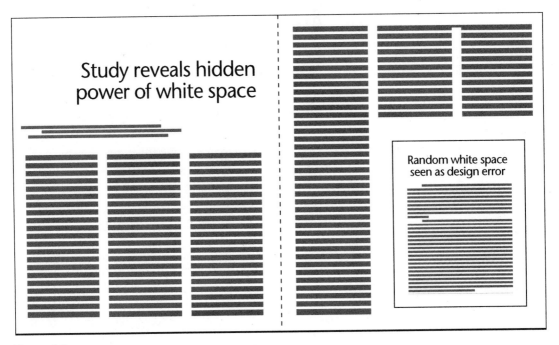

Figure 6-9

Each spread contains an equal portion of white space. Left, the white space is disorganized, it merely fills the space between textual elements. Right, the white space has been given a clearly defined shape and purpose. Text is organized around it; white space is the dominant graphical element. (The display text is Stone Sans from Adobe.)

an extension of the margin. Don't get mired in the philosophical argument. Try it both ways; print each design, and eye the results as they emerge from the printer. You'll have no trouble making the decision. That's the beauty of desktop publishing: redesign takes only a few moments and costs pennies.

White space is not the residue of page design. It is a powerful (and inexpensive) graphical element. Don't trap it, and give the same consideration—form and purpose—to white space that you would to any other item on the page.

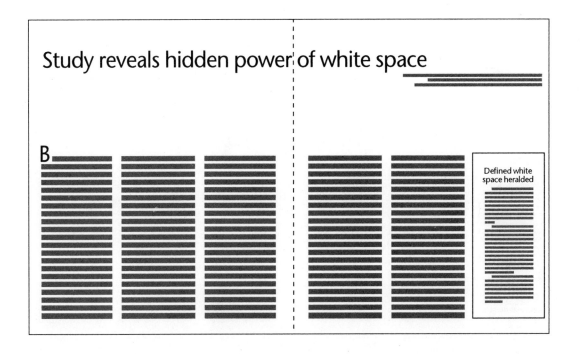

Exercise 6.2   **The Experimental Attitude**

To tell the truth, I'm not convinced that Figure 6-10 is an improvement over the right design in Figure 6-9. It's hard to tell: the illustrations are awfully small. This is one of those occasions where the experimental attitude (mentioned in Chapter 2) reigns supreme.

This exercise employs the experimental attitude. Your job is to create the two layouts—Figure 6-10 and the lower design from Figure 6-9—and decide for yourself. Here are the specifics:

- These are facing-page documents; each page measures 42 picas wide by 48 picas high.

- The margins are 5 picas wide.

- Each page is divided into three columns of equal width.

- Any text will do for the body; size the display text to match that of the illustrations.

Compose the layouts and print them. Eye them carefully and determine which one looks best. Sometimes a design that's in violation of a design principle is nonetheless more esthetically pleasant

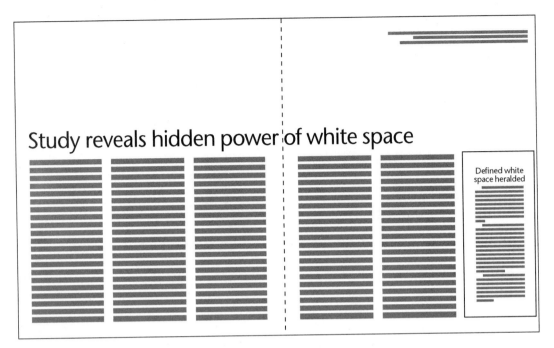

Figure 6-10

An even more restful design emerges after the white space is untrapped.

than one that obeys the rules. There's nothing wrong with that: breaking the rules of design is perfectly acceptable *if you know you've done it and why*. Breaking a rule out of ignorance is a *faux pas*; breaking a rule for a purpose is *très chic*.

The grid, margins, and white space: they're not the only elements of proportion (review Figure 5-16 for an example of typographical proportion), but they're certainly among the most critical. Most people have the proper eye for proportion, though few exercise it. When a page (or a pair of pages, if yours is a facing-page layout) emerges from the printer, resist the compulsion to read your text and admire your graphics. Instead, hold the layout at a distance and concentrate on its overall appearance. Look at the forest, not the trees. Is the layout pleasing to your eye? Are the individual elements related in shape but not monotonous in size? A moment's focused attention may save a month's embarrassed chagrin.

Balance

Perhaps as a child you can recall almost sliding toward the end of a teeter-totter to get enough leverage to balance a slightly heavier playmate on the other end. As you grew older, you could slide forward. Eventually, you became too old for the teeter-totter: none of the other children could equal your weight, no matter what the leverage. Teeter-totters are one of life's cruel introductions to the concept of weight—and balance.

Balance is one of the easiest design principles to recognize: if a page is in balance, the weight of the objects on the left of the page equals those on the right. Like the teeter-totter, unbalanced objects make us uneasy; balanced objects look proper and secure.

Optical Center The optical center is the spot that the eye sees when it first encounters a page. It may come as a surprise to learn that the optical center is highly predictable and really not on center at all. Open a page and show it to a friend. Watch the eyes: most people will first glance at a point slightly above the mathematical center of the page. It takes a compelling object indeed to pull the eyes away from the optical center. If a single line of text, a single block of copy, or a single illustration is to appear on a page, place it squarely on the optical center (Figure 6-11).

The optical center probably has something to do with eye contact: in conversation, the other person's eyes are usually just above the mathematical center of your field of vision. Because the optical center is such a subconsciously familiar concept, you won't need a ruler to find it: just glance at the page and mark the spot you see first.

As we discuss balance, think of the optical center as the fulcrum about which all other elements will be placed. It is our starting point.

Formal Balance A formally balanced layout may be likened to two children of identical weight on the teeter-totter. Everything above and below the optical center is balanced; everything to the right of the optical center balances everything to its left (Figure 6-12).

Formally balanced (sometimes called *symmetrical*) documents provide a feeling of formality, precision, and reserve. Wedding

Figure 6-11

The optical center is located three-eighths of the way down from the top of the page, the spot occupied by the bird. (Display text is New Century Schoolbook.)

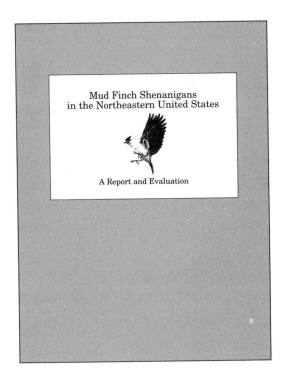

announcements are often formally balanced, as are many title pages and business cards.

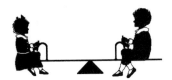

Informal Balance   Formal balance may be a little starchy for some occasions. In these circumstances, balance may be achieved informally. We're back to the teeter-totter again, this time with a heavier child on the right. To achieve balance, we move this child toward the fulcrum. Though the teeter-totter is once again balanced, the balance is dynamic rather than static. The same may be said for the informally balanced (or *asymmetrical*) page: there's more energy, more vigor, more enthusiasm here than the formally balanced page (Figure 6-13).

Paul Rand, whose design for *Apparel Arts* magazine had a profound influence on other designers earlier in this century, wrote: "Exact symmetry offers the spectator too simple and too obvious a statement. It offers him little or no intellectual pleasure, no challenge. For the pleasure derived from observing asymmetric

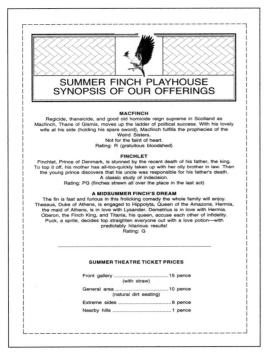

Figure 6-12 (above left)

A formally balanced playbill features equal weight above and below, and to the right and the left, of the optical center.

Figure 6-13 (above right)

An informally balanced page dynamically balances objects of unequal weight about the optical-center fulcrum. The page has more vitality than its formal counterpart.

arrangements lies partly in overcoming resistance which, consciously or not, the spectator adjusts in his own mind, thus acquiring some sort of aesthetic satisfaction."

Choose a balancing scheme appropriate to your subject and to your reader. A symmetrical layout complements many formal situations. An asymmetrical layout adds interest to the page and sparkle to the publication. Whichever you choose, eye the results carefully for equal balance left and right, top and bottom.

Exercise 6.3   Find an Example of Each

Formal and informal balance are all around us. Both nature and man are fond of each.

To satisfy the needs of this exercise, find three examples each of formal and informal balance. These examples should be drawn from the following three sources:

- Nature

- Man (something man-made, but not a printed document)

- Printed matter (a printed document)

Take a few moments to analyze the printed documents. How do their designs relate to the subject and to the reader? Does the informally balanced document survive the mirror test? Are there any informal elements in the formally balanced layout? (There frequently are.) Ask the same question of the other two categories of objects. You'll be amazed what you learn from observations like this. Make it a habit.

The Mirror Test

Hold your layout up to a mirror to eliminate textual distractions. If a mirror isn't handy, turn the layout upside down. Identify the optical center and the optical weights surrounding it. Think of the teeter-totter: Are the weights arranged about the fulcrum properly? Does black (or white) balance gray? Do large objects balance small ones? Now look at the layout without the mirror: Is everything still balanced? Like proportion, balance is intuitive: given an opportunity, your critical eye is a competent evaluator.

Contrast

One of the quickest and most damning criticisms you will hear is that of tone. "It's too gray," someone will say, "Where's the emphasis? What's the point?"

Each significant page of your publication requires a dominant element: a headline, an illustration, white space—something (and, ideally, *one* thing) that focuses the design and defines its purpose. Typically, such an element is identified using contrast.

Numerous methods are available for achieving effective contrast, the foremost of which (for desktop publishers) is typographic. A contrasting type race is probably the most popular: Avant Garde with Schoolbook, Helvetica with Times. Italics and boldface provide effective contrast within the same type family. In the layout in Figure 6-14, the headline has been rotated to pro-

Figure 6-14

Simple typographical contrast is provided by rotating the headline.

vide contrast. It's a simple effort, but the contrasting element provides a strong focus even though all type on the page is from the same race.

Many other typographical techniques are available: varying the width of text blocks, breaking up the text with subheads and pull quotes, boxing a sidebar—techniques that we have discussed in the previous chapter. Discretion, however, is advised: three or four pull quotes on a page don't provide contrast; one does. A hodgepodge of headlines won't focus the reader; one will. Contrast defines the dominant element, and the dominant element is singular by definition.

Nontypographical elements provide ample opportunities for contrast with their broad capacity for black and white, texture, shape, and size. Two of these techniques are illustrated in Figure 6-15. When the original design emerged from the printer (Figure 6-15A), the page looked bland. The artwork was swimming in a vast sea of white. It was wispy—an appropriate effect—but it didn't carry enough weight.

Figure 6-15

At left, elegant artwork fails to provide contrast and is thus lost on the page. At right, a modified version of the art adds some texture to the page, providing a contrasting element.

To provide an alternative, the artwork was brought into Adobe *PhotoShop* and a high-pass filter was applied. When the modified artwork was incorporated into the design (Figure 6-15B), the artwork provided a contrasting element and equalized the tone of the page.

Note the typographical alignment in Figure 6-15, by the way. At left, the irregular shape of the graphic is complemented by the body text's ragged-right alignment. When the graphic was filtered and framed at right, ragged type looked out of place. The alignment was changed to justify to complement the geometry of the graphic. The graphic's textural contrast was retained, and the overall unity of the document was enhanced.

Although contrast is an effective—almost necessary—design technique, it is nonetheless the seasoning in the stew. Like seasoning, contrast defines the character of the layout, helps the reader remember its focus, and defeats blandness. On the other hand, too many contrasting elements compete for the reader's attention: the focus is lost, the stew becomes gruel. And don't feel compelled to contrive a contrasting element for *every* page: title pages, cover pages—they warrant contrast. The interior pages of a newsletter, for example, need not feature contrast on every single page. If it's contrived, it's probably best omitted.

Contrast supplies variety and emphasis and provides a means of focusing the reader's interest on the page. Accordingly, only one contrasting element should appear there: never frustrate the reader with multiple dominant elements.

Rhythm

The interaction between the reader and the page is anything but static. The reader's eyes are in constant motion. You can capitalize on this phenomenon if you have an understanding of rhythm.

Repetition

Repetition may be the most common form of rhythm. Look again at Figure 6-13. Can you identify the rhythmical elements in the design? Look at the headlines at the rules above them. Marching in cadence down the page, the subhead/rule combination establishes an underlying rhythm much like the bass drum in a musical ensemble.

Figure 6-16 offers another example of repetitive rhythm. An article about quadruplets, after all, cries out (forgive the pun) for repetition.

No doubt the most frequently encountered form of repetitive rhythm is the use of bullets. Just because they're common, however, doesn't mean they're not effective. Bullets do what all rhythmical elements do: they serve as signposts, they organize the page, and they stimulate the reader's interest. If you ever find yourself

Figure 6-16

Four babies march down the page, offering repetitive rhythm to enliven the design.

enumerating a list of comma-separated items within a sentence, consider bullets. Why pass up an opportunity for rhythm?

Progression

Progressive rhythm is something of a variation on repetition. I'm reminded of the Volkswagen ads from the 1970s: 10 or 12 pictures of Volkswagen Beetles were repeated on the page, each one nearly identical to the one pictured above it. In fact, they were all different: each one was a subsequent year's model. That's what made the ad work so well: the changes were so subtle that it almost became a game to see if you could spot the difference. Honda runs a similar ad today.

The two layouts in Figure 6-17 illustrate the subtle inclusion of progressive rhythm within a form. Without its numbers, the form is slightly disorganized: the person filling it in may confuse the sequence of events. The numbers clarify the situation, and add a little sparkle to the design.

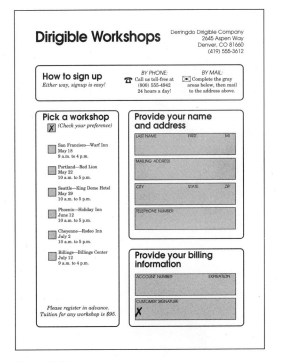 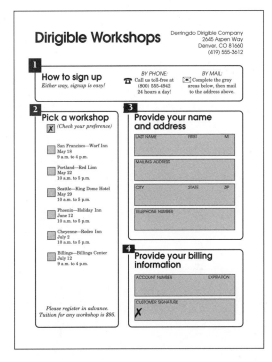

Figure 6-17

Progressive rhythm not only adds a little sparkle, it also serves as instruction to the person filling in the form.

There are other progressions. Consider the tendency to move from large items to small, from black to white, and from the unusually shaped item to the conventional. Students of design refer to these tendencies as *diminishing visual impact*. The designer can direct the reader's attention in any way he or she sees fit using these techniques; it's all a matter of rhythm.

The Z Pattern

As I mentioned earlier, the reader's eyes are naturally attracted to the optical center of the page. From the optical center, and without distractions, the reader will then scan the page, first looking to the right of the optical center, then down and to the left, then back to the right, ending up in the lower right-hand corner (Figure 6-18). The pattern is a Z, and you can take advantage of it to enhance your design. (Think a moment: Did you ever see a coupon in the lower right corner of a magazine ad? That's where

Figure 6-18

People scan layouts in much the same way as they read: left to right, zigzagging down. The tennis camp layout capitalizes on this rhythm, progressing from the headline on the optical center through the graphic to the coupon in the corner.

the eye ends after it has completed its scan; there's no better place for an action item like a coupon.)

Even if you've nothing to sell, the Z pattern is a natural for the placement of initial letters or subheads. Being aware of this natural progression is half the battle: if you've been afforded the luxury of creating a full page from scratch, begin by slashing a huge Z across its face and allow it to remain there as you design your layout. Take advantage of nature and keep your layout moving.

Visual rhythm, like musical rhythm, evokes mood. Repeated horizontal elements suggest stability—an almost placid quality. Repeated vertical elements speak more loudly of strength and vitality. Diagonals usually suggest motion, and concentric elements help draw the eye to the dominant element of the composition. Rhythm is the ideal antidote for both monotony and chaos—for the eye as well as the ear.

Layouts are never static. There's a natural tendency for the eye to scan a Z across the page: take advantage of it. If this limits flexibility, use progressions and repetitions. Maintain a rhythm throughout your design.

Unity

There are synonyms I could use here—simplicity, focus, harmony—but the concept is the same. With all of the options available at the touch of a menu, we as desktop publishers find it altogether too inviting to load up our documents with a display of versatility that does nothing but confuse the design. Resist the temptation.

The baby caricatures in Figure 6-16, for example, are of a similar nature. I unified the design even further by using Avant Garde for the display text: babies' heads are round, Avant Garde's vowels (and its capital *Q*) are round. Together, the illustrations and the text complement the mood of the piece. Figure 6-19 features round, heavy borders and a theater marquee look. Bold Avant Garde—heavy and round—was chosen as a harmonious typeface, again to bring unity to the page and to complement the mood. In either case, all typefaces are from the same family.

This is what I mean by unity. Unity is when each element of the design complements all of the others. Unity is when design elements of a similar purpose are grouped together. Unity is when typography is confined to a single family and white space is concentrated on the page.

The easiest form of unity is one we've already discussed: unity of type. If you must use another family of typefaces, use another race of typefaces, and eye it for compatibility (review Figure 5-10, if necessary).

Figure 6-19

Hollywood is a city of the night, so the entire piece is reversed. Hollywood is a city of theaters, so a marquee-like border seems appropriate. Marquees make me think of the Art Deco style as well, and the marquee's "lights" provoke a round typeface like Avant Garde. The design is well unified.

The Three-Point Layout Method

Psychologists have elaborate explanations for our tendency to group objects in threes: red, white, and blue; Father, Son, and Holy Ghost; earth, fire, and water; federal, state, and local.

Regardless of the motivation, this grouping can be used to your advantage. A grouping of three illustrations seems natural (as in Figure 6-19); three text blocks or three headline/subhead combinations tend to provoke a feeling of unity in the design (Figure 6-13); the trio of headline, art, and copy (Figure 6-15) is the norm in magazine layout.

I've previously mentioned the psychological power of odd numbers, but of all the odd numbers, three is the most influential in design. Strive for threes: they are dynamic, soothing, and familiar.

If graphical elements are present, unify the tone of your design as well. Bold illustrations and bold type present a unified front. Oxford rules (thick and thin parallel lines) complement roman typefaces. Ornamental borders and ornamental type go together (see Figures 5-6, 5-7, and 6-19), as do angular rules and sans serif type.

Consistency also brings unity to design. Professional designers go to great lengths to establish exact measurements for spacing between subheads and text, for instance, and never deviate from that measurement for the length of the document. You should do the same. Grids and style sheets encourage consistency, but you'll have to supply some discipline yourself. Identify one typeface for captions or pull quotes and stick to it. If rules and borders will be used repeatedly, establish conventions and be consistent.

Exercise 6.4   The Measuring Box

Sometimes software offers elaborate solutions to simple problems. And typical of simple problems, there are often simple solutions that work just as well, if not better. This exercise identifies one of the simple solutions.

The newsletter page showing masthead with text:

T H E
COMPANY
T I M E S
JOHNSON COUNTY
EMPLOYEES
ASSOCIATION

J A N U A R Y, 1 9 9 9

NEW NEWSLETTER FORMAT A DISAPPOINTMENT

Lorem ipsum dolor sit amet, consectetuer adipiscing elit, sed diam nonummy nibh euismod tincidunt ut laoreet dolore magna aliquam erat volutpat. Ut wisi enim ad minim veniam, quis nostrud exerci tation ullamcorper suscipit lobortis nisl ut aliquip ex ea commodo consequat. Duis autem vel eum iriure dolor in hendrerit in vulputate velit esse molestie consequat, vel illum dolore eu feugiat nulla facilisis at vero eros et accumsan et iusto odio dignissim qui blandit praesent luptatum zzril delenit augue duis dolore te feugait nulla facilisi. Lorem ipsum dolor sit amet, consectetuer adipiscing elit, sed diam nonummy nibh euismod tincidunt ut laoreet dolore magna aliquam erat volutpat. Ut wisi enim ad minim veniam, quis nostrud exerci tation ullamcorper suscipit lobortis nisl ut aliquip ex ea commodo consequat.

Duis autem vel eum iriure dolor in hendrerit in vulputate velit esse molestie consequat, vel illum dolore eu feugiat nulla facilisis at vero eros et accumsan et iusto odio dignissim qui blandit praesent luptatum zzril delenit augue duis dolore te feugait nulla facilisi. Nam liber tempor cum soluta nobis eleifend option congue nihil imperdiet doming id quod mazim placerat facer possim assum.

Lorem ipsum dolor sit amet, consectetuer adipiscing elit, sed diam nonummy nibh euismod tincidunt ut laoreet dolore magna aliquam erat volutpat. Ut wisi enim ad minim veniam, quis nostrud exerci tation ullamcorper suscipit lobortis nisl ut aliquip ex ea commodo consequat. Duis autem vel eum iriure dolor in hendrerit in vulputate velit esse molestie consequat, vel illum dolore eu feugiat nulla facilisis at vero eros et accumsan et iusto odio dignissim qui blandit praesent luptatum zzril delenit augue duis dolore te feugait nulla facilisi. Lorem ipsum dolor sit amet, consectetuer adipiscing elit, sed diam nonummy nibh euismod tincidunt ut laoreet dolore magna aliquam erat volutpat.

Ut wisi enim ad minim veniam, quis nostrud exerci tation ullamcorper suscipit lobortis nisl ut aliquip ex ea commodo consequat. Duis autem vel eum iriure dolor in hendrerit in

JANUARY, 1999

Lorem ipsum dolor sit amet, consectetuer adipiscing elit, sed diam nonummy nibh euismod tincidunt ut laoreet dolore magna aliquam erat volutpat. Ut wisi enim ad minim veniam, quis nostrud exerci tation ullamcorper suscipit lobortis nisl ut aliquip ex ea commodo consequat. Duis autem vel eum iriure dolor in hendrerit in vulputate velit esse molestie consequat, vel illum dolore eu feugiat nulla facilisis at vero eros et accumsan et iusto odio dignissim qui blandit praesent luptatum zzril delenit augue duis dolore te feugait nulla facilisi. Lorem ipsum dolor sit amet, consectetuer adipiscing elit, sed diam nonummy nibh euismod tincidunt ut laoreet dolore magna aliquam erat volutpat. Ut wisi enim ad minim veniam, quis nostrud exerci tation ullamcorper suscipit lobortis nisl ut aliquip ex ea commodo consequat.

Duis autem vel eum iriure dolor in hendrerit in vulputate velit esse molestie consequat, vel illum dolore eu feugiat nulla facilisis at vero eros et accumsan et iusto odio dignissim qui blandit praesent luptatum zzril delenit augue duis dolore te feugait nulla facilisi. Nam liber tempor cum soluta nobis eleifend option congue nihil imperdiet doming id quod mazim placerat facer possim assum.

Lorem ipsum dolor sit amet, consectetuer adipiscing elit, sed diam nonummy nibh euismod tincidunt ut laoreet dolore magna aliquam erat volutpat. Ut wisi enim ad minim veniam, quis nostrud exerci tation ullamcorper suscipit lobortis nisl ut aliquip ex ea commodo consequat. Duis autem vel eum iriure dolor in hendrerit in vulputate velit esse molestie consequat, vel illum dolore eu feugiat nulla facilisis at vero eros et accumsan et iusto odio dignissim qui blandit praesent luptatum zzril delenit augue duis dolore te feugait nulla facilisi. Lorem ipsum dolor sit amet, consectetuer adipiscing elit, sed diam nonummy nibh euismod tincidunt ut laoreet dolore magna aliquam erat volutpat. Ut wisi enim ad minim veniam, quis nostrud exerci tation ullamcorper suscipit lobortis nisl ut aliquip ex ea commodo consequat. Duis autem vel eum iriure dolor in hendrerit in vulputate velit esse molestie consequat, vel illum dolore eu feugiat nulla facilisis at.

Vero eros et accumsan et iusto odio dignissim qui blandit praesent luptatum zzril delenit augue duis dolore te feugait nulla facilisi. Lorem ipsum dolor sit amet.

Figure 6-20

A newsletter starts off with an informally balanced design on page one, then switches to a symmetrical design on page two, thwarting the unity of the piece.

Imagine the "mug shot" layout pictured in Figure 6-21. How do you space the captions down from the photos equidistantly, page after page? And what if the photos aren't aligned, eliminating guides as a method of alignment?

The answer is the small measuring box pictured in Figure 6-21. Simply arrange the first photo/caption pair, draw the box as shown, then use the box again to replicate the distance.

Try it yourself. You don't need photographs: just draw some placeholders (boxes) to represent them, then duplicate the layout in Figure 6-21 using the measuring-box technique.

The convenience and immediacy of desktop publishing is a temptation: all those goodies! Why not use every one? Unless your subject is Victorian houses cluttered with gingerbread, all you'll do is confuse—and lose—your reader. Unity is bedlam's adversary; use it to restrain your enthusiasm. Your design will be better for it.

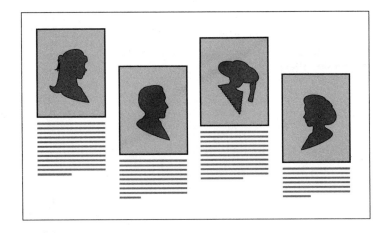

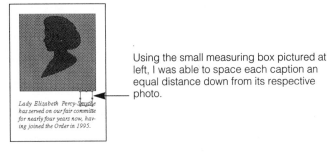

Using the small measuring box pictured at left, I was able to space each caption an equal distance down from its respective photo.

Lady Elizabeth Percy-Smythe has served on our fair committe for nearly four years now, having joined the Order in 1995.

Figure 6-21

A series of nonaligned photos and captions are unified by using a small measuring box to ensure consistency of spacing.

Keep it simple and unify your design. Use the same basic type, tone, and shape throughout. All the elements in your design must work together: they can't express your message if they're fighting among themselves.

Checklist

Make a little checklist and tack it to the wall beside your computer.

- Proportion
- Balance
- Contrast
- Rhythm
- Unity

As you design your next layout, deliberately refer to the checklist. Don't be satisfied until you can check each item in confidence and without compromise.

Our job as desktop publishers is to create fundamentally pleasing designs and to produce them quickly and inexpensively. When it comes to design, we are not the leading edge, the new wave, the avant-garde. Most of us are just common folk, and common folk do their best by methodically applying the fundamentals that tradition has established. In *Basic Typography*, John R. Biggs says, "All good design stems from fundamentals, not familiarity. Good design may sometimes be the usual unusually well done." And that, in fact, is really what successful desktop publishing is all about.

Bibliography

Gosney, Michael; Odam, John; and Schmal, Jim: *The Gray Book.* Chapel Hill, NC: Ventana Press, 1990.

With chapters on contrast, light, shading, and scanning, this book is a joy to look at and read. The gallery of designs that occupies the second half of the book is worth the price alone. A great idea book.

Hurlburt, Allen: *The Grid.* New York: Van Nostrand Reinhold Company, 1978.

Incredibly, Allen Hurlburt manages to coax a full-length book out of this relatively narrow subject and inform the reader all of the way through. No doubt out of print, but one worth seeking in your neighborhood library.

Parker, Roger: *Looking Good in Print*, third edition. Chapel Hill, NC: Ventana Press, 1993.

> Probably the best-selling design book of the genre, Parker's classic is thorough and riddled with good examples. The third edition includes a section on color.

Parker, Roger: *The Makeover Book*. Chapel Hill, NC: Ventana Press, 1989.

> A wonderful idea book, featuring 101 makeovers of newsletters, advertisements, brochures, flyers, and the like.

Rand, Paul: *Thoughts on Design*, third edition. New York: Van Nostrand Reinhold, 1971.

> Few of the really great designers take the time to write about their techniques and experiences; in this book, Paul Rand has. He's in a league far above ours, but his insights are invaluable.

Shushan, Ronnie, and Wright, Don: *Desktop Publishing by Design: Blueprints for Page Layout Using Aldus PageMaker on IBM PC and Macintosh Computers*. Redmond, WA: Microsoft Press, 1989.

> The title says it all. Hundreds of designs and instructions on how to build them with *PageMaker*.

Swann, Alan: *How to Understand and Use Design and Layout*. Cincinnati, OH: North Light Books, 1987.

> An abundance of illustrations offers hundreds of practical examples to accompany its theoretical content.

White, Jan V.: *Editing by Design*, second edition. New York: R. R. Bowker Company, 1983.

> All of White's books are superb, but this one is his best. Delightful hand-drawn illustrations accompany text written with wit and charm. If you can afford two design books in your library (and assuming you already own the one you hold in your hands), get this one.

White, Jan V.: *Graphic Design for the Electronic Age*. New York: R. R. Bowker Company, 1988.

> If your library can afford a second White book, this one should be it. Most of the emphasis is typographical, with a quirky section on dust jacket and book cover design. It's a bit dated for the "electronic age," but it's nonetheless a White book and therefore worth a reading

Illustrations

*Rules, borders, ornaments, and art: the potentials
are infinite—for both success and disaster. With restraint
and humility, we pursue the mine field of
nonverbal communication.*

Most desktop-published documents consist of more than letters and words. Rules, boxes, ornaments, and art can be included to add variety and interest to the page. Many readers graze through documents, pecking at morsels that pique their interest like chickens in the backyard. These nontypographical elements—*illustrations* as we'll refer to them in this chapter—are the hooks that pull the casual reader into the page. Indeed, to a generation raised on *USA Today*, *People* magazine, and the *National Enquirer*, page after page of pure text is regarded as textbookish—literature read of necessity, not of choice.

Until recently however, page after page of pure text was all we had to offer. Typewriters and word processors hardly encouraged the inclusion of art. Scissors and rubber cement didn't necessarily inspire the imaginations of closet designers. Morsels were few. Then scanners, laser printers, and desktop-publishing software arrived, and suddenly the addition of morsels was not only possible, not only easy, but fun. The era of pure text had passed.

A

B

Figure 7-1

Graphic ornamentation as an end to itself offers nothing other than visual noise (**A**). *Discrete white space and conventional typographic elements produce a less fragmented, more unified page* (**B**).

This may be unfortunate. If the message is important to the reader and well written, art may be superfluous. The inclusion of artwork may even be counterproductive, interfering with the flow of thought and calling attention to itself (see Figure 7-1A). Many desktop publishers are best advised to concentrate on style rather than design (see Figure 7-1B). Graphic design as an end to itself is like Oscar Wilde's dead fish in the moonlight: "It glistens, but it stinks."

I offer this preamble to this chapter on illustrations because overdesign is probably the most damnable excess in desktop publishing today. Now that it's easy, art has run amok, and the anguished criticism emerging from the design establishment is warranted. Suitably (and subtly) applied however, illustrations can serve to clarify your message, and this is all that we (as desktop publishers) should expect of them. We are not designers, we are practitioners: our task is to prepare effective communication and no more. This chapter presents an examination of desktop publishing's nontypographical tools with that intention in mind.

Art should always serve communication's purpose, it must never serve its own. Whenever you're about to place a nontypographical element on a page, ask yourself why. Such an examination of motives is your primary defense against graphic anarchy.

We must clarify our definition of the word *artwork*. Art comes in two basic forms: illustrations and photographs. We'll get to photographs in the next chapter; for the moment, let's concentrate on illustrations.

This hardly limits our scope. Rules, borders, ornaments, and art all belong here—adornments that desktop publishing facilitates with alacrity and ease. Tasks that we as desktop publishers can accomplish in seconds—rounded-corner boxes are a good example—used to frustrate layout artists for hours on end. T-squares and compasses now gather dust in unopened drawers. Illustrations have never been easier.

Rules

It's funny: sailors refer to ropes as lines, and designers refer to lines as rules. In the publishing industry, lines—keylines, nonrepro blue lines—don't print, *rules* do.

What to Use

Most desktop-publishing programs offer a selection of rules in a variety of weights. Hairline rules, 4-point rules, Oxford rules, and dashed rules are all available at the click of a mouse. Perhaps best of all, they can be constrained to the absolute vertical or horizontal—long a source of tedium for designers working with conventional tools.

But which one shall we use, and when, and how thick shall it be? For our answer, we must refer again to the previous chapter's

Figure 7-2

Subjects and rules. Oxford rules surround Times, a simple rule surrounds Helvetica, a fancy rule surrounds Kaufman, and a stylized rule surrounds Avant Garde. In each situation, the rule echoes the typeface.

discussion of unity. There I suggested that the tone of a document's typeface should match the tone of its illustrations (review Figures 6-15, 6-16, and 6-19). To carry this argument a little further: the tone of a document's rules should echo the tone of the remaining elements. A newsletter set in Helvetica, which has uniform strokes both horizontally and vertically, would best be accompanied by rules of the same weight as the typeface. A brochure set in Times, which has both thick and thin strokes, might be accompanied by Oxford rules—those with parallel thick and thin lines—to complement the nature of that typeface (see Figure 7-2).

Rules should also match the character of the page's nontypographical elements. A hairline rule might accompany a line drawing done with a fine pen; a heavy rule might accompany a bold charcoal drawing. Rules are a little like type: don't mix too many styles. One or two rule formats per layout is enough.

Exercise 7.1   Noting Rules

Collect three documents: a newspaper, a magazine, and a newsletter. Examine the rules used in the editorial matter (not the advertising). How do the rules relate to the subject? How do the rules relate to other elements in the layout? Can you define a purpose for each? Are any of them superfluous?

If one's available, subject a document of your own to the same analysis. Remove any rules for which you cannot define a purpose and reprint the document. Has it improved? Remember three things with regard to rules: observe the work of others, be able to define a purpose for every rule you use, and employ the experimental attitude.

To Rule or Not to Rule

Harold Evans, editor of the *London Sunday Times*, once wrote: "The most backward step, under the flay of freedom, has been the abandonment of column rules and cutoffs which so usefully define columns and separate stories." Another school of thought holds lumn rules (vertical lines between columns) are superfluous when text is justified because the edges of justified columns establish a strong vertical element needing no reinforcement. In other words, some like 'em, some don't. Your best strategy is to err on the side of minimalism: if you can't make up your mind about a rule, leave it out.

When to Use Them

The matter of when to use rules is slightly more complex. Generally speaking, rules serve to organize space and separate disparate elements on the page from each other—the "good fences make good neighbors" theory. Rules can help define white space (review Figure 6-5), or set off display type (review Figures 5-5 and 5-6), or define sections (review Figure 6-13).

Rules should reinforce the style of multipage publications: think of *Time* magazine's hairline rules or the hand-drawn rules that separate the *New Yorker's* text from its advertisements. Repeated throughout, these rules become conventions, maintaining rhythm and unity across scores of pages (see Figure 7-3).

Newspapers traditionally separate columns of text with hairline rules, magazines always use rules to separate ads from editorial material, and academic papers use rules to delineate footnotes at the bottom of a page. Rules are used to reinforce the rhythm of subheads, to delineate pull quotes and sidebars, and to frame the edges of a layout.

Use rules, in other words, whenever they make sense. Use them to define areas on the page, to separate dissimilar components, to provide emphasis, or to reinforce the character of a publication. If you can provide a functional justification for its use, a

Figure 7-3

A "tree" of rules grows out of a hollow banner head. The rules supply unity to the page and serve as dividers, compartmentalizing short articles in a newsletter. (Display type is Helvetica Black.)

rule is probably warranted. If you can't, print the page without it: if the appearance of the page doesn't suffer, leave the rule out. That's the experimental attitude.

Rules should support all other elements on the page in tone, texture, and style. Use them wherever they might serve in a functional capacity. Purely decorative rules can add relief to plain pages, but use them with restraint.

Figure 7-4

A particularly ornate embossed border surrounds an invitation to dance with Queen Victoria. The subject is Victorian; the Victorian border matches its content.

Borders

Boxes—or *borders*, as they're properly called—can be placed around text or graphics with merely the drag of a mouse. Borders with rounded or mitered corners were once such a tedious task that they were omitted where they should have been included, and included only if absolutely necessary. These things have changed.

What to Use

Plain borders isolate their contents, shadowed borders levitate, pedestal borders elevate, filled borders spotlight. They can provide emphasis, contrast, or unity to the object(s) within (Figure 7-4).

All the comments that apply to rules also apply to borders: choose a style of line that complements the subject and be consistent. Each border must serve a purpose; no border should call attention to itself.

Figure 7-5

Subjects and borders, clockwise from top right. The angularity of Futura dictates a square border, Palatino's rash Y insists on breaking out of its border, an ovoid border echoes the shape of ovoid Helvetica o, and the scooped transitions in the Schoolbook q suggest a scalloped border.

Borders also present an additional design factor: corners. Should corners be square or round? Once again, turn to the subject for your answer. The angularity of Times dictates a square-corner border, the roundness of Bookman or Avant Garde suggests rounded corners. A photograph of the New York City skyline is reinforced by the angularity of square borders, the soft features of portraiture should have rounded—perhaps even cameoed—borders (Figure 7-5).

When to Use Them

Unlike rules, the self-contained nature of borders tends to isolate their contents, surrounding them with a frame that says "this is different," especially if the contents are typographic. This is significant. Before you draw a border, be sure that isolation is the

> **Borders isolate their contents: use them to separate text, add color, or surround art. Consider your subject before drawing a border. The subject will usually provide the clues necessary for line and corner decisions.**

desired result. Often the subtlety of rules—used in pairs top and bottom or left and right—may be an appropriate alternative.

Use borders to

- Separate a part of the text from the remainder, for emphasis

- Provide some typographical color to an otherwise gray page

- Break text into smaller, more appealing groupings

- Provide an appropriate border for line art or photographs

Exercise 7.2   Exiting the Cosmos

It helps to break out of the electronic cosmos now and again, and this is a good time to do so. Asked to design a piece entitled "Decorating with Ferns," a friend visited her local grocery store, purchased a number of doilies, scanned them, and used the resulting designs for borders around the pictures of ferns that accompanied the article.

You've been asked to provide designs for black-and-white magazine articles on three subjects: cooking with eggplants, the manufacture of dominos, and the theory and design of golf balls. In each case, the featured subject will be pictured often and prominently.

For each of the three subjects, suggest a typeface for use as display text and provide border formats for the illustrations. Look for border ideas outside of your electronic universe: nature, art supply stores, junk shops—each is a fertile resource for ideas and perhaps even materials from which to construct the borders themselves. If you have a scanner, scan your materials and use your desktop-publishing system to construct a number of borders to accompany your design.

Ornaments

The availability of Adobe's Zapf Dingbats for PostScript printers and Microsoft's Wingdings for TrueType provokes a brief discussion of *ornaments*—those little splashes of nontypographical color that are often used for emphasis and character.

Pi fonts offer dozens of bullets, boxes, arrows, stars, checks, flowers, and symbols that can spice up your documents and enhance communication efficiency. Because they're simply type— like Times or Helvetica—they're available at the touch of a key: effortless, immediate gratification (see Figure 7-6).

Their convenience, however, sets a trap that always awaits the desktop publisher: overuse. Used sparingly and purposefully, ornaments complement and enhance many typefaces and add visual impact to documents. Used without conscience, ornaments litter margins and white space best left unmolested. White space, you'll remember, is a powerful design element. Novice desktop publishers often look upon ornaments as an opportunity to fill "wasted" space, with fragmented copy and visual distractions the typical result (review Figure 7-1A).

Use discretion, but look upon ornaments as a convenient, effective source of communication efficiency. Circled numbers can lend a "designed" feel to otherwise monotonous lists and instructions (review Figure 6-17). Pointing hands, snowflakes, and arrows can all be used as bullets (review Figure 5-30); boxes can be placed next to items on a list (and even checked, if desired); stylized quotation marks can set off pull quotes; and scissors can surround coupons, saying "cut here."

Ornaments can add character to a layout, but only when they're used with a clear concept of purpose and intent. The stylized heart and leaves of Figure 7-6 add sparkle to the piece and unify the text with the graphics, but always with a purpose: although the page abounds with ornaments, none have been used

Figure 7-6

We're sure Emily Dickinson would approve: properly used, Dingbats can unify a document and lend character that would otherwise be lacking. All ornaments—including the large heart—are Dingbats, appropriately chosen to complement not only the subject, but the Zapf Chancery typeface as well. Design courtesy of Adobe Systems Inc. © 1986 Adobe Systems, Inc. All rights reserved.

MISS EMILY'S
INTRODUCTION
SERVICE

Gentlepeople
We're delighted that you have chosen our services *After completing the enclosed questionnaire, please include the appropriate payment and return both to us*

Your friend
Emily Dickenson

① *Complete questionnaire*
② *Enclose payment*
③ *Mail to us*

for its own sake. Each ornament supports the theme or reinforces communication.

Figure 7-7

Line art achieves detail not with gradations of tone (as in photography) but with textures and patterns. These details are well suited to the monotonal environment of desktop publishing.

Use ornaments to reinforce the character of a document or serve as graphic signposts and enhance communication efficiency. They're subject to overuse, however—always question your motives before employing them.

Line Art

Though the desktop publisher rarely has the budget to hire an artist, line art is nonetheless very popular in the industry. There are two good reasons for this: there is an abundance of line art available for use without copyright infringements, and line art lends itself well to scanning (see Figure 7-7).

Line art is art without grays. Because grays are a problem in the desktop-publishing environment (a problem I discuss in the next chapter), line art is usually preferable to photography. Additionally, the absence of a gray background—and elimination of the need for borders in many cases—lends an openness and informality to the page that is not possible with photography.

Even more so than ornamentation, line art must always serve a purpose. Resist the temptation to fill "holes" with arbitrarily selected line art, no matter how humorous, elegant, or clever it may be.

Figure 7-8

Three early desktop-publishing tools, including high-end and low-end word processors and a high-volume output device. From "Harter's Picture Archive" by Dover Books.

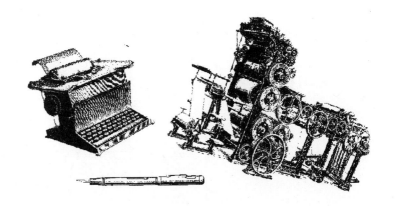

Clip Art

There's a gold mine in clip art out there, although most of it is in printed form. Hobby shops and art supply stores usually offer a number of titles. Most of these books cost less than $10 and offer hundreds of individual pieces of art (see Figure 7-8).

Before you buy one however, read the copyright notice. It's usually just inside the cover or soon thereafter. Typically you'll see a note that, in effect, says "go ahead and use this artwork as you wish, just don't use *everything* in this book to make a competitive product." Dover Books (see the endnotes to Chapter 5) usually grants permission to use 10 or fewer illustrations from one of their books in a single publication. Whatever the specifics may be, verify that the material you're about to use is free of copyright restrictions before you utilize it in your publication.

Scanners

Once the proper art is available, how do you convert it to an electronic format? The desktop publisher's favorite method is the scanner. Scanners convert practically any subject into the proper format for inclusion in desktop-published documents. Once in this form, artwork can be sized, cropped, bordered, and rotated—all electronically, using the appropriate software. Many desktop publishers consider a scanner to be a necessary component of their operation.

A scanner provides access to more than just clip art. Hand-held scanners (often found in the $100–$300 range) can scan

Figure 7-9

I projected, then hand-traced a photographic original and used the tracing to head a friend's column in the first newsletter I ever published.

wallpaper, textures (marble, granite), and even artwork you've done yourself. Because photographic production is such a problem (more about that later), you might want to try your hand at hand-tracing photographic material. Using an opaque or slide projector, even the most inartistic of us can trace an "artistic" rendering of a photograph, perhaps even enhancing the subject in the process. Armed with a pocket camera, I snapped a quick picture of my friend Willie (Figure 7-9), traced the snapshot with a pencil, and scanned the tracing.

In some situations, a scanned image is an improvement over the original. The original pencil strokes in Figure 7-9 revealed my lack of artistic confidence. The graininess of the scanned image not only hides the amateurism, it adds a coarse texture that actually improves upon the original.

Figure 7-10

A clip art city floats in a radial blend of grays. The design is furnished with Word for Windows 2.0, and appears courtesy of Microsoft Corporation.

Clip Art Services

A number of services have appeared offering clip art on disk, many of them in subscription form. Once every other month or so, a package arrives at your door with another couple of hundred images, ready for use (see Figure 7-10). No scanner is required. There are scores of providers, just look in the back of the latest computer magazine for their ads. Ask about copyright policies before you buy, and see the endnotes at the end of this chapter for a list of resources.

Clip art is available in either raster or vector format (read the next section, "Illustration Programs," for a discussion of raster and vector graphics.) Be sure you're buying a format you can use.

Copyrights

The federal copyright law is an attempt to stimulate creative endeavors by creating an economic monopoly for the originator of any creative work, whether it consists of music, words, art, or photographs. The U.S. Copyright Revision Act of 1976 clearly states that when you use someone else's copyrighted material, you must have the copyright holder's permission to do so. Moreover, section 106(2) further stipulates that only the copyright owner may "prepare derivative works based upon the copyrighted work." You can assume that this includes scanned images, even if they are modified using painting, drawing, or tracing software.

But don't trash the scanner yet. In this country, copyrights are granted from the moment of creation to fifty years after the creator's death. After that, the law assumes that the creative endeavor that it is trying to stimulate is beyond stimulation, and the endeavor falls into the public domain. In fact, anything created prior to August of 1906 is in the public domain, regardless of the longevity of its creator.

Aside from material in the public domain, almost everything printed is protected by copyright—*even if a copyright notice doesn't appear on it.* If you must use copyrighted material, write to the holder of the copyright for permission.

Because of its monotonality, line art may be the best form of artwork available to desktop publishers, and available it is, with an abundance of clip art in both printed and electronic form. It must have a purpose, however, and should never be used gratuitously.

Illustration Programs

All graphics come in two forms: *raster* or *vector*. Raster-based graphics (also called *bitmapped*) are the most common: they're what scanners produce. Vector-based graphics (also called *object-oriented*), on the other hand, offer more flexibility and potentially better quality (see Figure 7-11). Sound familiar? Computers handle text in exactly the same way, a matter we discussed in Chapter 3, "Selecting a Typeface."

A bitmapped graphic consists of a series of dots. When enlarged or reduced, however, the dots either become visibly large or overlap one another, producing either a graininess or a peculiar op-art effect called *moiré patterns*. Rotation causes problems as well. Bitmapped graphics, in other words, are best used at their original size and orientation.

A vector graphic is a series of strokes and arcs that together define the outlines of objects. A skyline of Manhattan might consist of hundreds of rectangles playing the parts of buildings, with thousands more rectangles serving as the windows into the buildings (review Figure 7-10). Because they can be manipulated mathematically, vector graphics size and rotate freely, with no loss of quality.

Tracing

Figure 7-12 examines a scanned, clip art graphic. It appears twice: as a raster (bitmap) of black dots, and again in vector format. The

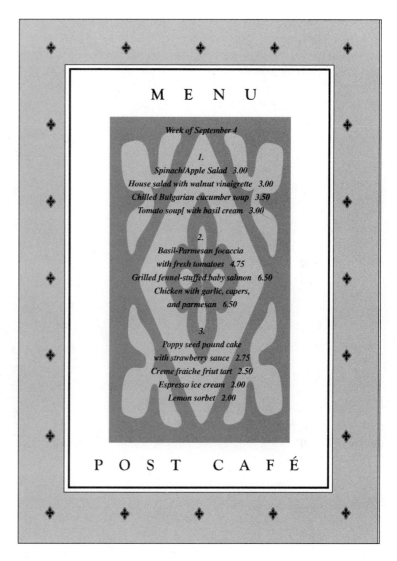

Figure 7-11

A wallpaper-like border complements a French restaurant's menu. Using an illustration program, the object-oriented border elements have been exaggerated and repeated to serve in the interior of the document as well. Design courtesy of Adobe Systems, Inc. © 1986 Adobe Systems, Inc. All rights reserved.

Figure 7-12

Raster vs. vector graphics. At their original sizes, the two graphics are difficult to tell apart. At 200% however, the graininess of the raster graphic becomes apparent.

Original size

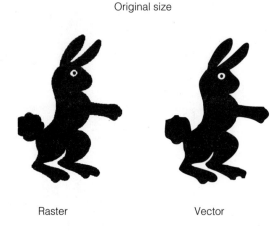

Raster   Vector

Enlarged 200%

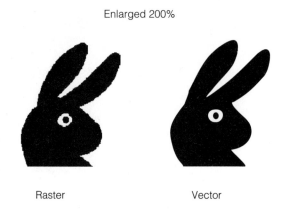

Raster   Vector

similarities are more profound than the differences, until the graphic is enlarged.

An enlarged map of black dots simply enlarges the dots, their number remains the same. An enlarged vector graphic is an arithmetic manipulation of the strokes and arcs that comprise the image. It's an unfathomable amount of work, but computers love math. Think of a compass drawing a circle: no matter how large the circle, its quality remains the same, only the size changes. We could print a billboard-sized image of the vector graphic in Figure 7-12, and the quality would remain the same.

Figure 7-13

Not bad, and certainly not very big, this wolf needs enlargement. Scan it, then trace the scan to obtain an infinitely sizable vector-based graphic.

You need to enlarge it; you may want to rotate it; you could just need a part of it. Only a vector-based graphic will do.

Scan it, then trace it with an illustration program.

Exercise 7.3   Scans and Traces

Figure 7-13 offers a fine little wolf to accompany the rabbit in Figure 7-12. I used these caricatures to illustrate a story on predator/prey interactions. Unfortunately, the original graphic was somewhat small (about the size you see in Figure 7-13), and I needed a cleaner version of it than my scanner provided. Additionally, I needed to stretch and compress the graphic (for use as the columns in a column graph), and I didn't want any jagged edges to develop.

The solution was to scan the graphic, then trace the scan using an illustration program. And that's what you're to do for this exercise: scan the wolf (for which you have my permission, but don't use it in any of your publications!), then use software to trace the scan and convert it into an object. Enlarge (and rotate, if you can) both the bitmap and the object, and compare the results.

That's why most vector graphic programs offer *tracing* functions. Simply put, the program overlays a bitmapped original with tracing paper and traces the image as a series of arcs and lines. The bitmap can then be discarded and the vector-based tracing used in its place. The vector-based rabbit in Figure 7-12 was

Blends and Masks

Most vector-based illustration programs offer spectacular *blends* (gradations of color or grays) and *masks,* where one opaque object is placed on top of another to mask part of the underlying object from view. Although these features may look spectacular on your screen, they're dickens to print, especially when they're printed on high-resolution imagesetters. Some won't even print at all.

The solution is to *rasterize* the vector-based graphic. Most illustration programs will do this: simply export (the Export command is usually found under the File menu) the graphic in the TIFF format. TIFF (Tag Image File Format) files are bitmaps and thus can't be enlarged or reduced reliably, but you can enlarge or reduce the graphic in the illustration program before it's exported, producing a bitmap that doesn't need to be resized. Try it: You'll save yourself a world of trouble when it comes time to print.

traced in *CorelDRAW!,* an object-oriented drawing program capable of producing quite elegant graphics (review Figure 2-7). Other popular vector drawing programs include Aldus's *FreeHand* and Adobe's *Illustrator.* All three programs include tracing commands.

Use illustration programs whenever ultimate quality and flexibility are required. They cannot equal the tonality of true photography or the convenience of scanned images, but their distinctive appearance and indigenous suitability to the desktop-publishing environment warrant consideration.

Modifying Text

Illustration programs allow you to specify rotation, body color, outline color and thickness, size, and distortion for letters just as you can for any other object. This exceptional flexibility allows you to create logos or initial letters that can be infinitely sized without fear of distortion or loss of resolution.

A *swash*—a fancy loop or extender attached to a letter—can also be added using illustration programs. The exotic typography in Figure 7-14 consists not only of exaggerated swashes, but highly distorted letterforms as well. This graphic could appear on flyers and billboards, ranging from playing-card size to 10 feet. This is an ideal application for illustration programs.

Graphics take time to produce using illustration programs, but illustration programs offer style and flexibility that aren't available in other types of programs. Although vector-based graphics will never replace bitmaps, and they will never equal true photography, they may be enlarged, reduced, rotated, skewed, or duplicated without loss of quality. Because of that (and because of their unique texture), illustration programs have created a new position in the spectrum of graphical possibilities.

Figure 7-14

Textual swashes and distortions (look at the word the) are most flexible when produced with an illustration program.

Resist the Temptation

As desktop publishers (and not designers), we must always exercise skepticism and restraint, especially with regard to nontypographical elements. Our tools are so convenient and flexible that the temptation to overdesign is almost irresistible.

Resist that temptation.

Instead, take an analytical approach to the inclusion of illustrations. As always, first consider the subject and the audience, then consider the application of graphics. How may they best be used to emphasize that which is important? Is there a tone or character to the document that graphics can reinforce? Might a nontypographical element be used to attract the browsing reader and make the subject appear irresistible? The answers are found in the dispassionate analysis of subject and reader. Such a vantage point encourages rational judgment—exactly what's required by those of us who haven't devoted a lifetime of study to the graphic disciplines.

Bibliography

Adonis Clip Art, 12310 NE 8th Street #150, Bellevue, WA 98005-9832.
  Subscription clip art service for the Macintosh and Windows.

Artbeats, PO Box 20083, San Bernardino, CA 92406.
  Professionally rendered EPS (vector) clip art. Numerous titles.

ArtMaker, 500 N. Claremont Blvd., Claremont, CA 91711.
  For DOS and Windows users, 250 PCX (raster) files rendered at 300 dpi.

Clipatures, Dream Maker Software, 7217 Foothill Blvd., Tujunga, CA 91042.
  Clip art collections in EPS (vector) format for the business user.

DesignClips, LetterSpace, 100 Wooster St., 2nd Floor, New York, NY 10012.
  A thorough library of graphic symbols collections in both TIFF (raster) and EPS (vector) formats.

Desktop Art, Dynamic Graphics, 6000 N. Forest Park Dr., Peoria, IL 61614-3592.

One of the larger subscription services, also offering *Print Media Service* and *Clipper*. Collections are published monthly and distributed along with *Ideas & Images*, a printed design guide.

Enabling Technologies, 343 South Dearborn, Suite 2000, Chicago, IL 60604.

Eight volumes of clip art containing over twelve hundred images in Macintosh and PC formats, raster and vector both.

FM Waves, 70 Derby Alley, San Francisco, CA 94102.

Both Macintosh and PC; raster and vector files of "clip art with an attitude" (their quote) on CD-ROM. Also available: *Graphic News Network*, a monthly subscription service.

FontHaus, 15 Perry Street A7, Norwalk, CT 06850.

In addition to alphabetic fonts, FontHaus offers a number of "picture fonts," including symbols and borders in the form of pi fonts.

Image Club, #5, 1902 11th Street S.E., Calgary, Alberta, Canada T2G 3G2.

Another of the large clip art services offering a prodigious collection of art, fonts, and photography.

Images with Impact, 3G Graphics, 11410 NE 124th St., Suite 6135, Kirkland, WA 98034.

A number of EPS (vector) collections of clip art.

Hedke, John: *The Windows Shareware 500*. Chapel Hill, NC: Ventana Press, 1993. (Macintosh users should see the endnote for Prevost.)

There's a wealth of clip art, fonts, utilities, and peer advice available from online services such as America Online and CompuServe. America Online, for example, offers over 30,000 Windows files, half of which are art and fonts. The CompuServe Aldus and Quark forums are the best place for support if you have *PageMaker* or *Xpress* questions. But you can't tell the players without a program, and this book whittles your thousands of online choices down to a manageable 500. If you're an online addict (and you should be—there are thousands of pieces of clip art and hundreds of inexpensive fonts available online), this book will pay for itself in a few months.

Lichty, Tom: *The America Online Tour Guide and Membership Kit.* Chapel Hill, NC: Ventana Press, 1993.

> Why mention this book here (other than to plug another of my books)? See the endnote for Hedke, above. America Online is without a doubt the best place to begin your online experience if you haven't done so already. This book includes all of the software you need to log on, 10 hours of connect time, and 400 pages of descriptions of what's available.

Metro ImageBase, 18623 Ventura Blvd., Suite 210, Tarzana, CA 91356.

> Metro is one of the leaders of printed clip art, and now, with over a dozen collections of 100 TIFF (raster) files, they're one of the leaders in electronic clip art as well.

Presentation Task Force, New Vision Technologies, Box 5468, Station F, Ottawa, Canada K2C 3M1.

> One of the first in the business. Most files are in CGM format for PC users.

Prevost, Ruffin, and Terrell, Rob: *The Mac Shareware 500.* Chapel Hill, NC: Ventana Press, 1993.

> See the comments under Hedke.

ProArt, Multi-Ad Services, 1720 W. Detweiller Dr., Peoria, IL 61615-1695.

> Another veteran of the printed clip art field goes electronic with EPS (vector) files on either disk or CD-ROM.

Totem Graphics, 5109-A Capitol Blvd., Timwater, WA 98501.

> Full-color EPS (vector) images,

Visual Arts, Electronic Pen Ltd., 4131 Cimarron Dr., Clarkston, GA 30021.

> Over 10 megabytes of EPS (vector) art.

Photographs

Ah, the photograph: its irresistible appeal, its brutal honesty, its efficient clarity. Why it's an ideal adjunct for the desktop publisher, and why moirés lurk behind every door.

T hroughout our formal education, we learn to associate reading with drudgery. "Read Chapter 14 before class tomorrow" spoils many a potential literary enthusiast. Television, *USA Today*, and *People* magazine are the predictable consequences of a society that has come to know the printed word as its adversary rather than its ally.

As desktop publishers, we must resign ourselves to this predicament and embrace the world of nonverbal communication. Our job is to package communication as attractively and effectively as possible, and our most alluring attraction is the photograph.

Photographic images lower the reader's resistance to literary content and provide a shortcut to effective communication. Selected properly, photographs illuminate, articulate, and define the subject. If we are to serve as effective communicators, photographs are a most worthy subject for a chapter of consideration.

Taking the Picture

As desktop publishers, we are usually involved with more than the layout of a publication. We write the stories, create the artwork, take the pictures, and design the layout. Of necessity, one of our responsibilities is that of photographic illustration, using the camera to clarify subjects already described editorially. Though the page-design concepts discussed in Chapter 6 apply to photographic design as well, black-and-white photographic concepts are the focus of this chapter (we discuss color in Chapter 9), and there's no better place to start than with taking the picture itself.

Selecting the Subject

A good photograph is one that supports and refines the message. Typically, the story is written, then photographs are taken to illustrate it. The first step is to evaluate the message. Is there some visual appeal about it that we can use to attract the reader's attention? Can a photograph help the reader understand a concept that is best described visually? Is there a sequence to the message that photographs might help define? Is there a mood that can be communicated or a personality that can be identified with a photograph? Photography can establish an atmosphere that can intrigue the reader and add appeal to the layout that would not otherwise be available. "Mood shots" are often tangential to the story and need not necessarily support it directly.

The next step is to play the part of the reader: read your story from the reader's perspective, and look for situations where the reader might benefit from visual clarification. If your newsletter is describing the failure of a building's heating plant and your readers are the clerical workers who work in the building, photographs of the faulty component might help them understand the cause of their discomfort (see Figure 8-1A). If your readers are the people who manufacture or maintain the heating plant, photographs of the freezing clerical workers might help establish a sympathy (see Figure 8-1B).

The Company Times

Volume 12, Number 11 — November, 1999

Heating plant on the fritz again!

Faulty valve may take a month to replace

Lorem ipsum dolor sit amet, consectetuer adipiscing elit, sed diam nonummy nibh euismod tincidunt ut laoreet dolore magna aliquam erat volutpat. Ut wisi enim ad minim veniam, quis nostrud exerci tation ullamcorper suscipit lobortis nisl ut aliquip ex ea commodo consequat. Duis autem vel eum iriure dolor in hendrerit in vulputate velit esse molestie consequat, vel illum dolore eu feugiat nulla facilisis at vero eros et accumsan et iusto odio dignissim qui blandit praesent luptatum zzril delenit augue duis dolore te feugait nulla facilisi. Lorem ipsum dolor sit amet, consectetuer adipiscing elit, sed diam nonummy nibh euismod tincidunt ut laoreet dolore magna aliquam erat volutpat. Ut wisi enim ad minim veniam, quis nostrud exerci tation ullamcorper suscipit lobortis nisl ut aliquip ex ea commodo consequat.

Duis autem vel eum iriure dolor in hendrerit in vulputate velit esse molestie consequat, vel illum dolore eu feugiat nulla facilisis at vero eros et accumsan et iusto odio dignissim qui blandit praesent luptatum zzril delenit augue duis dolore te feugait nulla facilisi. Lorem ipsum dolor sit amet, consectetuer adipiscing elit,

The main compressor distribution valve (above) must be replaced before we're warm again.

laoreet dolore magna aliquam erat volutpat. Ut wisi enim ad minim veniam, quis nostrud exerci tation ullamcorper suscipit lobortis nisl ut aliquip ex ea commodo consequat. Duis autem vel eum iriure dolor in hendrerit in vulputate velit esse

Nam liber tempor cum soluta nobis eleifendusme option congue nihil imperdiet doming id quod mazim placerat facer possim assum. Lorem ipsum dolor sit amet, consectetuer adipiscing elit, sed diam nonummy nibh euismod tincidunt

Inside:

Valve fritz 1
Long-range forecast 3
Workman's comp 5
Grievance committee ... 7
Dick & Jane announce baby 7
Newsletter awarded grant 9

Modern Comfort

The newsletter for today's heating-plant engineer — November, 1999

Distribution valve failure rate seen as threat to industry reputation

Lorem ipsum dolor sit amet, consectetuer adipiscing elit, sed diam nonummy nibh euismod tincidunt ut laoreet dolore magna aliquam erat volutpat. Ut wisi enim ad minim veniam, quis nostrud exerci ad minim veniam, quis nostrud exerci tation ullamcorper suscipit lobortis nisl ut aliquip ex ea commodo consequat.

Duis autem vel eum iriure dolor in hendrerit in vulputate esse molestie consequat, vel illum dolore eu feugiat nulla facilisis at vero eros et accumsan et iusto odio dignissim qui blandit praesent luptatum zzril delenit augue duis dolore te feugait nulla facilisi. Nam liber tempor cum soluta nobis eleifend option congue nihil imperdiet doming id quod mazim placerat facer possim assum.

Lorem ipsum dolor sit amet, consectetuer adipiscing elit, sed diam nonummy nibh euismod tincidunt ut laoreet dolore magna aliquam erat volutpat. Ut wisi enim ad minim veniam, quis nostrud exerci tation ullamcorper suscipit lobortis

Bundled against the cold, Jane Zapf-Bookman claims that productivity is down 50 percent and that she may never regain feeling in her left foot again.

tation ullamcorper suscipit lobortis nisl ut aliquip ex ea commodo consequat. Duis autem vel eum iriure dolor in hendrerit in vulputate velit esse molestie consequat, vel illum dolore eu feugiat nulla facilisis at vero eros et accumsan et iusto odio dignissim qui blandit praesent luptatum zzril delenit augue duis dolore te feugait nulla facilisi. Lorem ipsum dolor sit amet, consectetuer adipiscing elit, sed diam nonummy nibh euismod tincidunt ut laoreet dolore magna aliquam erat volutpat. Ut wisi enim

A

B

Figure 8-1

*A newsletter for clerical workers (**A**) might feature a photograph of a faulty heating-system component to document physical-plant problems. A newsletter for heating-plant engineers (**B**) might best capture the discomfort of system failure by picturing a clerical worker, bundled against the cold.*

Dominant Feature

As desktop publishers, most of our documents are informative; we're not producing coffee-table books or photo essays. Our photographs must communicate, and the most effective photographic tool in the pursuit of that goal is simplification. By simplifying your photograph, you expedite communication. If your photograph is an effective communicator and its statement reinforces the subject of the accompanying story, unity will be the result, and your layout will be the beneficiary.

In other words, once you've decided on the subject of your photograph, concentrate on it. If you're photographing an office worker who is torpid from cold, photograph the office worker's anguish. Exclude every other element from your photograph other than anguish. Amateur photography is littered with images of tiny subjects overwhelmed by colossal landscapes. Move in and fill the frame with your subject. Exclude distractions. Leave no room for doubt.

Analyze your story and your reader, then decide on suitable subjects for supporting photographs. Concentrate on those subjects as you take the photographs; strive for simplicity. Understand what your picture must say, then say it with certainty.

Background

If your subject is a person—a "mug shot" as they say in the publishing (and, unfortunately, the law enforcement) trade—take your photograph in a context that reinforces character. People love to look at pictures of people. It isn't that we're curious about appearance, we're curious about character, and the mug shot's primary responsibility is to express character. If your subject is a heating-plant engineer, include the heating plant in the background of the mug shot, capturing the profession as well as the person (Figure 8-2). People's workplaces are highly revealing of their characters. (So are their *hands*. Second only to the face, hands identify the subject's character, occupational background, and environment. Don't neglect to include them in your composition.)

The foreground might also be defined as "background"—a supportive element to the subject of the picture. Our office worker might be selectively photographed through the forest of her favorite houseplant, picturing not only the person, but her working environment as well (Figure 8-3).

Lighting

Strangely enough, light is the most frequent distraction in mug shots, especially light from flash bulbs. Placed too close to a wall and shot with a flash, your subject will cast a shadow monster, poised for the attack. Place your subject at least six feet away from walls, windows, and mirrors under these conditions (see Figure 8-4).

Figure 8-2

Photographed amidst the complexity of his heating plant, our engineer's picture tells us much more about him than would a simple mug shot.

We all know that windows and mirrors reflect flash and may obliterate the subject altogether, but certain less evident reflections can be just as distracting. Shot with a flash, the retina of the eye reflects an ethereal red (in color photos) or deathly white (in black-and-white photos). Smooth skin reflects flash light as "hot spots" of white—very necrophilic. The solution: bounce flash. If the ceiling is 10 feet or lower and relatively white, bounce your flash off of it, and allow two or three f-stops of additional exposure to compensate. If there is no ceiling, hold the flash away from the camera as far as possible to light from the oblique.

Finally, be wary of sunlight. Harsh sunlight casts strong shadows that may develop as black, a problem if the shadows appear under eyebrows or noses. Harsh sunlight also causes subjects to squint. Shoot in the shade.

Figure 8-3

The inclusion of her office environment (top) tells us much more about our office worker than a simple mug shot (below). The houseplant in the foreground frames the shot, softens the mood, and adds interest.

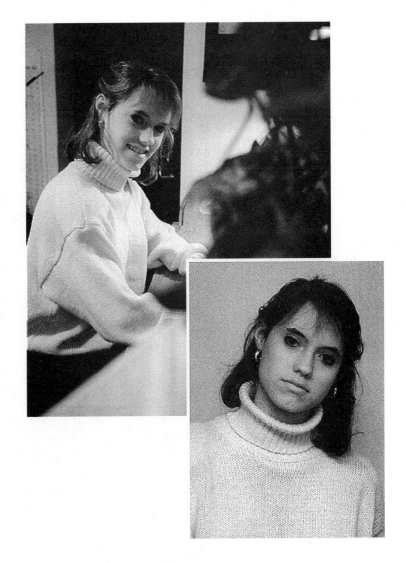

People look at pictures of people to judge character; mug shots should always strive to capture that character. Include a supportive background if possible, eliminate distractions, and shoot with reflected light.

Figure 8-4

Poor Helen Hall, she's overwhelmed by distractions, including the flash and even the photographer himself reflected in the mirror.

Exercise 8.1   Pictures in the Attic

Most of us have access to a pile of photographs we've taken over the years. Although it's a masochistic thing to do, haul that pile out and take a hard look at those photos with an eye for the design principles presented in this chapter. Is the dominant feature well defined? (Most snapshots are taken from too great a distance and no feature dominates.) Are there any distractions in the background? Is the lighting effective? Where is the light source?

Look for a good example and look for a bad example. Nearly every collection of photographs offers some of each. Why is the bad example bad? How would you change this picture if you could take it again? What's good about the good example? Is there any room for improvement?

Apply this kind of analysis to photographic layouts in the same way that you apply typographical analysis. Look for good and bad examples of lighting, directionality, and composition. Clip good examples for your swipe file. The most effective component of good design is awareness, and effective awareness is learned behavior.

Hang on to these pictures. We'll use them again in the next exercise.

Placing Pictures on the Page

Chapter 6 has already discussed the design principles that apply to the overall layout of the page. The inclusion of photographs should never disrupt those principles—indeed, photographs often provide opportunity to improve design.

Photographs present their own layout problems, however, and should never be placed on the page without regard for their content, captions, and significance.

Direction

People are rarely photographed full-face to the camera (excepting the law enforcement mug shot mentioned earlier, and this probably isn't your bailiwick). Generally speaking, people pictures face left or right. This directionality should always be respected and may even be exploited.

A cardinal rule states that people pictures should always look inward toward the page. No matter which way the original faces, you can always use software (or instruct the print shop if they're placing the photograph on the layout) to "flop" the image horizontally when it's placed in the layout. This is usually a good idea: people are made uncomfortable by pictures of people looking off the page. (*Watch out!* Mirrored images may result in violins bowed with the left hand, shirts buttoned from the wrong side, monograms spelling obscenities, or wedding rings on single people.) Review Figure 6-13: I had to reverse the direction of the finch there to keep it from flying off of the page. People looking up provoke curiosity (try it in a crowd); people looking off the page encourage investigation; people facing people are friendly; people with backs turned are not.

With the introduction of version 5.0, *PageMaker* included a button to flop graphic images (it's in the upper right corner of the Control Palette whenever a graphic is selected). Normally, however, flipping an image is best done by the scanning program that originally acquired it.

Design your layout with an awareness of the directionality of its photographs. This directionality should contribute to the rhythm of the page and may even establish its mood.

Grouping Photographs

Usually, a series of photographs of the same subject is more interesting than a solitary picture. If they're available, consider using several photographs, but don't pepper them about the page. Group them instead, playing with directionality and dominance within the group. Groupings are more interesting to the viewer, and they contribute an element of unity to the page as well (see Figure 8-5).

Be aware of the viewer's tendency to browse through your groupings from the left to the right. If there is an order or rhythm to your grouping, arrange it to take advantage of this tendency.

One caveat: If landscapes are involved, arrange your grouping so that the horizons are aligned. Landscape photographs are like windows in a wall. Looking at a wall of windows, we expect to see an aligned landscape extending across each window, regardless of their arrangement. Your reader expects the same of your photographs.

Size as a measure of importance. A grouping of pictures all of the same size is not only dull, it indicates a lack of commitment. As is the case with the photograph, there must also be a dominant feature of the group. If multiple photographs are to appear on the page, vary their sizes and allow one to dominate.

By varying sizes you emphasize your subject, leaving no doubt about dominance and subordination. If your story is about a harried heating-plant engineer, let his or her picture dominate the layout. Supportive photographs—of frayed insulation and torpid

Figure 8-5

A grouping of photographs tells the story far better than would a single picture. An odd number of photographs (always more interesting than an even number), sized and cropped to lend vitality to the arrangement and emphasis to the message, is always best.

clerical workers—corroborate the main theme and add detail. Signal the Big Idea with a Big Picture. The essence of editing, after all, is to understand the central issue and to focus the reader's attention on it.

Group, rather than scatter, multiple photographs. Decide upon the grouping's dominant statement, and size the photographs accordingly. Groupings provide unity and differing sizes provide contrast, adding interest and enthusiasm to your design.

Exercise 8.2   A Family Newsletter

If you still have that collection of family photographs you found in the attic during Exercise 8.1, scan them and prepare a layout using your desktop-publishing software. Follow the principles suggested in this section of the book. Remember to place the photos with an awareness of their directionality and group them, if possible, in odd-number groupings.

If you really do have access to some old family snapshots and a scanner, you might as well get some mileage from this exercise by writing a little family newsletter. Mail it to everyone concerned. Perhaps your sister in Toledo will remember you with a present next Christmas if you do.

Bleeds

Some artwork—rules and photographs especially—may be printed all the way to the edge of the page for effect, a procedure referred to as a *bleed*. Unlike line art, most photographs are surrounded by a frame of white space that confines the subject. Photographs bleeding beyond the edge of the page break out of that confinement, providing the illusion that there's more out there beyond the page. It is an effective illusion if the subject is appropriate. Landscapes are well suited to bleeding, mug shots are not.

Bleeds make their subject (and the page) appear larger, they break monotony, and they provide an undeniable direction to the layout. Though bleeds are effective, there are two good reasons for caution. First, consider the margin: margins provide unity to a multipage document and frame the contents of the page. Bleeds violate the margin. This is why bleeds are effective at attracting attention, but it's also why bleeds must be approached with caution. Is the subject appropriate? Is it worthy of the attention that it's going to receive? Will the bleed help or hinder communication? If the answers to these questions justify the bleed, don't be shy. Because you're going to make such a bold statement anyway, make a **BOLD STATEMENT**, don't whisper.

Bleeds with Laser Printers

Few laser printers are capable of printing to the edge of the page. Typically, a small margin is required left and right. (Review Exercise 2.1 if you're not familiar with your printer's limits.)

Many photocopy machines can print to the edge of the paper, however. So can most print shops.

Let's say that your photocopy machine can enlarge a page to 125% of the original. All you have to do is prepare your page normally—positioning the bleed slightly beyond the edge of the page with your desktop-publishing software—and print at the inverse of 125%, or 80% of normal. Place the result in the photocopier (or send it to the print shop), specify 125% enlargement and *voila!* Bleeds—right off the edge of the paper.

On a more practical level, a bleed may cost you too much money. Most printing presses can't print to the edge of a page—the press's "grippers" require an un-inked edge to handle the paper. To accommodate a bleed, the printer has to print on paper larger than the finished size and trim the edges later. This may require special paper and extra handling. Get a cost estimate from your printer before becoming too enamored with the thought of bleeds.

Captions

If there are many photographs (or illustrations) in your layout, most readers will graze on them before reading the accompanying story. With this in mind, write your captions—the short descriptive paragraphs that accompany artwork—to stand alone, independent of the body text. Taken as a collective whole, captions (you may also hear them referred to as *legends*) should tell a complete, albeit brief, version of the story, relying on the accompanying artwork for detail. Captions receive high readership: sell your story with them.

No photograph is so striking or so evident that it can run without a caption. Readers look at a photograph and then look for its caption. If the caption is missing or hard to locate, irritation and frustration set in; at best communication suffers, at worst you may lose the reader entirely. Thus, include a caption for each photograph, and place them closely together. There should be an adhesive quality between the two: the caption should appear just above, below, to the left, or to the right of the photograph. Leave no doubt about which caption refers to which photo.

Pick a contrasting type style for your captions, and stick with it throughout the publication. If there are many photographs, captions become an important design element. If their style varies from photograph to photograph, the unity of the design suffers. Usually, a self-effacing, light-body type style is used—italics are common, set no larger and often somewhat smaller than the body text. Let the picture do the talking; make the caption play a supportive role.

It's best to set your captions unjustified, with the straight edge of the caption aligned with a straight edge of the accompanying photograph. Avoid hyphenation: even though captions are often set in short, narrow columns of their own, an excessively ragged edge is preferred to the distraction of hyphenated words. Grazing readers prefer to gulp their captions without chewing.

Captions receive high readership. Include one with every photograph, and write it independently of the accompanying story. Assign captions a contrasting, supportive type style— unjustified and unhyphenated for maximum readability.

Technicalities

In the previous chapter, we considered line art and the other monotonal graphic elements that are well suited to desktop publishing. A photograph, on the other hand, consists of black and white and all the tones in between. Continuous-tone art like this requires an altogether different approach than that of line art—an approach that requires a thorough understanding of the medium.

Memory Requirements

Consider the memory requirements of a 5-by-7-inch image that is to be reproduced using a 300-dpi laser printer. Each square inch requires 300 multiplied by 300, or 90,000, dots. Our 5-by-7-inch image consists of 35 square inches, or 3.15 million dots. Because it requires a byte of memory to describe a dot in one of 256 levels of gray, our 5-by-7-inch, black-and-white image requires 3.15 megabytes of memory to display our picture. Although compression techniques enable us to *store* the picture (on a disk) in about a third of that space, all three megabytes have to be available if we want to display it on the screen and manipulate it using image-manipulation software.

Such a deal.

In other words, don't judge an image's memory requirements by observing its file size. Most images are compressed when they're stored, but they're all decompressed when they're brought into memory.

Printing Requirements

Desktop laser printers have a notorious problem printing grays. There's only one color—black—of toner inside them, so to produce grays, they have to *dither* the image—a process that's analogous to the screening process newspapers and magazines use to print grayscale images with black ink.

It stands to reason that some laser printers handle grays better than others. Cost is usually a factor: expensive printers usually print better grays than inexpensive ones. And even some of those printers that print beautiful grays print them in such a way that inexpensive printing processes—quick printing and photocopying—can't reproduce them.

This all falls back on one of the principles described in Chapter 2: Know your system. Know how well your laser printer can reproduce grays and how well your print shop can print them.

An alternative is to take the photograph to the print shop and ask them to produce a *halftone* for you. Halftoning involves a tried-and-true photographic process that guarantees accurate and reliable photographic reproduction under nearly any printing circumstances. The cost is about 10 dollars a page and a page can contain more than a single photograph.

So why bother with scanners and prodigious memory? In spite of the technological difficulties, there are nonetheless two good reasons for scanning photographs and including them in desktop-publishing documents.

First, consider the utility of a scanned photograph. Electronically placed in the layout, a scanned photograph can help us visualize the page. We can position it, crop it, and size it with our desktop-publishing software—all the while observing the results on the screen. We can try hundreds of layouts in minutes and print those that look promising in seconds. The expense is minimal. High resolution and a broad grayscale aren't necessary for these purposes. We can even scan the original as line art, without tonality. A low-resolution (inexpensive) scanner is all that's required, the memory requirements aren't prohibitive, and even a dot-matrix printer can print the image.

This flexibility is unique to desktop publishing. It's one of desktop publishing's primary advantages over conventional design. If you're going to include photographs in your publication, by all means scan them and include them in your rough layouts. Graphic artists with years of experience may be able to envision the impact of a photograph on a layout without seeing it there, but we cannot. If we're expected to design professional-quality layouts, we need all the help we can get.

That's reason number one: conceptualization.

Reason number two has to do with communication. Printers are notoriously rushed and can make decisions or mistakes that compromise the integrity of our designs. Wherever possible, communication—especially communication regarding the positioning, sizing, and cropping of photographs—must be as clear and comprehensive as possible.

There's no better way than to include properly positioned, sized, and cropped photographs in the rough layout. These images—regardless of their quality as long as they're recognizable—unambiguously provide contextual instructions to the printer. Simply print the layout complete with its rough images, write "For position only" in grease pencil or felt-tip pen right across each picture, and provide the print shop with both the printed layout and the original photographs. The print shop will screen the photographs (converting them to halftones) and paste the halftones onto the layout (or strip them into the negative) where you've indicated they're to go. Never again will Jane Zapf's photograph appear above Dick Bookman's name.

Moiré Patterns

Both *PageMaker* and *Xpress* size, crop, and rotate scanned photographs, a convenience that's especially evident when you con-

Figure 8-6

At right, a scanned image appears at its original size. Reduced by an indiscriminate value at far right, the image displays a moiré pattern.

trast it with the manual methods we had to use only a few years ago. Unfortunately, a reliance on this convenience can backfire.

All scanners convert images into a series of electronic dots. Certain settings—especially those that produce scanner halftones (as opposed to the settings that produce grayscale images) result in a series of black dots that, similar to printers' halftones, are nothing but black dots: no gray at all. At the other end of the process, your laser printer also employs a series of dots to simulate grays on paper. These dots—the scanner at the front end and the printer at the back—must be aligned or *moiré patterns* develop.

Let's say you've set your scanner to produce halftones, and the scanner produces dots A, B, and C. If these dots align exactly with dots A, B, and C at the printer, everything occurs as predicted. But what if you enlarge the image a bit? Scanner dot A still may align with printer dot A, but scanner dot B (which has been enlarged and is now slightly farther away from dot A than it was before) may no longer align with printer dot B. It might fall halfway between printer dot B and printer dot C, or perhaps it covers them both. Regardless, a new texture emerges in the finished product. The texture usually resembles some sort of a repeating pattern akin to wallpaper. It's rarely attractive, never intended, and always a problem. Such is the nature of moiré patterns (see Figure 8-6).

There are four solutions to the moiré menace, (1) If your scanner's software offers a halftone option, don't use it unless you intend to print the image at its original size. (2) Take the photograph to the print shop as mentioned earlier and ask them to provide a halftone *at the size required*. (3) Use an image-editing program like Adobe's *Photoshop* to size the graphic intelligently. If you provide *Photoshop* with the image size and resolution you want, it takes care of the rest. (4) Use the Control Palette (*PageMaker*) or the Measurements Palette (*Xpress*) to declare a percentage of enlargement or reduction that won't cause moirés. For this you must know the resolution of your scanned image and the resolution of your printer and follow this formula:

Image resolution ÷ output resolution x any whole number x 100 = scaling percentage

For example, if you wanted to print a 300-dpi image on a 1270-dpi imagesetter, you would divide 300 by 1270 (.2362) and multiply that by 100, or 200, or 300, or some other multiple of 100. Such an image should be sized to 23.62%—or some multiple of that value—to avoid moiré patterns.

Scanning Halftones

This chapter assumes that you are using original continuous-tone images. Photographs are actually composed of an infinite number of grays. Newspapers and magazines don't use gray ink to print photographs, they make halftone representations of originals. A series of tiny dots—all black—do the job: big dots for dark areas; little dots for light areas.

Scanning halftones is asking for trouble, legal as well as technical. They're legal trouble because most halftones appear in copyrighted publications. They're technical trouble because the scanning process converts an image into a series of dots, but if that image already *is* a series of dots, you're in effect trying to make dots out of dots. That's a bit like trying to make a sheep out of gabardine: the process simply doesn't work backward. If the original isn't a true photograph, leave the scanner on the shelf.

Scanned photographic images require an acute awareness of the system, including the printer. Treat them with awareness and understanding. Consider the traditional (halftone) alternative if you're not sure of the process.

Exercise 8.3   Moirés by Choice

You don't even need a scanner for this exercise, just your desktop-publishing program and a printer. The exercise uses employs a screen shot of your computer screen, something that both Macintoshes and Windows machines can do without any additional hardware. Screen shots are similar to scanner-produced halftone images.

1. Take a screen shot of your computer's screen. If you're using a Macintosh, press Shift-Command-3 (use the 3 key on the typewriter keyboard, not the 10-key pad). This will produce a file named Picture 1 on your startup disk. If you're using a Windows machine, press the Print Screen key. This will place a picture of the screen on the Clipboard, ready for pasting. (Some Windows machines require you to press the Print Screen key twice: test yours to find out.)

Magic Stretch

PageMaker offers a unique feature called Magic Stretch. In essence, Magic Stretch confines TIFF (bitmapped) images to only those sizes that won't cause moiré patterns when the image is printed. To invoke this feature, hold down the Command (Macintosh) or Control (PC) key as you size a graphic by dragging on one of its handles. Hold down the Shift key as well, to confine the graphic to its original proportions. Only certain sizes will be available when these keys are held down, and they're the only sizes that won't cause moiré patterns. It saves a bit of math.

2. If you're using a Macintosh, import or place the file named Picture 1 into an otherwise blank document that's open in your desktop-publishing software. If you're using a Windows computer, simply choose Paste from your desktop-publishing software's Edit menu. Again, a blank document must be open.

3. Repeat step 2 two more times, for a total of three images, all on a single page.

4. Use the Control Palette (*PageMaker*) or Measurements Palette (*Xpress*) to enlarge one of these images somewhat. Reduce one of the other images somewhat as well. Leave the third image at its original size.

5. Print the page and look for moiré patterns in the images. Don't be surprised if the original displays moiré patterns when it's printed. The resolution of your screen may not bear an integral relationship to the resolution of your printer.

Between Snapshots and Art

Photography encompasses a spectrum that extends from the informality of snapshots to the discipline of art. As desktop publishers, we must exclude these extremes and concentrate on the supportive role of photographic illustration. We must have a clear vision of our reader and our message and supply photographs that satisfy the needs of both.

In the layout, photographs must be given the same consideration as any other design element: the proportion, balance, contrast, rhythm, and unity of the page are all subject to the influence of its photographs, just as photographs are subject to these design elements within themselves.

Even the most appropriate photographs and the most effective designs can fall victim to inappropriate technology, however— a beguiling enticement that leaves most desktop publishers defenseless. Although electronically reproduced photographs offer an undeniable convenience, an awareness of the processes used by the scanner and by the printer is paramount to success.

Finally, a note of prudence. Don't become too enamored with photography. Remember that some subjects simply do not lend themselves to photographic embellishment. On occasion, photographs can be redundant, even anticlimactic. And if you can't afford it, if that which is available is of mediocre quality, or if most of your photographs are of the inside of your lens cap, don't jeopardize your publication. Professionally crafted typography, arranged on the page with proper rules and white space, is preferable to amateur photography any day.

Bibliography

Finberg, Howard, and Itule, Bruce: *Visual Editing: A Graphic Guide for Journalists*. Belmont, CA: Wadsworth, 1990.
Valuable information on the use of photographs in document design. This book also provides a glimpse into the journalistic changes that have been prompted by desktop publishing.

Pattison, Polly; Pretzer, Mary; and Beach, Mark: *Outstanding Newsletter Designs*. Available from Polly Pattison, 5092 Kingscross Road, Westminster, CA 92683.
This fully illustrated book lives up to its title's promise.

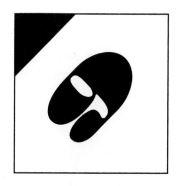

Color

With all the hulla blue going on,
let's go out and paint the town vermillion

Few industries have undergone as extensive or abrupt a change as the color prepress industry has in the past decade. Traditional photographic color prepress—the separation of a color image into its primary color components for process color printing—has been eliminated by an electronic process that uses the very programs we've discussed in this book: *Xpress*, *PageMaker*, *Photoshop*, and a few others.

This massive industry shift has provoked a skewed perception by the general desktop-publishing marketplace regarding the significance of color. Color is to Aldus and Quark as automobile racing is to Ford and General Motors: whoever leads the race wins prestige and sales, yet few buyers will use the product for that purpose. Unfortunately, the general market for desktop-publishing software hasn't yet made that distinction. Most desktop publishers feel feverishly compelled to use color. It's the thing to do. That's like feeling compelled to race your 1991 Escort in the Indianapolis 500.

Relax, Mario Andretti. Taken quantitatively, 99 percent of the documents produced by desktop publishers are black-and-white.

193

Blue Moons

The term *blue moon* refers to a second full moon occurring in the same month as the first. As I write this chapter, it's nearly the end of August, 1993, and in a few days we will experience a rare and genuine blue moon. The first full moon this month occurred on the 2nd; the second will take place on the 31st. A blue moon: how appropriate an event for the writing of a chapter on color!

Ninety-nine percent of the driving you do in your 1991 Escort is pretty tame as well. You'll only encounter a drag race from a green light once in a blue moon, and even then you'll probably stumble and falter and perhaps even embarrass yourself a bit. Color is a similar experience for many desktop publishers.

Why Use Color

Indianapolis 500 or not, there are occasions when your motivation (and budget) suggest the use of color. Understand, however, that color is a powerful element. A blind friend of mine once described humans as a "visual species" (a poignant and uniquely perceptive observation, I thought), and more than most creatures, our visual perception is dominated by color. In *Designing with Color* (see the endnotes), Berry and Martin claim that color stimulates 40 percent more interest than black and white—a power to be used with caution and respect.

In other words, have a game plan. Begin with an understanding of why your document warrants this kind of authority. A number of reasons come to mind.

Emphasis

Whenever color is included in an otherwise monochromatic design, it's usually the first thing the eye notices. The *fovea centralis* is a small pit in the retina where detailed visual observation occurs. Because the fovea is such a tiny area, the eye rarely lingers. In its quest for the acquisition of maximum information, the eye roves, following one of the paths described in the rhythm section of Chapter 6. If this natural inclination is disturbed—if the initial area of attention is poorly defined or if the subsequent path is ambiguous, you've lost your initial advantage.

Understand that establishing emphasis with color isn't difficult—color is what the eye wants to see first—as long as you allow one element to dominate, color it wisely, and then offer the eye a clear path to follow from there on. Work with a single focal point in mind, and retain a sense of direction throughout the design.

Figure 9-1

The RGB color-editing dialog box from Quark Xpress for Windows. The color wheel in the dialog box matches the color wheel shown in Figure 9-4.

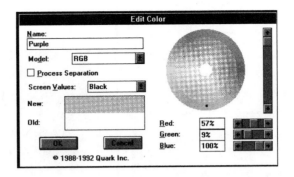

Color Models Desktop publishing provides three different methods—so-called *color models*—to define and reproduce any particular color. Two of these have to do with machines.

The *RGB* color model relates to *additive* color—color that emanates from its source. This would be a rare event—most color is reflected from objects; few objects emit colors of their own—were it not for television. Indeed, RGB is the television standard, and even though a television set can produce a nearly infinite variety of color, it does so using only the three primary emitted colors: red, green, and blue (see Figure 9-1). At intensities of 100%, red, green, and blue produce white.

The *CMYK* color model relates to *reflected* (or *process*, or *subtractive*) color. By combining various percentages of cyan (a blue-turquoise color, pronounced *sy'-an*), magenta (a purplish red color), and yellow inks, we are able to produce the same infinite variety of colors on paper that television does on screen. In theory, only cyan, magenta, and yellow are required for the printed (reflected) representation of all colors, but in practice it takes so much cyan, magenta, and yellow ink to represent black that smearing, drying time, and cost become a factor. And because most printed pages contain text (and thus a lot of black), a fourth color of ink is added to the color model—black—to expedite the situation. They don't call it CMYB (*B* for black) however, because there's a tendency to associate *B* with blue. Instead, they chose *K* (for *chroma*, the ancient Greek term for color saturation), thus CMYK—the standard for the printing industry (see Figure 9-2).

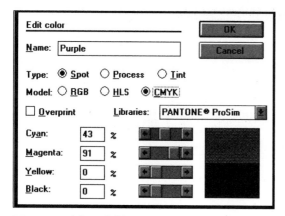

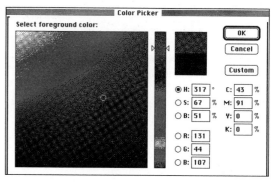

Figure 9-2 (above left)

The Edit Color dialog box from PageMaker for Windows defining purple using the CMYK color model.

Figure 9-3 (above right)

The Color Picker dialog box from Adobe Photoshop for the Macintosh. Purple is represented numerically in all three color spaces. The vertical shaded box represents hue; the large shaded box represents brightness (100% top, 0% bottom) and saturation (0% left, 100% right).

The third color model relates neither to television nor to printing presses, but to the human perception of color: *HSB*, or *hue*, *saturation*, and *brightness* (see Figure 9-3). *Hue* is what we usually think of when we speak of color: red is a different hue than blue. *Saturation* is a bit like adding or removing pigment. Unsaturated blue is baby blue. Removing *brightness*—also referred to as *tone*, *value*, or *lightness*—is a bit like adding black paint to a color. Navy blue is blue with less brightness.

Color Saturation   We're still talking about emphasis, and as long as we continue to talk about the perception of color (as opposed to the reproduction of it), we must refer to the HSB color model.

Of the three factors, saturation is the most effective when it comes to emphasis. A fully saturated color usually expresses more emphasis than one that's pale, regardless of the color itself. Unsaturated colors are perceived as passive or washed out.

In summary, remember that saturation is your best ally when it comes to providing emphasis. The principles relating to contrast, balance, proportion, and rhythm apply here as well. A single, fully saturated color element will almost always become the design's contrasting element: balance it with other, more moderate elements, set it in proportion to them, and develop a rhythm that reinforces its celebrity.

Purple: Uniquely Man-Made

I used purple as my example in Figures 9-1, 9-2, and 9-3 because as a color, purple is an anomaly. Of all the hues, purple doesn't occur in nature. The rainbow represents nature's colors—all hues, fully saturated, lightness depending on environmental conditions— ranging from red (always on top of the rainbow) to violet (on the bottom, if the rainbow is fully defined). Purple is actually a blend of red and violet, which would put it below violet on the rainbow. Violet, however, is the rainbow's bottommost color; thus, purple is uniquely man-made.

For effective emphasis, consider a fully saturated color that's allowed to dominate the design. Remember that the eye is constantly on the move, however, and provide it with a path to follow once it has observed your focus.

Decoration

Decorative color is best accomplished with a bit of pluck. Candor and honesty belong here. This is no place to be timid. I'm not encouraging chromatic anarchy: don't slash at your design with random acts of color. Make your marks intentionally, but make them with an eye toward the subject and the reader.

Hue plays a leading role in the decorative abstract; saturation is of lesser importance. Indeed, because saturated colors tend to dominate the design, larger areas of less-saturated colors serve better as decorative elements than do saturated colors, even if the saturated areas are small. Choose hues that complement the subject: browns and greens are natural; grays, blacks, and purples are exclusive; primary colors are active; violets and pinks are romantic.

Consider coloring rules, borders, and elements. If you're limited to a single second color, remember that you can simulate multiple colors by shading the one you have. *PageMaker's* Element menu provides access to shaded fills; choose Modify from the *Xpress* Item menu for the same effect.

Whereas color for emphasis may be limited to smaller areas, decorative color areas are usually large (as large as the paper itself—we'll discuss colored paper in a few pages). Small areas of decorative color are often lost on the page; large areas work more effectively.

Figure 9-4

The color wheel.

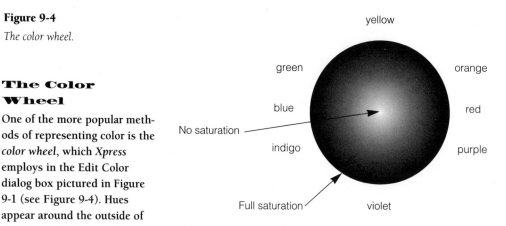

The Color Wheel

One of the more popular methods of representing color is the *color wheel*, which *Xpress* employs in the Edit Color dialog box pictured in Figure 9-1 (see Figure 9-4). Hues appear around the outside of the *Xpress* circle, traveling counterclockwise following the rainbow's "Roy G. Biv" convention (red, orange, yellow, green, blue, indigo, violet). Purple—the man-made color mentioned earlier—completes the circle by appearing between violet and red. Saturation extends radially from the center of the wheel, with the lowest degree of saturation at the center. Imagine dimming the lights as you look at the wheel to conceptualize brightness.

Colors appearing opposite one another on the wheel are referred to as *complementary* colors. Actually, that's a bit of a misnomer: in their purest form, complementary colors often vibrate or buzz when they appear side by side. On the other hand, colors adjacent to one another on the wheel harmonize quite nicely. Three points on the wheel that are equally spaced—think of the points on the Mercedes star logo—are known as a *triad*, an especially effective color combination.

Consider decorative color as you would consider the color of upholstery in a room. Like upholstery, decorative color is often muted and abundant, and it should always contribute to the unity of the design.

Clarification

Used as an articulator—infrequently and in small sizes—color provides an effective exclamation point. Think of warnings printed in red, colored diagrams with matching colored references in the text, red negative values in spreadsheets, or the colored terms in help files on which you click for a definition.

To function effectively as a clarifier however, color should be used sparingly and at full saturation. The areas of color should be small and singular: red warnings lose their impact if yellow, orange, and brown all appear on the same page.

Exercise 9.1   Product Identification

Advertisers have known for years that color, used repeatedly and saturated fully, stimulates memory, and therefore product identifi-

Test Those Tints

Working with a rich maroon secondary color, a friend sought to reinforce the elegant mood of her design with a number of shades, ranging from 20 to 60 percent. Proofed on her laser printer, the design looked handsome. She rubbed her hands in anticipation when it went to press, anxious to see the impact the maroon would provide.

When 4,000 copies arrived on her desk, she was aghast to discover her maroon document riddled with pink! Indeed, orange, red, reddish brown, and brown inks all tend toward pink when they're shaded. There's no such thing as "light maroon," it's a contradiction of terms.

Test a shaded design either on your system's color printer or on a color printer at a local copy shop. You might have to provide color separations (both *PageMaker* and *Xpress* offer this option in their Print dialog boxes, though you'll need a PostScript printer to separate using *Xpress*) for the print shop: call ahead and tell them that you just want to proof a color layout. They'll tell you what they need.

Critique the proof mercilessly. Does the design represent your intent? If an error in judgment was made, be thankful that 4,000 copies of that error don't sit on your desk at the moment, mocking your lack of foresight.

cation, as effectively as the product's name or logo. Quickly now: Name the colors that come to mind when I mention Coca-Cola, Ford, John Deere, IBM, Apple, or Kodak. (Kodak, by the way, experimented with blue in place of their trademark yellow in 1914 and sales dropped significantly.)

For this exercise, take an hour to cruise a department or grocery store and make notes regarding the use of color found on the shelves. Few places are as competitive for attention as display shelves at retail stores. Madison Avenue devotes its best to package design, and that includes color. What works? What doesn't? How do colors relate to their products or to their products' markets? Do any colors appear more frequently than others? What kinds of colors (primary, secondary) predominate?

Very little ground remains to be broken regarding the use of color. Thousands of expensive studies have been commissioned, and the results of those studies are most apparent in product packaging. Observe and be wise.

Color clarifies information by relying on either convention or repetition. If color is to serve this purpose in your publication, use it sparingly, in small areas, and at full saturation.

Continuity

Think of blue Helvetica bold subheads. Microsoft is fond of this technique. Blue subheads march throughout the length of their manuals, establishing effective signposts for the reader and facilitating subject location. To reinforce the effect, 4-point rules appear at the top of each page, providing continuity even for those pages that don't contain subheads.

Two Ball in the Side Pocket

Table 9-1 is based on Faber Birren's *Color Psychology and Color Therapy,* a reference that's not only thorough, but lucid and entertaining as well. Birren worked as a consultant for years, first in Chicago and later in New York. One early client was New Brunswick, the pool-table people. The problem: people were not buying pool tables for home use. Birren found that it was a matter of color psychology. American women would not have the green-topped tables in their homes, he learned, because they associated this color with pool halls and gambling. Birren recommended changing the color of the table, and sales flourished.

Nowhere is color more evident as an element of continuity than in road signs. Quickly: Name the color used for stop signs, warning signs (curves ahead, yield), and informational signs (New York 63 mi). Primarily because it is used infrequently in road signs, blue is especially effective at identifying rest stops along the interstate system.

Color is especially effective as an element of continuity in design. A single color is best for this, and use it for no other purpose. Be particularly consistent, and choose a color that's readily identifiable but not too loud.

Mood

Interestingly, the emotional effect of color isn't entirely subjective. Quickly: What's your favorite color? What was your favorite color when you were seven? Are the two answers the same? Probably not. Color preferences are well documented and predictably objective. Children prefer colors with longer wavelengths: red, orange, and yellow. After several years (I won't humble you with an enumeration of an exact amount), preferences shift toward color with shorter wavelengths: blue, indigo, and violet.

Long-wavelength colors are generally referred to as *warm*; short-wavelength colors are *cool*. Muted blues, oranges, and reds are often associated with the American Southwest; greens, yellows, and browns are associated with nature (and the military, for those who are acquainted with the military's camouflage color schemes); primary colors are associated with children; and blues are invariably considered pure.

Table 9-1 presents most of the primary colors on the color wheel and the psychological effect they have on us. Refer to it the next time you're unsure of the emotional impact of color.

Table 9-1   Unsure of the Psychology of Color? Consult this table.

	General Appearance	Mental Assoiacations	Direct Associations	Objective Impressions	Subjective Impressions
Red	Brilliant, intense, opaque, dry	Hot, fire, heat, blood	Danger, holidays, the flag	Passionate, exciting, fervid, active	Hilarity, exuberance, safety
Orange	Bright, luminous, glowing	Warm, metallic, autumnal	Halloween, Thanksgiving	Jovial, lively, energetic, forceful	Hilarity, exuberance satiety
Yellow	Sunny, incandescent, radiant	Sunlight	Caution	Cheerful, inspiring, vital, celestial	High spirits, health
Green	Clear, moist	Cool, nature, water	Clear, St. Patrick's Day	Quieting, refreshing, peaceful, nascent	Ghastliness, disease, terror, guilt
Blue	Transparent, wet	Cold, sky, water, ice	Service, the flag	Subduing, melancholy, contemplative, sober	Gloom, fearfulness, furtiveness
Purple	Deep, soft, atmospheric	Cool, mist, darkness, shadow	Mourning, Easter	Dignified, pompous, mournful, mystic	Loneliness, desperation
White	Spatial—light	Cool, snow	Cleanliness, Mother's Day, the flag	Pure, clean, frank, youthful	Brightness of spirit, normality
Black	Spatial— darkness	Neutral, night, emptiness	Mourning	Funereal, ominous, deadly, depressing	Negation of spirit, death

---

Color can establish the mood of a design, perhaps more effectively than any other design element. Choose your colors wisely, ensuring their congruity with the subject and the reader.

Where to Use Color

Color can take many forms in desktop publishing. There's colored ink, of course, but there's colored paper, too. You can color rules and borders, pictures, text, and business graphics. Let's examine each.

Figure 9-5

The PageMaker PANTONE selection dialog box (top) and the Xpress equivalent (bottom).

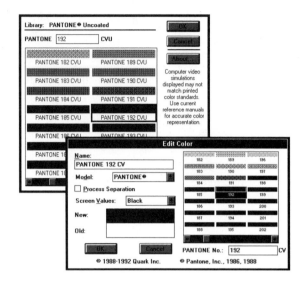

The PANTONE Color-Matching System

What do you do before you buy five gallons of Sherwin-Williams to paint the living room? No doubt you begin by consulting some color samples from the paint store. You bring a few of them home, hold them up next to the couch and the drapes, and pick a color that you like based on your living-room environment. Then it's back to the store where the paint people mix up your chosen color according to the formulas Sherwin-Williams provides.

Choosing colored ink is no different than choosing living-room paint. Using a color swatch book, you pick a color based on your document's environment: the paper, the reader, and the subject. When you find a color you like, you take it to the print shop where they mix up ink based on their formulas to match your chosen swatch.

continued

Paper Stock

Lots of paper colors are available. Check with your print shop; they will have a number of colors in stock and can special order others if you don't see what you need. There will no doubt be a small surcharge (and some might proffer an environmental argument), but the expense is usually small and the effect—if it's deliberate—often validates the fiscal compromise.

Colored paper is misused more often than it's used properly, however. More often than not it's the product of the designer's mood: "I'll bet they'll pay attention if I use this chartreuse paper!" Colored paper always represents a compromise in readability (lessened contrast), so its use must be justifiable.

For maximum effect, use a second color of ink whenever you use colored paper. With a sample of the paper stock in hand, grab your PANTONE color swatch book (see sidebar) and find a color of ink that works well with the paper. It should be a dark color with plenty of saturation. Both the color of the ink and the color of the paper should relate to the subject and the reader; consult Table 9-1.

continued

Unlike the living-room scenario, however, print jobs often involve competitive bidding. Because a number of potential vendors are involved, your color swatch and the printer's formulas must adhere to some kind of standard. It's as if Sherwin-Williams, Benjamin Moore, and Fuller-O'Brien all used the same swatch book and mixed their paints according to the same formulas. (Wouldn't that be nice? Then you could get competitive bids of living-room paint, secure in the knowledge that you would receive the color you want, regardless of who supplies the paint.)

The standardized color-matching system used in the printing industry is the *PANTONE Color-Matching System*. Nearly every printer in this country relies on it, and both *Xpress* and *PageMaker* can apply PANTONE colors to your documents (see Figure 9-5).

Unfortunately, your computer's monitor isn't a very accurate device when it comes to displaying color. You need a swatch book, and PANTONE will be happy to sell you one. All art supply stores carry them, and they're expensive: typically $65 or more. If you're going to print in color, you must oblige this expense. Specifying colored printing ink without a PANTONE swatch book is like selecting a living-room paint with your eyes closed.

Exercise 9.2   The PANTONE Color-Matching System

Raid your swipe file (if you have one by now), or collect a few desktop-published documents, looking for those printed with a second color. Compare that color with a PANTONE color swatch book. No doubt you'll find an exact match.

Now try to determine why the designer chose that particular color. Does it relate to the reader or the subject? Perhaps it was chosen to complement the color of the paper. It may be a corporate color, or a seasonal color, or just a token of the designer's whimsy.

Photographs

So far I've been able to avoid the spot color vs. process color discussion that this chapter requires, something I can't ignore any longer.

The PANTONE sidebar describes the *spot* color method. Spot color inks are mixed according to formulas: if you want PANTONE 192 (a chestnut red), the printer mixes the inks and prints that color directly on your paper. Usually only one or two of these colors appears in a design (in addition to black), thus the expression *spot* color.

The alternative is *process* color. Typically, process color uses four colors of ink: cyan, magenta, yellow, and black. By printing these colors in combinations, any color can be realized. Magazines use process color almost exclusively: all printed color photographs are printed that way. Successful process color is a marriage of operator experience, sophisticated software, and calibrated equipment. Any one if these factors is well beyond the scope of this book. We're discussing spot color in this chapter, and spot color only.

Halftones   *Halftones* are photographs printed with one color of ink. We discussed most of their design considerations in the previous chapter but neglected to mention one: color. There's no reason why a halftone must be printed with black ink. Printed with brown ink on buff-colored paper, halftones look like the old "sepia-toned" photos—the kind you can still buy at country fairs in the booths where they take your picture in period costume. Printed with blue ink on white paper, halftones take on a cold, mechanical feeling.

Unfortunately, most inks change character when they're not printed at full saturation. Although a halftone may be printed with a fully saturated color of ink, the halftone process itself mixes a considerable amount of the paper's color into the photo. The results can be devastating.

Before you run 10,000 copies of a halftone printed with colored ink, print it once in black and take the results to a copy shop that offers a color photocopier. Ask them to print a copy of the halftone in the color and on the paper you plan to use. Most print shops can do that—even if the original is black-and-white—and the charge rarely exceeds a dollar.

Printing monochrome halftones with anything but black ink is risky business. Although special effects are possible, proof the design before going to press.

Duotones   A far better alternative to the colored monochrome halftone is the *duotone*. Duotones are halftones printed with two colors of ink, one of which is usually black. The addition of black ink eliminates the potential for the ghastly unsaturated colors that monochrome color halftones usually provide, yet the character of the second color is retained.

Duotones make particularly good sense in documents where a spot color has been selected that properly complements the subject and the reader. Under these circumstances, either all of the document's photographs can be printed as duotones, or just a few,

Figure 9-6

The Duotone Options dialog box from Adobe Photoshop *for the Macintosh. Note the Dot Gain value at the bottom center.*

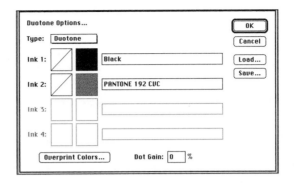

Dot Gain

Duotones are tricky because of an anomaly known as *dot gain.* Dot gain occurs when the tiny dots that comprise the halftone spread a bit when they're printed on paper. Factors like the paper's absorbency, the viscosity of the ink, the type of press, and the drying method all contribute to dot gain. With two inks, however, one may provoke more dot gain than the other, and the printed result may not match the intent, even if the duotone was proofed.

Good software can compensate for dot gain (see Figure 9-6). Ask your press operator what kind of dot gain you should expect, provide your software with that number, and the result will probably not displease you.

with the duotones providing the distinction necessary to isolate those pictures that require special emphasis.

Exercise 9.3   Duotone Trials

This exercise assumes you have a scanner (or a scanned photograph), access to Adobe's *Photoshop* or some other program that's capable of making duotones, and a few dollars for making color photocopies. That's a lot of assumptions, but if you have what it takes, you'll be all the richer with some duotone experience in your repertoire.

Open the graphic in *Photoshop*, and choose Duotone from the Mode menu. When *Photoshop* asks you to pick a second color, pick one that flatters the subject or invokes a mood. Use a PANTONE color swatch book for this. The screen will update to preview the printed image.

Save the document as an EPS file, import (*Xpress*) or place it (*PageMaker*) into a blank document in your desktop-publishing software, then print the separations. Take these to a copy shop with a color photocopier, and ask them to print one separation in the PANTONE color (some color photocopiers don't know about PANTONE colors but can "learn" any color—take your PANTONE swatch book with you) and the other in black, both on the same piece of paper. *Voila!* Instant duotone proofs.

Figure 9-7

The Xpress *(top) and* PageMaker *(bottom) character-formatting dialog boxes. Note that each provides the option of applying color to text.*

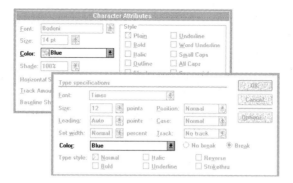

Text

Colored text is an option in both *Xpress* (Character Attributes, under the Style menu) and *PageMaker* (Type Specifications, under the Type menu), and each program features color as an attribute for inclusion in styles as well (see Figure 9-7).

Colored text rarely exhibits the contrast that black text offers: you'll need to increase its point size and stick to simple letterforms. Again, consider only smaller text blocks: coloring something as large as a headline provokes an emphasis that may not be intentional.

If the text is recurring—subheads, running heads, and the like—make the color a part of a style and use the style to format the text. It's easy to neglect a single subhead, for example, when you're looking down the barrel of a deadline; styles ensure consistency.

As the only colored element on the page, colored text appears to be highlighted. If colored text is to serve as a repetitive element of the design (rather than as a highlight), unify the design by applying the same color to a nontextual page element as well. A colored subhead, for example, might be accompanied by a rule of a similar weight. Colored callouts in illustrations might find their match in a colored illustration border.

Colored text rarely exhibits the contrast black
text does, thus it must be set in a larger size and
a font of less complexity. Use styles to ensure
consistency, and accompany colored text with
colored rules or borders to ensure unity.

Borders, Rules, and Ornaments

This is fertile ground for the application of color. In multipage
documents, colored rules and borders establish a rhythm and provide continuity from one page to the next. In single-page documents, colored rules and borders can serve as simple decorative
elements (a thin colored rule between columns, for example), or
as emphasis (a fiery red border surrounding a warning), or as a
convention (a stylized blue question mark in the margin next to
a paragraph that answers—or asks—a question). In multiple-sec-
tion documents, uniquely colored page borders or folio lines for
each section are effective.

Random thoughts come to mind:

- Use a saturated color for rules and ornaments. Choose a color
  that's not too dark (it'll be hard to distinguish from black)
  and not too light (it might disappear altogether). If the color
  must be light, apply it only to heavier components on the page.

- Unless emphasis is the goal, unify the page by including more
  than one element with the contrasting color. A single colored
  element—rule, border, ornament, or text—calls attention to
  itself. Multiple colored elements are perceived as aspects of the
  design.

- Be consistent. If you're using a colored folio line on page 1, be
  sure the folio lines on all of the other pages are the same color
  as well.

- Background tints—panels of color in the form of filled
  boxes—can easily dominate the page if they're too bright. On

the other hand, their mass can be used to balance another dominant element, if that's what's needed.

- Consider text surprinted over a colored background tint as you would any other surprinted text. Make it larger than normal, and use a font with simple letterforms.

- Unless the color is dark and saturated, colored ornaments and line art should be simple in design and bold in stroke. A delicate filigree printed in yellow, for example, won't be seen at all.

- Screened to 20% or so, colored artwork (again, the simple variety) serves well as a phantom—an almost subliminal graphic serving as a background to the design. Phantoms are a bit like watermarks, and like watermarks should never interfere with readability. Use the photocopier test mentioned earlier in this chapter to test a phantom before going to press with it.

Adding color to rules, borders, and ornaments is so easy it's often overdone and rarely very startling. It is nonetheless an effective technique for ridding a page of boredom. Whenever color is to be included, test your design before going to press.

Exercise 9.4 **Thermal-Transfer Colors**

This exercise describes a process with which all desktop publishers should be familiar. It requires a product named *Desktop ColorFoil* (PaperDirect sells it—see the bibliography at the end of this chapter) or something similar (LetraSet makes a similar product called *Omnicrom*). Most art supply stores carry these products, which are strips or sheets of colored material that transfers to paper when subjected to heat. The heat is usually supplied by a laser printer, set to print a blank page.

What's interesting about these products is that they only transfer color to paper in the areas where there is already toner, either from a laser printer or from a photocopy machine. By selectively adhering strips of ColorFoil to a black-and-white, laser-printed original, you can replace the black toner with the color you've chosen, and there are hundreds of colors available.

A design similar to that pictured in Figure 6-13 is ideal. A number of rules segregate this design, and they're ideal candidates for colorization.

Following the directions supplied with the product, colorize a few of the rules on the layout and set the results aside. Do it again, colorizing additional areas. Use different colors for each of these scenarios. After you've done a half dozen or so, arrange them side by side and critique the results.

Nearly every industry that mass-produces expensive products starts with a prototype, and that's what you're producing when you use ColorFoil in this way. It's almost immediate, always convenient, and frequently a salvation.

Business Graphics

Business graphics—bars, charts, and pies—usually appear in one of two forms, as presentations or as artwork. Presentations (slides and overheads) are not the subject of this book. As artwork however, business graphics are frequently included in desktop-published documents, and often they appear in color.

Association   Coke and IBM have spent years developing a color association with their products. You might consider the same strategy, albeit on a smaller scale. If you're running a series of business graphics comparing your product with another, assign your product a dominant color (perhaps the only color other than black), and use it consistently.

━━━━━━━━━━━━━━━━━━━━━━━━

Business graphics often benefit from the addition of color to develop association, declare differentiation, establish hierarchies, and promote emphasis. Proceed with caution, however. Develop the graphic in monochrome first; add color only after the graphic serves its purpose without it.

Differentiation   Color is especially effective at providing differentiation. An organizational chart, for example, might show managerial personnel in red and clerical personnel in blue. A word chart might assign a lighter color to explanatory text and black to major heads.

Hierarchies   Here's an opportunity to use gradations of color—a single color printed at different intensities, or "fills," as desktop-publishing software refers to them. An area chart might stack its layered hierarchy with saturations—fills—ranging from 20% to 100%. If multiple colors are an option, hierarchies are best indicated in the Roy G. Biv (rainbow) order of colors.

Emphasis   Here's another opportunity for gradations of a single color. You might emphasize one line on a bullet chart, for example, by printing it at full saturation, with the others printed at 60%. One segment of a pie chart printed in color is sure to attract attention.

Regardless of the technique, proceed with caution. Business graphics are often adorned with too much color. Most specialists in business graphics claim that a graphic must first be made to work in black and white before any color should be added. You might adopt that strategy as well: develop your graphic in monochrome—using blacks, whites, and grays—then replace the grays with colors one at a time. It clarifies thinking.

The Experimental Attitude (Revisited)

Color is becoming an increasingly convenient and affordable method of enhancement. All desktop-publishing software now offer it, few systems remain with monochrome monitors, and high-quality color printers are in the same price range that black-and-white printers were only a few years ago.

Resist the compulsion to buy all of these goodies if you don't already own them. Color's evocative quality is available without traditional color at all: no colored ink, no colored paper—yet it's color just the same. *Tonal* color refers to the various shades of gray that can be achieved with a single color of ink (usually black) on a single color of paper (usually white).

A design can seem blacker—more lively and assertive (or perhaps more solemn and severe)—through the use of bold elements: thick rules, heavy borders, dense screens, and bold typography. On the other hand, a design can seem lighter—more informal, colloquial, or vernacular—by providing wide margins, extra white space, or by eliminating rules and borders. Body text size can be reduced by a point or so and its leading retained. Look at the two forms pictured in Figure 9-8: the "color" in each design becomes apparent when the two are compared with one another.

In our design courses, we first require the student to master effective monochromatic design. We study composition by taking (and observing) photographs in black and white. We emphasize the principles of proportion, balance, contrast, rhythm, and unity. Thousands of effective designs emerge at this phase of learning, and many students feel comfortable stopping here, realizing that color is neither their medium nor a necessity. Don't feel bad if you won't be using color in your designs: Ansel Adams got along just fine without it; so can you.

If color is on your agenda however, subject it to the same scrutiny as you would any other design element by holding it to the light of subject, reader, and system. Design your document first without any color, then add it carefully, challenging every stroke. Like any new toy, color is subject to overuse—an error that is made all the more apparent by color's sheer power and authority. Include it only when you can clearly identify its purpose.

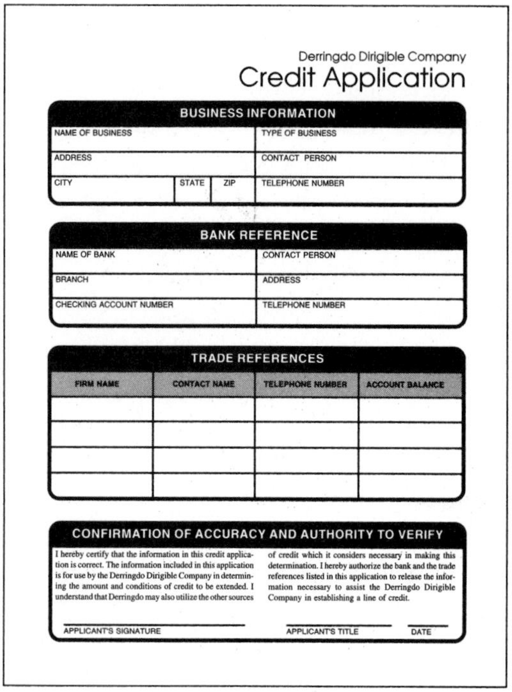

Derringdo Dirigible Company

Credit Application

BUSINESS INFORMATION

NAME OF BUSINESS			TYPE OF BUSINESS
ADDRESS			CONTACT PERSON
CITY	STATE	ZIP	TELEPHONE NUMBER

BANK REFERENCE

NAME OF BANK	CONTACT PERSON
BRANCH	ADDRESS
CHECKING ACCOUNT NUMBER	TELEPHONE NUMBER

TRADE REFERENCES

FIRM NAME	CONTACT NAME	TELEPHONE NUMBER	ACCOUNT BALANCE

CONFIRMATION OF ACCURACY AND AUTHORITY TO VERIFY

I hereby certify that the information in this credit application is correct. The information included in this application is for use by the Derringdo Dirigible Company in determining the amount and conditions of credit to be extended. I understand that Derringdo may also utilize the other sources of credit which it considers necessary in making this determination. I hereby authorize the bank and the trade references listed in this application to release the information necessary to assist the Derringdo Dirigible Company in establishing a line of credit.

APPLICANT'S SIGNATURE APPLICANT'S TITLE DATE

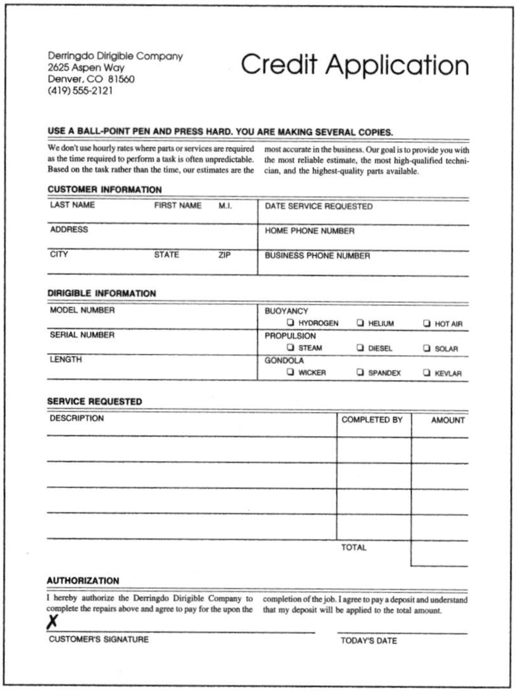

Derringdo Dirigible Company
2625 Aspen Way
Denver, CO 81560
(419) 555-2121

Credit Application

USE A BALL-POINT PEN AND PRESS HARD. YOU ARE MAKING SEVERAL COPIES.

We don't use hourly rates where parts or services are required as the time required to perform a task is often unpredictable. Based on the task rather than the time, our estimates are the most accurate in the business. Our goal is to provide you with the most reliable estimate, the most high-qualified technician, and the highest-quality parts available.

CUSTOMER INFORMATION

LAST NAME	FIRST NAME	M.I.	DATE SERVICE REQUESTED
ADDRESS			HOME PHONE NUMBER
CITY	STATE	ZIP	BUSINESS PHONE NUMBER

DIRIGIBLE INFORMATION

MODEL NUMBER	BUOYANCY ❑ HYDROGEN ❑ HELIUM ❑ HOT AIR
SERIAL NUMBER	PROPULSION ❑ STEAM ❑ DIESEL ❑ SOLAR
LENGTH	GONDOLA ❑ WICKER ❑ SPANDEX ❑ KEVLAR

SERVICE REQUESTED

DESCRIPTION	COMPLETED BY	AMOUNT
	TOTAL	

AUTHORIZATION

I hereby authorize the Derringdo Dirigible Company to complete the repairs above and agree to pay for the upon the completion of the job. I agree to pay a deposit and understand that my deposit will be applied to the total amount.

✗

CUSTOMER'S SIGNATURE TODAY'S DATE

Figure 9-8

Dominant borders and heavy rules lend the design on the left a darker "color" than the more restrained design on the right.

And finally, we return to an attitude first promoted at the beginning of this book: Don't include color in a design without first experimenting with it. Professional designers have worked with color for years. They understand its impact, and they know where each of its land mines is planted. Most of us do not. Accordingly, our best defense is experimentation. Fortunately, technology is ready to assist us in the form of accessible and affordable color photocopy machines. Find a good one in your neighborhood, make the acquaintance of its best operator, and use them both to test your designs before they go to press.

Bibliography

Berry, Susan, and Martin, Judy: *Designing with Color*. London: Quarto Publishing, 1991. (Published in the United States by North Light Books, Cincinnati.)

Only 15 pages of text; well over 100 pages of examples. Compares colors and layouts as cool and warm, passive and active, feminine and masculine, neutral and artificial, and so on. This is the best way to learn color—by looking at it and comparing designs.

Birren, Faber: *Color Psychology and Color Therapy*. Secaucus, NJ: The Citadel Press, 1961.

There are lots of color theory books, but most are too elementary or too complex. This one walks the middle of the road, writing in a conversational style with laboratory citations to lend authority to every observation.

The Color Resource Catalog. The Color Resource, 708 Montgomery Street, San Francisco, CA 94111-2104. 1-800-827-3311.

There's no better way to steer your way through the new technology maze than by reading books from this catalog. A phone call is all it takes to get on this mailing list.

Kuehni, Rolf G.: *Color: Essence and Logic*. New York: Van Nostrand Reinhold, 1983.

Exceptional pedagogy and occasional pedantics mark this scholarly volume. Although you may not want to become a color engineer or psychologist, read this book nonetheless. A little formal education gives you a perspective that's invaluable in document design.

The PaperDirect Catalog. PaperDirect, 205 Chubb Avenue, Lyndhurst, NJ 07071. 1-800-272-7377.

Call these people and ask them to put your name on their mailing list. They offer the widest selection of specialty papers (and the Desktop ColorFoil system mentioned in this chapter) of any shop in the country, and they're as near as your telephone.

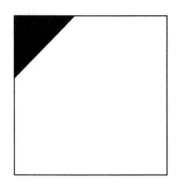

Glossary

ascender   The part of a lowercase letter that rises above the main body. Compare with *descender*.

bad break   In composition, starting a column or a page with an orphan or ending a column or a page with a widow. See also *widow* and *orphan*.

baseline   The invisible line that all characters in a line of type "sit" on. Excepting descenders, no part of any character extends below the baseline. Typically, leading is measured from baseline to baseline. See also *leading*, *mean line*, *x height*, and *descender*.

baseline alignment   The alignment of baselines across the column gutter of multiple-column documents or across the page gutter of facing-page documents. See also *gutter* and *baseline*.

baseline leading   The method that measures leading from baseline to baseline. Common now to all desktop-publishing applications. *PageMaker* defaults to a variation of this method called *proportional leading*.

beard   Going back to the days of movable type, the beard was the part of the *stamp* or block of type that extended below the descender or above the ascender. Also known as the *shoulder*.

bitmapped   The term used to describe graphic or textual images produced by a pattern of individual dots, or "bits." Photographic and freehand graphics are often bitmapped. In this context, bitmapped is synonymous with *raster*. Contrast with *vector* or *object*.

bleed   An extra amount of printed image that extends beyond the trim edge of the sheet or the page.

blurb   Typically, a blurb is a short capitulation of the body text appearing just above or just below the headline for that text as enticement for the reader.

body type   A type used for the main part or text of a printed piece, as distinguished from the heading. See also *text*. Contrast with *display type*.

boldface type   A name given to type that is heavier than the text or body type with which it is used.

bracket   In typography, the transition from a vertical stroke to a horizontal serif. Bracketed designs feature a semicircular transition not unlike shelf brackets.

brilliance   In typography, a typeface designed with high brilliance features extreme contrast between its thick and thin strokes. New-style designs such as Bodoni feature high brilliance. See also *contrast*.

bullet   In typography, a bullet is any character that appears at the beginning of a paragraph that distinguishes that paragraph as one of a series. Bullets are often large dots, but any character will do: numbers, letters, or fancy designs from pi fonts. See also *pi font*.

CMYK   In printing, a method of printing all possible colors using only cyan, magenta, yellow, and black inks.

color separation   In photography, the process of separating color originals into the primary printing color components (cyan, magenta, yellow, and black) in negative or positive form.

complementary colors   Colors appearing opposite one another on the color wheel. Most complementary colors vibrate or beat against one another visually when they appear adjacent to each other, and thus aren't really complementary at all.

continuous tone   A photographic image that contains gradient tones from white to black.

contrast   In typography, a design featuring a variation between thick and thin strokes. In design, contrast is any element that appears in contrast to other elements on the page. See also *brilliance*.

copyfitting   In composition, the calculation of how much space a given amount of copy will take up in a given size and typeface. Also, the adjusting of the type size to make it fit in a given amount of space.

crop   To eliminate unwanted portions of a graphic or page.

crop marks   Printed lines outside of the image area to identify its perimeter. Used as a guide for trimming paper.

descender   The part of a lowercase letter that extends below the main body.

display type   Type set larger than the text, or body, of the document. Generally, display type is defined as that that appears in sizes larger than 12 points. Contrast with *body type*.

dot gain   Depending on paper, ink, and a number of other factors, tiny dots of ink tend to expand as they're absorbed by the paper when printed. This tendency—*dot gain*—is significant in halftone printing as it tends to cause images to print darker than originally intended. See also *halftone*.

duotone   Monochrome photographic images can assume a significant embellishment (or change) of character by printing the highlights of the image in a second color. This result is known as a *duotone*.

em   In composition, a unit of measurement exactly as wide as the point size being set. So named because the letter *M* in early fonts was often cast on a square body.

em dash   A dash the width of an em. Typically, the em dash is used as an article of punctuation. See also *em*.

en   One-half the width of an em. Often used as the distance occupied by a space.

en dash   A dash the width of an en. Properly used, an en dash signifies continuance, as in August 17–19. See also *en*.

finial   In typography, a *finial* is the small knob found at the termination of the top stroke of the lowercase *c*, *f*, and *r*. Look for finials at the termination of the lower strokes of the lowercase *j* and *y*.

flush left (or **right**)   Type set up to align at the left (or right) edge. This body of text is set flush left. Justified type is set flush left and right. Contrast with *justify*.

folio   The page number or any other element that repeats on every page.

font   A complete assortment of letters, numbers, and punctuation of a given typeface and type style.

galley   In the days when text was sent to a typesetting shop, it returned in the form of a galley, or a long narrow strip of paper, cut to column width. Galleys were cut into column-length strips and pasted onto the layout mechanically.

greeking   Nonsense text used for copyfitting. Greeking contains no words, but otherwise looks very much like text, complete with words, sentences, and paragraphs.

gutter   The blank space, or inner margin, from printing area to binding. Some refer to the area between columns as a gutter as well.

hairline   A thin printed rule, typically measuring 0.25 point thick. See also *rule* and *point*.

halftone   The reproduction of continuous-tone artwork, such as a photograph, through a crossline or halftone screen that converts the image into dots of various sizes. Contrast with *continuous tone*.

HSB   A method of defining color by describing its components of hue, saturation, and brightness. This method is most accurate at describing color as the eye sees it. Compare with *CMYK* and *RGB*. Also known as *HLS* (for hue, lightness, and saturation.)

imagesetter   The direct descendent of the typesetting machine, the *imagesetter* sets not only type, but every other element of the page as well. In effect, a laser printer is an imagesetter, although the term is usually reserved for devices capable of printing at resolutions greater than 1200 dots per inch.

justify   The process of setting all lines within a body of text to the same length, producing smooth left and right margins. Contrast with *flush left*.

kerning   The process of removing space between pairs of characters so that they appear closer together. Contrast with *letterspacing* and *spacing*.

keyline   An outline drawing of finished art to indicate the exact position, shape, and size for such elements as halftones, line art, and the like.

kiss   The process of kerning characters until they barely touch, or kiss. Compare with *TNT*.

ladder   Used when a number of hyphens appear sequentially along the right edge of a body of text, as "a *ladder* of hyphens."

leader   Rows of dashes or dots used to guide the eye across the page. Used in tabular work; typically referred to as a *tab leader*.

leading   The distance between lines of type, measured in points.

letterspacing   The process of adding space between pairs of characters so that they appear farther apart. Contrast with *kerning* and *spacing*.

ligature   A single letter replacing a combination of letters (usually two) that don't fit together well. Typical ligatures are *fi* and *ff*.

line art   Graphics composed of pure black and pure white are often referred to as line art, especially if they represent art produced with pen or pencil. Contrast with *halftone* and *continuous tone*.

M   Abbreviation for quantities of 1,000 sheets of paper. Do not confuse with *em*.

mean line   The line described by the tops of most characters exclusive of ascenders. Compare with *baseline*. See also *x height*.

moiré   The undesirable pattern caused by incorrect screen angles of overprinting halftones. Moiré patterns also develop when certain bitmapped (raster) images are reduced or enlarged on the layout by desktop-publishing software.

new style   In typography, a style of design featuring significant contrast and small, lightly bracketed serifs. Bodoni is the most common representative of this era. Contrast with *old style*.

object   In graphics, the term used to describe graphic images composed of lines, arcs, ellipses, and rectangles—the so-called objects of object-oriented graphics. Synonymous with *vector*. Contrast with *raster* or *bitmapped*.

oblique stress   A characteristic of old-style typographic design, *oblique stress* describes a slant to the left most evident in characters with round letterforms, such as the *o*, *e*, *b*, *d*, and *p*. See also *old style*.

old style   In typography, a style of design characterized by oblique stress, bracketed serifs, and light contrast. Bembo, Garamond, Goudy, Janson, and Caslon are examples. Contrast with *new style*. See also *oblique stress*, *contrast*, and *bracket*.

orphan   The last line of a paragraph appearing at the top of a page or column. Orphans are easy to confuse with subheads. Contrast with *widow*.

PANTONE   A trademark for a system of color definition based on color swatches and mixing formulas published by PANTONE. This system is the most commonly used color-matching system in the United States. Also called PMS, for PANTONE Matching System.

phantom   A design element—typically a graphic—lightly printed on the page so that text can be printed over it.

pica   Unit of measurement used principally in typesetting. One pica equals 1/6 of an inch.

pi font   A font with no traditional letters and numbers, composed instead of fancy bullets and ornaments. Zapf Dingbats and Wingdings are typical pi fonts. See also *sort*.

point   Unit of measurement, used primarily for designating type sizes and leading. One point is equal to 1/72 of an inch. Twelve points equal a pica.

point size   Term used to describe the size of text. Measured from the top of the stamp to the bottom of the stamp. See also *stamp*.

process color   In printing, the use of four colors of ink (cyan, magenta, yellow, and black) to reproduce all visible colors.

proportional leading   A leading specification unique to *PageMaker* whereby two-thirds of the leading specification appears above the baseline and one-third appears below. This method is *PageMaker's* default. Compare with *baseline leading*.

ragged right (or **left**)   Type that is set with an even left (right) margin and an uneven (ragged) right (left) margin. See *flush left*. Contrast with *justify*.

raster   Graphic or textual images produced by a pattern of individual dots. Photographic and freehand graphics are often raster. In this context, raster is synonymous with *bitmapped*. Contrast with *vector* or *object*.

raster-image processing   The conversion of all page elements—text, graphics, and objects—into a bitmapped (or raster) image at the printer's resolution for final presentation on the page. Raster-image processing may occur at the printer or in the computer, but it must occur eventually before the page may be printed. The device that does the processing may be an independent unit (as is the case with most imagesetters), in which case it's known as a *RIP*, or Raster Image Processor.

register   Fitting of two or more printing images (usually color separations) on the same paper in exact alignment with each other.

register marks   Crosses within circles applied to original copy prior to photography. Used for positioning negatives in register.

reverse   Any element printed in the same color as the paper. Reversed text, for instance, is usually white on black.

RGB   A method of defining color composed of the three emitted, or additive, colors: red, green, and blue. In combination, these three colors produce white. All television systems (including color computer monitors) use this system. Compare with *CMYK* and *HSB*.

Roy G. Biv   A memorization technique for remembering the colors of the rainbow in order, from top to bottom: red, orange, yellow, green, blue, indigo, and violet.

rule   In printing, *rules* are lines that print. *Lines*, on the other hand, are lines that *don't* print, such as guidelines.

runaround   Type set to wrap around a graphic or another element of the design. *PageMaker* refers to this as *wrap text*.

running head   A headline or title repeated at the top of each page. See also *folio*.

scanner   A device that systematically scans images and converts them into electrical signals for use by a computer.

screen   A grid pattern with opaque lines crossing each other at right angles, thus forming transparent squares or "screen apertures." Continuous-tone images photographed through such a screen emerge as a pattern of black dots, varying in size according to the brightness of the image. See also *halftone*.

screened print   A print made with a halftone screen to simulate shades of gray. See also *halftone*.

serif   The short cross strokes at the ends of the main strokes on many letters of some typefaces. Times has serifs. Helvetica (a sans serif typeface) does not.

shoulder   The part of an individual character that extends above the face to the top of the stamp, or below the face to the bottom of the stamp. See also *beard* and *stamp*.

sidebar   A short article, usually ancillary to the subject of the body text, accompanying a longer story. Sidebars are usually placed at the side (or top, or bottom) of the primary story, thus the term *side*bar.

sidehead   A subhead placed at the side of—rather than above—the text that follows it.

signature   Multipage masters, all appearing on one sheet of paper. When folded (and sometimes cut or trimmed), signatures assemble into the pages of a multipage document. Printing large signatures such as this takes advantage of full press capacity.

small caps   An alphabet of small capital letters, approximately the size of lowercase letters, intended for use with larger capital letters.

sort   In publishing years ago, a *sort* was an individual character of a pi font. Publications that required a number of sorts often caused the printer to run out, thus the old saying: Out of sorts. See also *pi font*.

spacing   The uniform addition or removal of space between words and/or characters in a body of text. Contrast with *kerning* and *letterspacing*.

spot color   Usually, a second color of ink applied to a monochrome document (though some documents feature three or more spot colors). Spot color inks are usually mixed to the customer's PANTONE specifications and are not a combination of CMYK inks. Compare with *process color*. See also *CMYK* and *PANTONE*.

stamp   The individual block (usually made of lead) used in movable type printing containing the face of an individual character of type. See also *beard* and *shoulder*.

stress   A slight backhand slant applied to certain characters—usually circular—to aid in character recognition. A characteristic of old-style fonts. See also *contrast* and *brilliance*.

surprint   To print text (though graphics may apply) on top of a background screen, color, or phantom. See also *screen* and *phantom*.

swipe file   A file you should maintain of ideas and designs to supply inspiration and motivation.

text   The body matter of a page or book, as distinguished from the headings.

thin space   A space, usually a quarter of an em wide. Thin spaces are frequently placed on either side of an em dash. See also *em* and *em dash*.

TNT   Tight Not Touching. The process of setting type so tight that characters almost, but not quite, touch. Compare with *kiss*.

tracking   The uniform modification of the kerning table (or font metrics) associated with a particular font. Psychologically speaking, the eye prefers to see letters more tightly set in large point sizes than in smaller ones. Tracking obliges this preference by tightening text appearing in larger point sizes.

transitional   A period and style of typographical design characterized by increased brilliance and more sharply bracketed serifs than old-style designs, and the near elimination of oblique stress. Compare with *old style* and *new style*.

triad   Three colors spaced equidistantly around the perimeter of the color wheel. Triads are usually perceived as pleasant color combinations.

vector   A type of graphic composed of computer-defined graphic routines (called *primitives*) such as lines and arcs. Vector-based graphics are the highest quality graphics, capable of infinite scaling without loss of resolution. See also *object*. Contrast with *bitmapped* and *raster*.

widow   The first line of a paragraph appearing at the bottom of a page or a column. Contrast with *orphan*.

Windows   An operating environment whereby familiar interface attributes—a pointing device, pull-down menus, scroll bars, and, of course, windows themselves—become the environment common to all programs designed for operation within the system. Windows is a trademark of Microsoft. Both Windows and the Macintosh operating environment are based on interface concepts first discovered at the Palo Alto Research Center in the early and mid-1970s.

x height   The height of all lowercase characters exclusive of ascenders and descenders, extending from the baseline to the mean line. The height of the lowercase *x* represents this distance most effectively in most font designs. See also *baseline* and *mean line*.

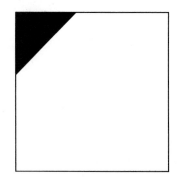

Index